HIGH COUNTRY
. . . .
The Solo Seeker's Guide to a Real Life

HIGH COUNTRY

. . . .

The Solo Seeker's Guide to a Real Life

David M. Alderman

INNER
OCEAN

Library of Congress Cataloging-in-Publication Data

Alderman, David M.
    High country : the solo seeker's guide to a real life
    / David M. Alderman ; foreword by Jean Houston. --
    Makawao, Hawaii : Inner Ocean, 2001

    p. ; cm.

    Includes bibliographical references.
    ISBN 1-930722-00-1

    1. Self-actualization (Psychology) I.
    Title.

BF637.S4 A43 2001
155.2--dc21   CIP

CIP information

        Inner Ocean Publishing, Inc.
        P.O. Box 1239
        Makawao, Maui, HI 96768-1239

Cover design: Bill Greaves

Cover photos: Imagine Bank

Interior page design: Bill Greaves

Typography: Debra Lordan

Editing: Joan Wilcox

Permissions granted for the use of the Orphic Sacramental Bowl drawing on
page 198 from *Masks of the Gods* (copyright © 1968 by Joseph Campbell) by
Viking Penguin, a division of Penguin Putnam, Inc. Diagram of Transactional
Analysis on page 112 from Games People Play (copyright © 1964 by Eric
Berne) by Random House, Inc.

Printed in the United States by Central Plains

9 8 7 6 5 4 3 2 1

DEDICATION

This book is dedicated to my children, Christian and Bryna, in hopes that they may someday find their own way to the High Country.

HIGH COUNTRY

. . . .

The Solo Seeker's Guide to a Real Life

TABLE OF CONTENTS

ACKNOWLEDGMENTS

My enduring thanks to Bret Thomas Alderman, writer and seeker, my great and dear friend, who refused to let me stop believing in the value of *High Country* and its eventual success, and without whom this book might not have been. Deep gratitude as well to John Nelson, who saw in the rough manuscript a gem, and whose vision was a brilliant flash of inspiration for me; thanks to Jean Houston for her encouragement and invaluable assistance; and to Joan Wilcox, without whose intelligence, expertise, and patience I never would have been able to make the new stone shine. Thanks also to all of my students and clients for all that they have taught me, and to my wife, Charene, for helping to sustain a place where I could do the work I love for all these years.

Above all, I owe an impossible debt of gratitude to all of those who have come before me. To Carl Jung, Lao Tzu, Chuang Tzu, and the innumerable unnamed who have kept the lineage of Spirit alive in all cultures of the Earth throughout the ages.

Namasté

DMA

Olympia, WA
May 2001

FOREWORD

. . . .

by Jean Houston

In reading this potent parable of human possibilities, I am moved to paraphrase Robert Browning and say, "A man's reach must exceed his grasp or what's a metaphor?" In *High Country,* David Alderman offers us a journey into Meta realms that exceed our grasp yet lure us into the Essential Self we may have forgotten we had. Here is the game of lost and found played on mythic terrains of mind and imagination. Here are guides to inner worlds like Carl Jung, Abraham Maslow, Joseph Campbell, and Fritz Perls raised to the status of numinous borderline persons and allowed archetypal power as they guide the traveler through the high country of his or her essential being. Here, too, is the new physics of world and consciousness rendered accessible, the laws of the universe shown to be the laws that govern the self in its deconstruction and renewal. Here is the New Story wherein psyche and science, the shadowed and the true self journey toward the farther reaches of Human nature and come home to luminous possibilities. Here is myth made modern, archetypes made actual, the transcendent function realized in body and time.

Alderman's work testifies to the fact that all over the world myth is bursting through. Most of us were raised in print culture wherein principles of continuity, uniformity, and repeatability were elevated over the more organic principles of discontinuity, simultaneity, and multiple associations. Now the mythic flavor of the more ancient, organic perspective returns, and chaos theory becomes lauded as the way things work. We look for flow patterns rather than for linear cause-effect explanations. Resonance has become far more important than relevance, and nothing is truly hidden anymore.

In order to prepare for these world changes, the human psyche is manifesting many different singularities of itself as it helps the planetary movement toward convergence and transition. Psyche is moving at remarkable speeds past the limits most of us have lived with for thousands of years into an utterly different state of being. The contents of the psyche are manifesting at faster and faster rates—a dreamlike reality in which it is difficult to tell anymore what is news and what is drama, what is matter and what is myth. We live in chaos, which we may have created in order to hasten our own meeting with ourselves.

All over the world, in virtually every culture I visit, I find that images that were relegated to the unconscious are becoming conscious. Happenings that belonged to extraordinary experiences of reality are becoming more common, and many of the maps of the psyche and its unfolding are undergoing awesome change. David Alderman portrays this phenomenon in his depiction of the protagonist's travels to a high country where the self undergoes the mysteries of a transformational journey—through the crevices of social habits and the ice caves of personal compulsions to those high plateaus where daily life is transcendent experience. Thus does the author assist in the creation of the new story in which myths and metaphors are recast, and the human fabric and all our ways of knowing are seen anew.

It is our privilege and challenge to witness and assist a new story coming into being. As actors in this new story, we are seeing the rise of new archetypes, or, perhaps, the evolution of old ones. Alderman, for example, gifts us with Nu Lao Tzu, a trickster guide reminiscent of the wily genius of the Taoist Immortals.

The fact of the matter is that we are required to work with myth and archetype in order to open up the story to changing conditions everywhere in the world. Patterns of millennia have prepared us for another world, another time, and, above all, another story. At the same time, exponential change, unlike any ever known in human history or prehistory, has confused our values, uprooted our traditions, and left us in a labyrinth of misdirection. Factors unique in human experience are all around us—the inevitable unfolding toward a planetary civilization, the rise of women to full partnership with men, the daily revolutions in technology, the media becoming the matrix of culture, and the revolution in the understanding of human and social capacities. The Zeit is getting Geisty as the old story itself is suffering a sacred wound in order that it, too, may grow and address the multiples of experience and complexity of life unknown to our great-grandparents.

Since the new story, the new mythology is not yet in place, it is up to us, separately and together, to carry out the work of re-envisionment. This book, weaving as it does so many realms of knowing and experience, is a testament to that act of re-envisioning. But can one ever really change, or even invent a myth? Go beneath the surface crust of consciousness of virtually anyone, anywhere, and you will find repositories of the imaginal world—the teeming terrain of myth and archetype: holy men and wise women, flying horses, talking frogs, sacred spaces, death and resurrections, the journeys of the heros and heroines of a thousand faces. Having taken depth probes of the psyche of many people the world over, I know this to be so. I know that in the West we have moved from the Promethean myth—of snatching fire from heaven—to the myth of Proteus, the shape-shifter. The sea god Proteus was capable of taking on all manner of shapes, forms, and purposes at will. This is us today; suddenly, like Proteus, we have to become protean— highly resilient and creative, able to adapt to the ever-changing story—especially in the light of constant challenge, and ever-present peril. Myth serves as a manner of explanation, but it is also a mode of discovery, for myth is the coded DNA of the human psyche. It is the stuff of the evolving self that awakens consciousness and culture according to the needs of time and place. It is the promise of our becoming.

How then can we change patterns so deeply woven into the structure of our psyches? Up until recent decades, I doubt that one could have done much more than alter certain details. Now, however, in a time of whole system transition when everything is deconstructing and reconstructing, the story of who and what we really are requires its own redemption. It is as critical a task as one could attempt at the beginning of the millennium—how to actually go about changing the dominant myths by guiding people into the realms of the psyche wherein they have the power to change their own essential story. Along with this author, I work on the premise that, all over the world, psyche is now emerging, larger than it was. We are experiencing the harvest of all the world's cultures, belief systems, ways of knowing, seeing, doing, and being. What had been contained in the "unconscious" over hundreds and thousands of years is up and about and preparing to go to work. What had been part of the collective as the shared myth or archetype is now finding new rivers of unique stories flowing out of the passion play of individual lives.

With so much more history, with so much more experience behind us and within us, we have achieved what is surely an extraordinary evolutionary achievement—the ability to continuously receive, re-create, reframe, and extend our experience. This new protean capacity of the self is virtually a new structure in mind, brain, and psyche–that grants us the capacity to view ideas be they social, intellectual, political—or philosophical and spiritual sets—with a freedom that was not ours in the past.

Our creative capacity has grown exponentially, as has our capacity to deal with complexity that would have driven our forebears quite mad. As our ability to discern perspectives in space and time—both outer and inner—have grown, so has our ability to orchestrate our personal mythology.

What is emerging the world over is a technology of the sacred, a high art form as well as a once and future science. It finds its theory and practice in the teachings of the mystery schools of old, in shamanic training and initiations, as well as in the modern laboratories of consciousness research and the cutting edges of psychotherapy. While global computer networks and other information superhighways give us access to the world mind, there are arising groups of artist-scientists who are providing us with the "high ways" to the world soul. The author of this book is surely a major explorer and guide to this ultimate journey.

Since culture is everywhere being newly reimagined, nothing is more necessary than a rebirth of the self. These are times that are meant to breach our souls, unlock the treasures of our minds, and, through the divine act of traveling the *High Country*, release the purpose, the plan, and the possibilities of our lives.

INTRODUCTION

. . . .

High Country

One hundred twenty years ago, the T'Peeksin and the Squaxin Indians hunted deer where my house now stands. All the local tribes would gather in summer on the sandy beaches at the mouth of the Deschutes, just down the hill from here, for potlatches and to harvest the bounty of the water and the woods. At night, they traded stories of the hunt, of sacred, ancient days, and of the Spirit that created and abides in all that is.

I like living here because a certain sense of the old wilderness and wonder still remains. Better still, there are trails not two hours' drive from where I live that lead into a wilderness untouched even by time. A day's hike from one of those trailheads will get me into the high country, where I can become totally immersed within the unspoiled world of nature. There, I can remember my true inner nature, too.

For me, the high country is any place above the timberline. Alpine fields in early summer are the most serene and pure arenas for the senses that I know. The summer breeze there is so smooth and thin it somehow slips between slight stalks of camas and lupine without touching, and the vast expanse of space beyond the ridge tops seems to open me to my true self from deep inside.

Of course, not everything about high-altitude hiking is beautiful and fun. Up there, you have to deal with Life and

Nature on their own terms, even if you get scared or worn out. There is no place to hide from Life in the high country, and no one to carry your load but you. There are real dangers in that wilderness, from bears to lethal cliff-side trails; yet even these can open you to real life in ways you might never expect, if only you can keep your fear from overtaking you.

My son, Chris, and I were dramatically reminded of this aspect of the wilderness on our last hike together, now many years ago. We had hiked all day and made camp at about seven thousand feet, between a pair of tiny alpine lakes, well above the timberline. From our campsite, we had an unobstructed view of the North Skokomish River valley and the entire range of foothills leading down to Hood Canal, a vista of over one thousand square miles.

A full moon rose early and high in the cloudless August sky, shining like daylight, but with a mysterious silvery hue, on the whole vast wilderness out there below us. I found the moonlit landscape entrancing and spiritually inspiring. Chris, then twelve years old, found it spooky and ominous.

I wanted to get away from the campsite, to find a solitary place to meditate in that magic, but Chris would not leave me alone and followed me wherever I went. He was afraid that a bear we had seen during the day might come back and eat him. Eventually, I gave up on the notion of meditation and, grudgingly, walked with him back to home base.

As we sat in the brilliant moonlight with a small candle lantern flickering before us for comfort, we began to hear something moving not far from the tent. Something heavy and slow. The candle flame was blinding us to the bright night, and we could not see well beyond its immediate light—but something was definitely out there.

Closer and closer it came, at an agonizingly methodical pace. We watched and listened, both of us feeling uneasy and alert as owls. Then it came into view, not ten feet from where we were sitting: a huge blacktail stag of regal bearing and uncompromised dignity, grazing the high alpine meadow in cover of darkness.

Our shared fear resolved into wonder, as Chris and I sat for another half hour or so watching that royal monarch meander around our shelter, checking us out and sampling the tough young shoots fostered by the nearby ponds. When the buck left, we went to bed and slept until dawn. That magical beast had raised both of us above our fantasies of hope and fear, and brought us face-to-face with a vision of real life that outstripped anything we might ever have imagined.

This story is, I think, a good reflection of what happens to each of us in our everyday lives. You and I, all of us, tend to miss the most magical parts of our lives out of fear and what psychologist Karen Horney calls "the tyranny of should."[1] That fear often comes from beyond our conscious knowing, as an unnoticed remnant of unresolved childhood pain or some such unexamined assumption. Our notions of how life should be, even in the realm of our spiritual ideals, may often actually keep us from experiencing the depths that real life has to offer. Sometimes the candle that we light for comfort blinds us to the magic of the night.

Yet there are moments when Life presents each of us with unforeseen opportunities to break through our preconceptions into a more immediate experience of being truly alive. Unexpectedly, we are faced with a situation that appears entirely unworkable, and we are forced to just sit down and look at things as they actually are, for better or for worse. How we choose to respond at times like these can make all the difference between living life unconsciously, in fear, or ascending to a new, higher vista of our true relationship with Life and with the Universe in which we live.

Those of us who choose to heed this call to the high country of our own lives will find ourselves embarked upon a deeply spiritual journey, in which we are challenged to reach beyond our given limits toward real, creative living. This personal quest for truth, and for a meaningful relationship to Life, is, in fact, at the very root of all enduring myth and religion. It demands that we learn how to face the unknown in ourselves and in the enormous Universe, and say "yes" to the life we were given—sorrow, loss, love, joy, and all.

In the Judeo-Christian tradition, to say yes to Life is to say yes to the will of Jehovah. In Islam to say yes is to yield to the will of Allah. Buddha's doctrine of acceptance of the world just as it is was a resounding yes to Life, in all its impermanence. Lao Tzu, the legendary Taoist sage, said yes to Life as an expression of the mysterious Tao, the Great Way, whose nature exceeds all formal understanding. The ancient Greeks and Romans said yes through their great mythologies and art and science. The Pagan way says yes to Life as Nature.[2]

Each of these traditions represents a vision of our Human place within the Universe which has survived the test of time, because they speak to an intrinsic Human need for meaning and self-understanding. They help define what it means to be wholly Human. They offer images of our proper relationship to Life, that act as signposts on the pathways of the high country of Life and Human Nature.

Spirit in the Modern Age

The high country of our Human Nature is that level of awareness at which we experience our essential selves as real and alive within the Universe. The ancient Chinese word for such an essence is "tao". When we let go of our conditioned ways of being and our fear of who we are, we automatically come to an unconditional acceptance of our own true natures. That is what we might call finding our own tao.

The concept of a personal tao includes the notion that the whole Universe has a certain essence, a universal Tao. The life force that moves in you is understood to be exactly the same Life force which regulates the orbits of the planets and of the countless galaxies through their own rhythmic cycles. Your Human Nature is seen as an intrinsic part of the natural Universe in which you live.

In modern times, however, both Life and Human Nature

seem to have become mere objects to the scientific eye. Life has become something we must conquer and control, whereas Human Nature has become something we must guide, train, and contain for our own good. All the cultures of the world are being melded into one by the vast reach of our technology and its global web of influence. The new icon of our age is now the artificial monolith: the skyscraper, the space shuttle, the nuclear reactor. Progress is our mantra.

Over the past five hundred years or so, the great religious myths and visions of the Human place in Life have all fallen from their high stations of leadership in the great cultures of the world. In their place has grown a more pragmatic, scientific view of our Human place in Life, a view that seems, at first impression, to lack the inspirational and religious tone necessary to elevate our vision of ourselves beyond the common plane.

Yet there *is* a vision of the natural unity of Life even within the objective perspectives offered by science. The language and the point of view have changed, but the Universe to which our modern science is devoting its attention remains the same, in essence, as the world rendered so poetically in the concept of the Tao. Signs of the Transcendent linger still.

Modern science tells us that the Universe exploded into being out of Nothingness with a Big Bang about fifteen billion years ago. According to this vision of Creation, the whole Universe as we know it began from a singular point so dense that even time and space were inseparably bound together. Before Creation, so our modern science theorizes, there were no such things as time or space or matter or energy: there was only a Formlessness of infinite potential, called a singularity. Everything that is came from this one point of creation. That includes you and me and everything else that ever lived. We are the distant relatives of stars. This is the Creation story of our modern scientific "myth."

Of course, this scenario suggests that there must have been some force or principle at work before anything came into existence. It demands, in fact, that there must be some sort of

Transcendent Law of Nature at work in the Universe: an effective force or principle that has existed since before the origin of time and space, and that still functions as an essential organizing principle for everything that is, including Life and Human Nature.

It is to this transcendent, unifying principle that the Chinese refer with the term Tao. From the ancient Taoist point of view, the Universe and everything in it exists as a dynamic flux of opposites in union—starting with the birth of all that is from Nothingness. They call these complementary opposites in union the yin and yang of things.

We can see the yin/yang dynamic of the transcendent Tao in everything our modern science has "discovered" about nature—in an uncanny sort of symmetry between matter and energy, particle and wave, time and space, the observer and that which is observed.

The essential principles of the transcendent appear, in fact, in all our sciences, even down to the union of the conscious and unconscious aspects of our psyche, which is the core concept of modern psychology. The Transcendent shows up everywhere, in both Life and Human Nature.

Thus, our modern science appears to be blazing its own trails toward the Transcendent, even though that may not be its conscious intention. Our very Human Nature seems driven to find new pathways to the higher truths of Life. The call of the high country rings forth in us, and we each must find an answer.

Every one of us, every Human being, is embarked upon a journey through the high country of Life and Human Nature simply by the fact that each of us is living and thus part of all that is.

Most of us will never even realize that we are on a journey of this kind. We will experience the hills and valleys of our lives as events that come to us from the "outside" world, never realizing how often our inner lives create the challenges with which we each are faced, or how those challenges might lift us to a higher point of view of our lives and of what it means to be Human in the Universe at large.

Our eyes closed, or fixed on our relatively tiny personal objectives, we may never think to question the true nature of Reality, or the relative reality of our own existence. Yet every compulsion and addiction, every love affair and passion, every hatred, fear, sorrow, and joy that we experience as Human beings reflects the nature of the entire Universe in which we live and calls to us to stop, look up, and make for higher ground.

The Universe in which we live is all of a piece. Everything that happens to each of us is happening to the Universe, although the impact of our lives is less than that of dust upon the ocean. Likewise, what happens to the Universe happens to us. The Universe is not somewhere "out there"; it is right in our front yards, in our living rooms, in our kitchens, in our very beings. There is no space where the Universe is not.

Thus, there are forces at work in each of us that are Universal. The gravity of every star and galaxy exerts a force upon us, and our bodies exert a pull on each other. What happens in our little worlds and on our lonely green planet is always and only a practice of the laws by which the whole Universe lives, all of a piece.

Yet there are also laws that transcend the entire Universe, from which the Universe itself was fashioned. The Universe came into being at some point, and there is a point at which it ceases to be; such are the laws of time and space. Before the Universe began, what? Where it ends, what beyond that? Something that is a Nothing; a Nothing that is the birth and the boundary of all that is. A Reality that transcends all that is, yet that gave birth to and sustains it.

Any name or image that pretends to contain or define such a Reality, such a Force, must fail or fall into illusion. The Transcendent, by definition, transcends all formal description and all reasonable definition. It is the Form of the Formless, the Divine, if you like. That is as far as Human minds can go. Yet the signs of the Transcendent are everywhere within the natural world, even within us. The Universe is its child, and we are the children of the Universe.

Thus, there are not only Universal laws of nature at work in our lives, but also Transcendent Laws of Nature. As Carl Jung has noted, there is even a Transcendent Function in the Human psyche, by which our perspectives on ourselves and our lives are naturally elevated beyond that of our isolated egos, through a catalytic union between our conscious awareness and our unconscious: a union of the opposites within us.

Both quantum physicists and ancient Taoist masters would agree with Jung. Wherever we attempt to see the subtle nature of our world, a union of opposites appears that transcends our limited, personal perspectives. The world contained within the Universe we see is not the real world in total.

From this point of view, anyone who accepts the world strictly as it appears to the conscious mind must certainly be seen as mistaken. There *is* a higher order to the world, and it is functioning in each of us at all times in our psyches and in our material realities. The questions are, can we muster the awareness to perceive that higher ground and will we give the effort that the journey there demands?

The trail of the Transcendent is everywhere. The high country of Human Nature is an ever-present part of that terrain. All we need do is to look for it, and the telltale unity of opposites presents itself to elevate our vision of the world in which we live beyond the confines of our isolated selves, into a realm of ultimate connectedness and innate, unified beauty.

We are about to embark, within the pages of this book, upon a trek of the psyche and soul, into the high country of Life and Human Nature, along a pathway of the modern age. This pathway is also of the spirit. As such, it will be home to many spiritual advisors and guides; a place of mystical awareness and real magic. Here, the spirits of high country travelers from ages past—from Carl Jung to Lao Tzu, from Freud to Buddha— are apt to appear and speak with us, as guides through their particular terrain. The things that these fellow travelers say to us within the pages of this book will not be quotes from some book they have written or from some speech in the long dead past, but accurate reflections of the "spirit" of their visions of the world.

Each of these and countless other trails into the high country of Life and Human Nature, both modern and of ages past, offers a slightly different perspective, depending upon its point of departure and its point of view. Yet they all are looking at the same terrain and often cross or come within sight of each other; and they all maintain essentially the same goal. This book simply offers a tour of one such pathway. If you would like to come along, welcome.

The unity of opposites is everywhere, and we can start our expedition from wherever we are: there is no place where the Transcendent is not. So, if you are ready, let us begin our extended expedition of the mind, into the high country of Life and Human Nature.

PART ONE
· · · · · · · · · · · · · · · · · ·
Yang

"Whatever is born, Arjuna,
whether it moves or it moves not,
know that it comes from
the union of the field and
the knower of the field."

Krishna
Bhagavad Gita
13:26

CHAPTER ONE

· · · · · · · · · · · · · · · · ·

A Union of Opposites: The Physics of Tao

Yang and yin are elemental principles of reality.
If you can discover the yang and yin of anything,
you will find its elemental nature.
You will find its "tao."

It is the last hour before sunrise. The moon has gone down and the dark is as dark as can be. We sit at base camp, awaiting enough daylight to travel. I nearly always begin in the dark when I trek into the high country. It seems to be simply the nature of the journey, considering the distance we must travel.

At any rate, it might be good to take a little time like this, before we start on the long journey before us, to check our gear and to think about where we are headed. Before we begin, therefore, I would like to offer a few tips from what I have learned in my years as a high-country traveler.

First of all, there really are spirits haunting the dark woods through which we each must pass on our way to the high country of our Human Nature. The malevolent spirits are fed by our fear; the helpful ones tease us to play as they dance in the trees. They often whisper things we should remember, and so it is good to bring a notebook or journal and to keep it handy.

Of course, it is wise to carry a good light into the high country. In the trip that we are about to start, our light is our awareness. Any preconceptions that might be attached to the way we see things will act as filters on that light, will color and dim everything we look at, making it difficult for us to move along. As time goes on, the sun will come up, adding another, more transcendent light to our quest.

We should take a moment now to clear our minds and adjust our assumptions. Appreciating the high country takes a sense of presence. Breathe in deeply the sweet forest air. The sun is coming up. It is time to get going.

The ground in the mountains is wetted with dew at sunrise, and the dead, fallen leaves yield perfumes as they feed the tall trees, which stand vibrant with life through the seasons. Up here, no loss is wasted, and nothing falls without purpose. Because this is so, the realm of nature will endure eons after all human culture has vanished.

These trees stand day and night in the forest, and live out their lives in the absolute rhythm of Nature. If we watch our breathing, we will find that it follows a natural rhythm as well, as it rolls in and out without ceasing. We breathe in the life of the space all around us, and we exhale a part of our physical being into the world. It connects us with Life in the same way the seasons do trees.

This understanding marks our first step toward the high country of our Human Nature. In this realm, the sweet scent of decaying leaves is not simply a pleasurable treat for the senses. It subtly evokes the miracle of transformation. Somehow, this rotting matter is turned into life in the tree. It transforms automatically into pure energy there, and in the sweet air we are breathing. The new leaves that glisten above us give off a constant supply of clean oxygen that we also take in and somehow metamorphosize into a human consciousness.

How does this happen?

As I look around at all the living things that surround us, a question insists itself upon my brain, like a light, steady breeze. It's worth a note in my field journal.

*Field note: Every living thing depends upon the nonliving
world for its life: on air, water, and the dead matter called
food. Question: At what point does the air that I breathe and
the water and food that I put in my body become part of me
and "alive"?*

I do not have an answer.

Yet this one simple query has moved us further still up the
trail toward the high country, for it brings into question the
whole of our natural world. We have transcended already the
everyday world as we see it from habit, and are now looking
down upon it from a different perspective.

A sense of electrical energy suffuses the entire atmosphere
as we begin to sense the world's intrinsic unity. The air is alive
with the crackle of static vitality, as though only awaiting
something to which to give its charge. Is this magic, or is it the
way real life is? Are we simply too dull and distracted in everyday
life to perceive this aliveness around us, or is something mystical
happening?

As I ponder these questions, the hairs on the back of my
neck begin to prickle up. I hear something rustling above me,
up in the trees. Then a creaky old voice.

"Hello, there. A very nice day for a hike, is it not?" comes
a voice from the sky. I look up, and to my amazement I spy a
small, aged Chinese man, who has somehow ascended a young
alder tree to the top.

The trunk of the tree at the point where he rests could not
be more that two inches thick, yet it seems to support him with
ease. He is chewing a strip of red cedar bark with gusto and
obvious delight. There is mischief and a mysterious depth in
his eyes. Who is he?

He takes the bark out of his mouth and leans forward,
toward us. As he does, the tree bends like a prayer to just above
head level. It seems certain the old man is going to fall and
break every bone in his thin body, but he remains unconcerned
and supremely relaxed as he lets himself down to the ground

soundlessly from about seven feet in the air. How did he do that?

"Oh, my new friends," he answers as though he can read our thoughts, "everything in the world supports everything else. Why should not this fine young tree support me, if I let it?"

Okay. But eating cedar bark?

"Things are not as they seem on the surface, my friends," the man says, apparently reading our minds once again as he pulls a half-finished woven cedar basket from out of nowhere. "Some things are made to be chewed but not necessarily swallowed. Don't swallow everything you chew on up here. You need to be discriminating. See what things are before making them yours." And with that advice he begins weaving the softened cedar bark into his sturdy ware.

We cannot be certain whether the old man is talking about plant life or ideas, but before we can answer he says, "Up here, in the high country, there is no clear boundary between the world and your idea of it. That is the fun of the place."

This is too much. I look at the alder once more, craning awkwardly to try to spot some device or gimmick that has let the old elf ply his balancing trick. He notices my incredulity right away, of course, and sets me straight with a kind, chiding air.

"Ah, the tree again. Yes, I see. You think this is some kind of magic or trick. Well, it is. And then again it is not. The Universe creating itself is magic. The rest is a question of balance." And with that the old trickster nimbly scales the alder again, so quickly and so straight that its leaves do not even quiver.

"Oh, oh, I am falling!" he says in mock terror as he leans just so slightly toward us once more, the tree bending in its obedience to physics beneath the slight weight of the man. Then he drops to the ground as before, and bends deeply in a bow as though grandly receiving applause.

"Allow me to introduce myself," he says calmly. "My name is Nu Lao Tzu. But you can call me Mr. Nu."

Nu Lao Tzu? How is that spelled? I wonder. Is it *Knew* Lao Tzu, or *New* Lao Tzu, or really just plain Mr. Nu?

"Spell it anyway you like," he says, although I have not said a thing. "Each suits me as well as another."

I recall various Taoist legends about masters who became so unified with the Tao that their personal life force can never be exhausted. It is said that some of them could fly and walk through walls. I suspect that this spry, ancient-looking man is one of those Taoist immortals. At any rate, he seems to speak in the general spirit of Lao Tzu himself, the original author of the *Tao Te Ching*.

He falls in with us just as naturally as though he had been with us from the start, although clearly he is more than a simple traveling companion. His eyes are calm, yet lively, and his breath and body smell of wildflowers and smoke. He has a lithe and sturdy way of carrying himself, as though his body knows before his mind does just where he might be headed. Clearly, Mr. Nu is in his element up here. He invites us to his cabin for some tea.

As we walk with the old man, a vaguely familiar trail opens up. It seems to parallel the trail we started on, but moves through an old-growth forest as ancient as any I've seen. "Come on," says Nu Lao Tzu. "I know a shortcut." It seems that we are off on an adventure.

A Cup of Tao

Old-growth timber of some foreign variety impinges the edge of the trail as it meanders through the thick forest. This trail must be extremely old. Even the youngest of these trees seem ancient.

Every now and then we pass spur trails, some of which seem to lead toward our modern route, but they are all marked with weathered signs, hand-lettered in Chinese and they give me no clue as to where we are headed. The only thing that seems certain is that we are rapidly gaining altitude.

With every step further along this pathway, that vague yet inspiring experience of the unity of nature with which we began our day's journey is becoming more clear and specific. I notice it first in the rhythm and balance of walking: the way that we swing between our left and our right legs without ever breaking our stride. Also, the trees seem to strain straighter upward, as though to draw our attention to the fact that they, too, are balancing acts of the opposites: earth-diving roots and sky-clambering branches. The world seems to sing with a specific rhythm that I had not noticed before, swinging into and out of itself.

"This place was once known as the Spirit of the Valley," Mr. Nu says as we walk.[1] "This is the most ancient of trails, where the first yin and yang were discovered. Everything here now is filled with that Spirit."

Here, the sky appears to reach to the ground where we walk, filtering seamlessly through the limbs of the trees. Where does space end and objects begin? I look at the bright, sunlit sky, at the vast "empty" space up above, and suddenly spy a white crescent moon in the blue. Day and night in seamless and yet ever-changing union. It is as though the very Universe has opened up to us, displaying its heartbeat, its own ancient core.

At first, I find this dance entrancing and exciting, but as we move more deeply into this terrain of thought, it becomes confusing. The trees, unions of opposites themselves, come to appear as appendages of the Earth, which itself becomes a mere object in space, so that there is no absolute down or up for the roots of trees and their branches to point to. The rhythm of these opposites in union soon becomes entirely unmanageable, as the once simple relationships appear to overlap and extend into infinite space.

By the time we reach Mr. Nu's cabin, I am feeling a little confused (a common form of high-country altitude sickness). As a modern, Western thinker, I am used to seeing things in terms of constant, objective relationships. Up here, there appear to be none.

As we sit on a few small, hard benches in front of Mr. Nu's cabin, the morning sun shines upon us through the trees. The old man offers us empty cups, and then settles with a sigh into a little chair near our benches. Has he forgotten our tea? I look at my cup, wondering. Mr. Nu begins sipping at his empty cup with savor. What is he up to now?

"Ah," he says, satisfied. "A perfectly good cup of Tao." He holds up his cup and admires it. He moves the cup slowly in circles, as though it were filled with precious liquid and he was a connoisseur describing the essential components of a fine wine or tea. He glances at us mischievously, as though he knows what we are thinking. He seems to have an uncanny range of intuition. Or perhaps he has hosted so many travelers that he knows all the questions by heart. At any rate, what he says next goes right to the core of the issue for me.

"The whole Universe is in this cup. The whole Tao," the old man declares as he continues to slowly turn the cup. Then he shows us the inside of his cup, almost like a magician about to do magic.

"The inside of the cup is yin. It is in shadow. Its nature is receptive. It holds things and keeps them in a constant state. It is deep, its exact shape is difficult to determine, and so it is also subtle.

"The outside of the cup is yang. It is bright compared with the yin inside. Its nature is to contain the inside by remaining firm against all other forces. The inside moves inward. But the outside moves outward. It is the handle by which the inside is made usable. It is the outer form of the cup that determines the shape of the inside.

"The two, yin and yang, seem so different in nature, yet together they create the tao of 'cup.'"

Like most of us, I have heard of the terms used in similar ways in the past. Still, Mr. Nu's object lesson seems worth a note in my book. Since we are taking a break anyway, I dig out my journal and make a few sketches to help me remember the main points.

Field note: Yin is the subtle, receptive quality; yang is the firm, the directive force. You can't have one without the other. Together, they make up the tao of things.

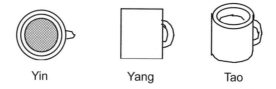

Yin   Yang   Tao

Question: At what point does the yang of the cup become yin?

"At the lip," says the old man, who has somehow slipped up behind me without notice. "The lip of the cup is its mystery. The lip of the cup is the secret of tao. How can opposites become united, and where does one end and the other begin? No one knows, and not even the most precise measurement can find the answer."

A little disgruntled, I write in the margin:

The lip of the cup is an area of ambiguity.

"Aha! Very good!" Mr. Nu exclaims. "You are very good with names, you modern folk. Yes! Area of ambiguity. I like that very much. We Easterners say only 'realm of don't know,' but I like area of ambiguity. Very scientific!"

I suspect Mr. Nu is making fun of me, but I can't be sure. The fact is, I, too, like the term, because it takes the pressure off trying to define yin and yang as facts or objective concepts. After all, where *is* the point at which the roots of trees leave off and become trunk, or trunk becomes limbs? Where does the air that we breath in leave off and become our life's blood, or that blood change into consciousness?

"Yin and yang are not facts," the old man explains patiently. "They can never be defined with boundaries. They are elemental principles of Reality. Everything that is has yin and yang in it, and exists as yin or yang in its relationship to the rest of the Universe.

"If you can discover the yang and yin of anything, you will find its elemental nature. You will find its 'tao.'"[2]

With that, the kettle begins to whistle from inside Mr. Nu's cabin, and he gets up to make our tea. He returns in moments with an old ceramic pot in hand. As he pours, he makes his point.

"Now, the tea is yin to the whole cup, which is yang by relationship. But the cup itself was yin to its maker. Yin and yang are not facts, they are ideas about relationship — the primal relationships that make up the created Tao. Ultimately, relationship is not about things in themselves, but about the space between."

This gives me pause. We sit and drink our tea in silence, the ancient realm of nature standing testament to what the old man has said. The sun begins to crest the nearest hill, and sheds light everywhere. At length, Mr. Nu speaks.

"You know, your own science myth is very wise in this way. It speaks of the Universe beginning in a state of perfect symmetry, like the water of a warm, still pond: everything just part of everything else with no divisions. There was no space between anything: everything just pure potential. I think you call it singularity.

"Then, bang! Everything comes into being by expanding, making space between things. Like when, in deep winter, pond water freezes into so many crystals.[3] Everything breaks into not quite perfect symmetries, just slightly off balance so that everything keeps moving and moving. Very Taoist," he adds, nodding his head in evident contemplation.[4]

How does this small, ancient man know about quantum physics? Surprised, I ask him.

"Oh, those guys?" he replies. "Those physicists? They come up here all the time!

"They really crack me up, too. Sometimes they talk like they discovered the Universe. Like everyone in China just wandered around looking at the ground for seven thousand years!

"Ha! Very funny." He chuckles, slapping a knee. "Oh, but

very smart, too," he adds, almost in consolation, as though being careful not to offend us.

"Come with me," he says, rising from his chair and setting off up the path. "I will take you back to your own path and you will see." And with that we are off again, leaving our tea cups behind and taking a spur that, unlike the dark, wandering trail of Lao Tzu, cuts straight through the forest to its destination.

Echo Ridge: Tales of the Transcendent

It seems that, for Mr. Nu, the *discoveries* of modern science appear simply as the latest mythic image of a Universe whose true nature can never be captured by the mind. The way he talks, we might think that modern science has been studying Tao all along and simply has not yet noticed. He seems quite amused at what we modern folk find amazing and surprising about the nature of Reality as it appears up here, on the borders of the high country. From his perspective, the unity of All That Is seems completely self-evident in nature, and obviously can never be captured in concepts or objective images.

I have to admit that he seems to have a point. Everything I know about the scientific view and modern thought points toward their unavoidable collision with the unformed and the uncertain. We can describe what things look like, but we can never speak directly to their innermost nature. Whenever we get close to the essential truth about the Universe we see, we seem to lose the trail and can only stand in awe. I make a note.

Field note: Science doesn't really explain anything. It can only describe what it sees. How do you explain a tree? According to science, the original nature of All That Is rests in a No-thingness before time began: no separate 'things' at all; perfect symmetry.

Every thing science "explains" refers, ultimately, to that No-thingness. Once science gets to that point, it starts talking in metaphor.

Oddly enough, as soon as I write this, the trail we have

been traveling brings us to the very edge of a sheer drop-off. Far below, thousands of square miles of ancient, twisting canyon spread out before us. Its source and its eventual destination lay somewhere beyond our view, so vast and archaic is its construction. The canyon's rock walls, untold ages old, are covered with what appear to be petroglyphs from the ancient religions and myths of the world. There are huge mythic beasts, sun gods, mythic heroes, and cabalistic signs that we cannot interpret.

The vast canyon echoes with whispering hymns of creation from ages past, all mingled together like the currents of the wind, or of the breath of time. One thing is singularly clear: we have come to the edge of the world that can be seen by reason and thinking alone.

On the rock face nearest us are more recently carved symbols and images, evidently left by modern-day travelers. Many of these images are inscribed with signatures I recognize: Stephen Hawking, Fritjof Capra, Heinz Pagels, and Gary Zukav, to name just a few. Each symbol and image points to some truth beyond what it can literally convey. Each speaks the language of metaphor and of pure symbol—the timeless tools of myth, of the science myth.

Some of the images are in the form of equations, which mean nothing to us. Others, I recognize. One image in particular enthralls me. I recognize it as a Feynman diagram of what is called a "virtual particle." I copy it into my notebook.

Field note: A Feynman diagram illustrating how a virtual particle known as a pion (π) arises from and returns to a nucleon (n) without altering the nucleon at all.

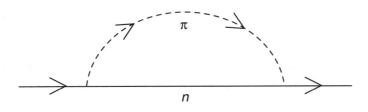

Virtual particles are actually the forces whereby "real" particles repel and attract each other. I remember reading about them in Capra's *Tao of Physics*. Like most types of energy at the quantum level of physical reality, virtual particles are forces that look like forms, energy that looks like matter. Opposites in union.

What is really interesting about virtual particles, though, is that they travel such short distances, appear so briefly, and move so quickly that they exceed the energy conservation laws of sub–light-speed physics. They use up no mass or energy when they leave the parent "real" particle, and add no mass or energy when they return. That is to say, they literally create their own existence out of nothing.[5] In this sense, they can serve as a sort of primary symbol for the transcendent nature of Reality as a whole. We could even use it as a map to the high country.

"Ah yes," says our guide with real admiration as he peeks at what I have drawn in my journal. "This is a very good picture of 'All That Is.'

"Every thing arises from Tao and has no real form of its own at all, yet every thing seems so real when we look at it. But nothing is separate from any thing else."

I smile at his innocence. "Actually, it's a diagram of a virtual particle," I reply a little patronizingly.

"Actually, it is a picture of *you*," responds the man, smiling oddly.

I pass off his comment without too much thought, and the old man's smile vanishes as if it were a mirage. He takes on a look of such focused intensity that he frightens me to my very bones. Mr. Nu's voice is suddenly cool and solid as wet rock.

"Do you believe somehow that the appearance of every single separate form in the entire Universe is an illusion except the image you have of your own self?" His stare pierces me.

When I do not answer, he leans closer, so close that I can feel his breath against my face. "Do you? Do you really think that? This self that you forget you carry with you everywhere, do you think that it alone in all the Universe is not a 'virtual' reality?"

I step back, desperate for some distance from that stare. If I am not real, how can he be talking to me? How can I be feeling his sweet breath upon my face? Why is he pushing me this way?

Another step back, and the ground begins to give way beneath me altogether. The truth of the old man's words has me by the gut, but I am fighting hard against it. Teetering at the edge of the cliff behind me, I struggle for my balance and begin to fall. Everyone seems awestruck at what is happening, paralyzed by this sudden turn of events, and unable to react quickly enough to save me.

"Help!" I scream, barely catching hold of a root that protrudes from the bank. "Help me!" I scream again, my body dangling above the canyon abyss.

But Mr. Nu just stands there, surprised as I am, and looking at me in an odd way, as though curious to see what is going to happen to me next. He disappears for a moment, while others in our group stand nearby and call words of encouragement. A moment later, Mr. Nu reappears with rope in hand, but he makes no move to drop it to me.

Terrified, I cannot bring myself to look down. I just want up, but I am losing my grip. I want out of here!

"Let go," the old man says to me. "What are you holding on for?"

Is he *crazy*? Is he *evil*? Is he, after all, one of the dark spirits of the deep woods?

"Let go," he says again. "What are you holding on for?"

"Stop *saying* that!" I scream, wailing, certain I am about to die. "I'm holding on to life, you idiot. I'm going to die."

"You are in illusion," he says matter of factly, as he backs away. The crazy old man backs away! My grip is almost gone. I know that I will have to let go soon. So I do, accepting, for a fleeting instant, what Life has allotted me.

With one last wail, I fall—a full four feet onto a rock ledge below.

Mr. Nu looks down at me. I am crumpled on the ledge, panting with exhaustion.

"What were you hanging on for?" Mr. Nu asks for the third time, appearing truly puzzled. "I could not throw this rope to you until your hands were free to catch it. Here. Catch."

He drops the rope down. I catch it as it swings through the air and I climb up. Shaken, I rest on the cliff side, feeling embarrassed and sullen. Some of my fellow travelers gather round to make sure I'm okay, but I don't want to talk to anyone right now. Mr. Nu sits with me a while before he speaks again.

"What were you so afraid of?" he asks.

"I thought I was going to fall and *die!*" I answer him, incredulous.

"Then, it was your imagination that so frightened you?" he asks, calm as ever.

"No," I answer indignantly.

"Well, then, did you die?" He is smiling now.

"No," I answer again, really getting angry.

"Your fear, my friend, was caused by your idea of the situation, not by the reality of it. If you had looked closely at the situation, you would have been able to let go and not have to go through all this."

"Oh really? And what if there had been no ledge and I actually died?"

"I do not know. Do you? Have you ever fallen to your death before?"

"Not that I recall," I answer facetiously.

"Then I still maintain that your fear was a product of your own imagination." With that he rises and walks away.

"What do you *mean?*" I call to him, in anger and frustration, just before he walks out of earshot.

He walks back my way. "My friend, everything that is yet to happen is real only in our idea of it. Everything that happened in the past is real only in our attitude toward it. Everything that is actual and real passes before we can think or feel about it at all. Only the present is real, and it cannot be held to any kind of form."

Still hurt and feeling ashamed of my own panic, I want to rail against the old man's philosophizing. But I cannot. We have all seen that the world of separate forms is an illusion, even in the eyes of modern science. I cannot concede, however, that I, also, am unreal.

"The person that you believe yourself to be is not the true self," our guide responds. "The world that you believe you know is not the real world. Both are only virtual realities, exactly like the particle you drew a while ago."

Mr. Nu turns up the trail and points out a high mountain range that I had not noticed before. He looks at each person in our hiking party, one by one, making certain that everyone listens to what he is about to say. My fall has sobered us all, and everyone's eyes are on our aged leader.

"The entire range of human awareness is right in front of you," he says gravely. "Beyond it rests the high plateau of real life. If you would like to go there and you are willing to face whatever you must face, then I can show the way. It is up to you."

CHAPTER TWO

. . . .

Meaningful Perception:
The Self as Process

The apparent world of separate things
is ultimately an illusion.
Human beings create the world of form
through their conscious awareness of it.
Otherwise, the Universe is whole, complete,
and undivided as to separate things.

If I am not who I perceive myself to be, who or what am I?
This ancient question seems to echo down the canyon of the
ages. It is a question that every one of us must answer for
ourselves if we are ever to get beyond our own projected image
of the world and into some kind of higher truth. It is up to
each of us, alone, to decide whether we will face our fear and
forge into the unknown in our lives.

I know that some of us have already decided on our course
before the question arises. Some force inside of us is pushing
us toward a higher vista on our lives, and so, without much
hesitation, we fall in with Mr. Nu as he moves up the trail, toward
the true high country of our Human Nature.

Some of our party, however, may not accompany us any
further, preferring not to risk the treasured insights they have
gained thus far, or feeling the need to rest and get acclimated to

the heights before they move on. Such a decision is intensely personal. It does not mean the journey has ended. Each one of us will find our way into our own high country in good time, one way or another. It is enough that some of us have chosen to move on.

As we leave the security of the world that we tend to accept as real in and of itself, the question of our personal identity becomes more urgent. If the whole world, including us, is not the dance of separate forms that we perceive, then what is it? And what are we? Is there no formal reality to us as individuals at all?

As usual, our aged guide appears to sense these questions before anyone can voice them. As though by way of a response, he directs our attention to where we are, right here, right now.

"Right now, we are leaving Echo Ridge and crossing the borderland between the perceived Universe and the Human perceiver," Mr. Nu points out as we move on together. "This realm is very interesting. This is where Human Nature itself begins—in the act of perceiving.

"Think about it. You each are only your experience of being. Imagine you had no experience of being at all. What if your body did not respond to its own inner perceptions, your brain did not perceive anything, your consciousness was wiped out? What are you then?" The answer seems so obvious that no one ventures to speak. There is just silence and a mild breeze over our ears, as we hike across this meadow toward the distant mountain range. Complete silence.

"Very good. That is right! You are dead. Why? Because people are really only their experience of being. You *are* your awareness."

This seems difficult to take in at first. We think of ourselves as *beings* not *seeings*. Yet we cannot argue with his logic: being dead is defined by the apparent lack of awareness on normal Human levels. Indeed, a major question in modern science is, *how* dead is dead? We have "dead" people living for years on respirators and with the aid of intravenous feeding tubes. Their bodies continue to operate on their internal sensitivities to blood pressure, heart rhythm, and other physical functions. So a lot of people think of them as (potentially) living. It is only when the body loses even its most basic awareness, and ceases to respond effectively within its own closed system, that the person is considered *really* dead.

As we contemplate the truth of what Mr. Nu has said, we each become keenly aware of our breathing and of the movement of our bodies. No one speaks, and the sound of our feet shuffling along the trail reminds us of the transience of our lives. How tenuous our existence is, hanging as it does by the thin thread of consciousness.

This understanding moves us quickly up the path toward the mountain range before us. Soon, we are standing at its foothills, surveying the four main formations that make up the range. As we look around, we notice that a great many paths converge here, each attempting its own route through the terrain. Some of the trails are old and well worn. Some are barely used any more. A few, like the one that we are on, are fairly new.

"These mountains are very old," Mr. Nu says. "The Buddha called them the 'Four Foundations of Mindfulness,' because they represent the four realms of conscious Human awareness that must be mastered in order to attain enlightenment."

Mr. Nu points from one peak to the next, as he continues. "Buddha referred to them as awareness of *the mind and thoughts*; awareness of *the heart and feelings*; awareness of *the body and senses*; and awareness of *the subtle principles of life*," he says, pointing to each peak in turn.[1]

"These days you just call them *Thinking, Feeling, Sensation,* and *Intuition*. But they are still the same things that they always were. They are the four ways of seeing by which we Human beings create and perceive the world of separate forms.

"The four modern names were Carl Jung's idea. I do not think he realized that Gautama had already named them. Still, I think the new names are okay because they make the whole thing easier to talk about.

"Personally, I would never have thought to bother with names at all, but now I think it is a good idea," the old man continues as we walk.

Although I find the formations that Mr. Nu is pointing to quite interesting, I can't concentrate on what he is saying. I have to interrupt. "Do you mean to say that you know Carl Jung? Carl Gustav Jung?" I ask, excitedly.

"Yes, Carl Gustav Jung. You know him, too?" Mr. Nu answers innocently. "He spent his whole life up here, mostly. In fact, he is still here in spirit. You want to meet him? Let's see if he's around," Mr. Nu says, scanning the horizon.

"Hey, Carl!" The old man calls with surprising force. "Hey Carl, you still up here?"

Hardly a moment passes before we hear a response.

"Yes, yes, of course I am still up here. Where else would I go, you old Taoist ninny?" A voice in a clear, brusque Swiss clip resounds from nowhere.

For a moment, I wonder whether this "spirit of Jung" will really only be that—a disembodied voice. That would be okay, but I was really hoping Carl Jung might join us, maybe even give us a tour of the Range of Human Awareness. After all, this is the terrain he made famous.

"So you want a tour," the voice calls again. Shivers run down my spine. Whoever is speaking—Carl Jung or not— appears to be reading my mind just like our Mr. Nu seems to do. I look more closely in the direction from which the voice originates. Sure enough, a man appears in the distance: a stout figure saunters down the trail toward us. He is smoking a black pipe from which streams a thin wisp of white smoke. With his white mustache, wire-rimmed glasses, and piercing eyes, he certainly looks like Carl Jung.

He stops and waits for us, leaning into his walking stick, which is carved with archaic designs. He seems totally unhurried and apparently at home here, in the high terrain. When we reach him, all he says is, "Come along, then," and he turns up the trail without ceremony. As we follow the man into his famous stomping grounds, he and Mr. Nu take the lead, laughing and talking like old friends.

Carl Jung and the Tao of Conscious Awareness

The mountain air is thickened by the smell of cavendish and peppermint, as the mid-morning sun starts to peek through the tops of the trees. As we draw near to the first of the four main formations in the Range of Human Awareness, I notice a change in my own awareness. My rational mind becomes keen and unusually active. What is going on here? I wonder.

The foremost of the four peaks seems to rise above all the others, as though it bears no direct relation to the world below. It seems wholly abstracted from the natural lay of the land, though it clearly arises from the same range as the other three peaks. Its rigid, angular shape is intriguing, indeed, thought provoking.

My mind begins rattling with all kinds of highly abstract speculations, thoughts wholly detached from the basic reality of our actual situation. I find myself in the grip of a series of deep philosophical questions. The weight of the questions begins slowing me down. That's when I notice that everyone else seems to be weighted down now as well.

When Mr. Nu and Carl Jung notice our pained expressions, they turn to each other like two wrinkled twins and wink. "Thinking!" they declare in unison.

They turn from us to the jagged formation that has captured our conscious attention. "Oh," I say, sheepishly, a little embarrassed at my own self-seriousness. Yeah, I get it. "Thinking."

Neither Jung nor Mr. Nu seems interested in making a big deal of my total absorption in this one peak, though. They are more interested in the lay of the entire range.

"Thinking tells us *what* a thing is," the good doctor explains. "Thinking is a psychological response to the world that we perceive whereby we organize and *quantify* our sense perceptions. It is not, of course, as direct a means of perception as, say, physical sensing, but operates in coordination with the senses to create our human vision of the world, in the form of ideas."[2]

Then he directs his gaze, and our attention, to the next peak over. Its shape is more rounded than that of the first, but it shares Thinking's abstract appearance. This peak must be the one named Feeling, I surmise.

"Feeling is in some ways similar to thinking, in that it, too, is an abstraction of our direct experience," Jung says, confirming my hunch.

"Your embarrassment on being caught up in your thoughts just now," he continues as he turns his attention toward me, "had a certain 'abstracted' quality, in that it referred to a personal *evaluation* of your own perception—what I would call a 'feeling tone' style of perception. Feelings tell us *how* things are."

While some of us might like to linger here, entranced by the realm of pure feeling, Jung and Mr. Nu keep moving. They know better than to become too enamored with any one aspect of conscious awareness. We follow their lead.

As we draw nearer still to the vast range before us, I scan the four peaks in an effort to regain my bearings and to understand more clearly the concepts that Jung is offering. I can see literally what Jung has been saying: how the aspects of conscious awareness known as thinking and feeling seem to stand out from the other two peaks, Sensation and Intuition.

As I gaze at the vast range before us, Mr. Nu sidles up to me and whispers conspiratorially. "Do not mind Carl. He still wants to make a science out of all of this. He does not like the notion that his science is also a myth."

Mr. Nu's comment irritates me. This is Carl Jung he's talking about, one of the great minds of the twentieth century. I want to defend Jung, but I restrain myself. I realize that I am experiencing an emotional reaction to a rational statement. I try to calm down.

I take a moment to think about what Nu has just said, and I realize that Mr. Nu might well be right in his assessment of Jung's blind spot, considering what we saw back at Mr. Nu's cabin: how the Universe actually exists as an unbroken whole, and how our ideas about Reality—even Jung's great ideas—are essentially myths that can never describe the true nature of Life. I don't like to admit it, because Carl Jung has been one of my personal heroes, but I manage to think better of my own emotional response to Mr. Nu's comment and so regain control of my feelings.

"Very good!" Nu Lao Tzu offers in congratulations. "You got it!"

Got what?

"You have understood that you can create and direct your own experience of Reality in thought and feeling! That is very important," he says, raising his eyebrows and nodding his head in exaggerated excitement.

Jung has chosen to ignore Nu Lao Tzu's theatrics, and has moved on to the next function of our conscious awareness, sensation. I hurry to catch up with him and the rest of the group. I get there just as Jung is describing the next peak.

"Our physical senses can only tell us *that* a thing is," Jung says, as he points out the third peak in the range. "Our senses receive information in a more immediate manner than do thinking and feeling, responding to whatever presents itself to be perceived. But they cannot manipulate that information.

"Physical sensing is much more immediate a form of perception than is thinking or feeling, although without it we might not have much to feel or to think about."

The peaks of the Range of Human Awareness loom over us now. They seem so close that we could touch them. The three peaks that Jung has described—Thinking, Feeling, and Sensation—create a sort of descending ridge, each peak progressively more "down to earth," and thus more in direct contact with the realities of the whole realm, than the one that precedes it. Clearly, thinking and feeling are two of a kind, in that they are more "directive" perceptual modes, although feeling is not quite as removed from the general terrain as is thinking. Then comes physical sensing and then…what?

"Intuition!" Jung and Mr. Nu shout in unison, although I had not said a thing, yet. How do they do that—answer my questions before I've even voiced them?

"Intuition!" they repeat. Again, I find myself becoming a bit irritated with them, but Mr. Nu apparently has had enough of my ill temper. He locks onto me with that steely stare of his and walks sternly toward me.

"Do you still think all of this is some kind of a magic act?" he asks, as though he can hardly believe anyone could be so dense. For a moment he seems stumped as to how he might get his point through to me. Suddenly, he brightens up. All trace of his own irritation has vanished. "Do you know anything about jazz?" he asks, twiddling his fingers as though playing "air sax."

At first I am too stunned that the old elf has even heard of jazz to answer. Fortunately, I regain my senses before I really insult him. Naturally, there must have been many great jazz musicians who found their way into the high country on their own paths, but "yes" is all I can manage to say in reply.

"Well," Mr. Nu continues, barely giving me time to voice even that thought, "do you think that jazz musicians *think* the notes before they *play* them?

"Of course not," he answers for me. "Who could think that fast? They play from a more subtle knowing—from intuition, that subtlest, most mysterious and receptive of all points in the Range of Human Awareness."

Jung nods in agreement, stepping forward to add his own insights on this, his favorite aspect of conscious awareness.

"That is why I have called intuition the *instinctive* function of conscious awareness," Jung adds, draping a fatherly arm over my shoulder. "Intuition is capable of grasping whole situations all at once, and of producing quite spontaneous understandings in the form of inspirations or just common hunches. You cannot conjure up an intuition like you can a thought or feeling, but intuition is a very active part of Human Nature. It functions all the time in our dreams, in our creative acts, and even in our personal relationships."

I must admit, intuition is just as much part of the way I experience life as is any of the other functions of conscious awareness. I might not be aware of it as much as I am the others, but that may be because it is so subtle and ubiquitous. I am deeply impressed by the wide Range of Human Awareness that somehow functions as a unit to create the Human experience of being. What a vista!

As Jung and I stand side by side, admiring the view before us, Mr. Nu gets an impish gleam in his eye, and whisks Jung's fancy walking stick out of his hand. He waves it as though it were a magic wand, in a broad sweeping motion, toward the vast range before us.

"These four ways of seeing make up the tao of our conscious awareness," says old Nu in a hushed tone of wonder and awe.

He is still teasing me, but I can see that he also wants me to understand something important. "Thinking and feeling are more directive, more yang, than are sensing and intuition, which are much more yin, or receptive, in nature," he says, as he turns to face me. "Do you see?"

Yes, I finally get it, I think. Intuition and physical sensing tend to see things as they *are*. Feeling and thinking tend to speak of how we *prefer* them to be and how we *think* of them. Intuition and physical sensing give us visions *of* the world. Feeling and thinking give us visions *about* the world.

It occurs to me, however, that there is also a yin/yang dynamic between thinking and feeling, and between sensing and intuition. That is when I start getting my high country sickness (confusion). I need to write this stuff down.

Field note: If intuition and physical sensation are the yin of our conscious awareness, then feeling and thinking are the yang. Yet intuition is more yin than any other mode of conscious awareness, and thinking is the most yang in character. This creates a yin/yang dynamic even within the receptive and directive modes of conscious awareness.

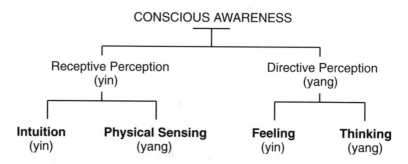

CONSCIOUS AWARENESS

Receptive Perception
(yin)

Directive Perception
(yang)

Intuition
(yin)

Physical Sensing
(yang)

Feeling
(yin)

Thinking
(yang)

"Hey, nice chart!" exclaims Mr. Nu as he peers over my shoulder, standing on tiptoe like a kid at the circus. "You have drawn the yin and yang in Human Nature. But remember, yin and yang are not facts. They are elementary relationships. So even yang elements will have both yin and yang aspects to them. All the yin and yang you have here, in this chart, is part of one big yang. It plays the part of the Creative in our Human Awareness. These four ways of seeing *create* the world as it appears to our conscious human mind."

Mr. Nu moves on, leaving me to ponder what he has said. I realize that I may be falling behind our leaders, but I am not the only one. The creative nature of our human awareness is something we all seem to have trouble keeping in mind.

Yet we have seen for ourselves that the world of separate forms that we think of as real is, in part at least, a creation of our own perceptual limitations. The real Universe is one seamless whole; we just can't see it all. We cannot see the energy everything gives off, or the microwaves, radio waves, and innumerable other energies that unceasingly move through us and through the entire Universe. If we could, the world would look like the static-filled screen of a TV that doesn't have an antenna. Yet we are so accustomed to assuming the objective nature of the world that we have to be reminded that the world we see is not, in essence, the world as it really is. I make a note.

Field note: Our conscious awareness creates a world of form for us from the seamless web of being that is the real

Universe. Conscious awareness is the creative "yang"of
Human perception: the form—making aspect of our Human
existence.

I am beginning to see more clearly what old Mr. Nu was trying to tell me back at the cliffs of Echo Ridge, when I was hanging onto that tree root for dear life. My conscious awareness creates all kinds of images out of the universal flow of Life. It no doubt even creates the *self*–image that I tend to think of as the true and real me. Yet I am much more than the image that I have of myself, and the Universe is so much more than that which I can see.

I can see now that it was not my literal death that Mr. Nu was trying to get me to face. It was the death of my self-image, and of my preformed idea of the world. Perhaps that is really what we all fear most—the death of who we think we are, and the loss of a way of life that we have come to cling to as an idealized image in our minds.

Clearly, Reality is always something more than the apparent forms that we perceive. Inside the realm of yang and the apparent is always the more subtle realm of yin, the realm of the receptive, which sustains the outer world of form. Thus, even in our Human Nature, there must be a yin aspect to balance and sustain the yang of our conscious awareness.

This yin realm, however, is nowhere to be seen among the formations which make up our conscious awareness. Indeed, there seem to be several pathways in the high country of Human Nature that end right here. They seem to assume that all we are is our conscious awareness and that life should be lived solely on the basis of what can be seen, touched, understood through reason, or in some way given form.

Many of these trails lead straight up to the top of one or another of the great peaks of conscious awareness, proclaiming pure reason, pure ecstasy, pure passion, or pure intuitive vision as the ultimate of human experience. The problem with these pathways, of course, is that they all lead right back down again.

They do not take us through the whole terrain of our Human being, but only up to one peak experience or another, and then return us neatly to our starting place. They are trails made for tourists.

Yet everything that we have seen as true of real life so far suggests that there *must* be something more to the Range of Human Awareness than only these four formations. Every step along the way up to this point has demanded a right foot *and* a left, an outside *and* an inside—for every yang, there is always a yin.

And so the questions come up automatically, as we push on into the great depths of the vast range known as Conscious Awareness: What is the "big yin" of our Human Nature? What is the subtle, "aformal" aspect of Awareness, of our innate Human being?

Nonconscious Awareness: The Space between Things

It seems clear to the entire group that, despite the attractiveness of shorter trails, the only way for us to gain a truly panoramic perspective on our own nature is to thoroughly explore the entire range of our awareness. We cannot learn what we need to know by climbing *over* this range, as other trails appear to do. We must find our way *into* the heart of this terrain.

We need now to find our way through the subtle valleys, not to the high peaks, of our Human Awareness. The path that we must choose, therefore, is one that will allow us to explore the space *between* the various peaks that make up the Range of Human Awareness. This trail needs to take us through the core of our Human Awareness. We all know that such a journey will be difficult and dangerous, dark with heavy mists and shadows; but we must face whatever we find along the way if we are ever to reach real life.

Before we even get to the first valley, however, at the base of that jagged peak known as Thinking, we come upon something so unexpected none of us could have predicted it. In a clearing up the trail from us stands Mr. Nu, wearing a small pair of dark-rimmed spectacles and sporting a fake goatee. He is reading a book. As we cluster around him we realize that it is *A General Introduction to Psychoanalysis*, by Sigmund Freud, and that the book is upside down. The odd little man appears oblivious to this fact, as he scans the pages with exaggerated dignity.

When Jung sees Mr. Nu performing this charade, he cracks up altogether, but manages to pull himself together and seat himself on a nearby log. Shaking his head in disbelief, he buries his face in both his hands. "Oh Nu!" is all he can say.

Mr. Nu is unperturbed and launches into a lecture that obviously is intended to mimic Freud himself.

"An idea that is pr-r-resent in my mind," he begins, trilling his *r*'s and speaking a strange accent halfway between Chinese and German, "may diz-appear and then r-r-return again, as one might say, by memory. But where did the idea go that I forgot and then r-r-r-remembered? We must az-zume that it was somehow *latent* in my consciousness. That is to z-zay that it was 'unconscious.' Thus, ideas and feelings and sensations and so forth that are pr-r-resent in us but of which we are unaware may all be called unconscious."[3]

Having given us a very broad hint of our next lesson about Human Awareness, Mr. Nu snaps the book shut, tucks it under his arm, and heads up the trail, disappearing down the path, into the dark valley beyond. Jung looks mortified—as much, apparently, at himself for finding the impression funny as at Nu Lao Tzu for his performance. He tries to set things straight with us by giving his old mentor, Sigmund Freud, his due.

"Before Freud," he explains to us, "there had never in the history of human thought been so precise and practical a vision of the unconscious aspects of the human mind. It was he who recognized that the unconscious exists as a real and active aspect of the psyche, whose function it is to store and to retrieve what he called the latent contents of our awareness.

"Freud discovered that the unconscious speaks through a process of association—in the latent meanings of our dreams, and in the metaphoric images of what we used to call hysterical reactions, but that are now more generally referred to as neurosis in all its diverse forms."[4]

What Jung seems to be describing is actually a nonconscious awareness; not the unconscious as a vast wasteland, but as an "aformal" realm of pure potential similar to the "Nothingness" from which our Universe blossomed at the Big Bang.

This notion is roiling around in my brain as we begin to move once more toward this first fog-laden valley, a difficult pass between Thinking and Feeling. Realizations and memories begin coming to my mind from "nowhere," tingled up into conscious awareness by thoughts and feelings that bear association to them. I think I am getting the picture. I want to get clear about this, but the group is moving on already, toward the first valley. I try to make a few notes anyway, holding my journal as steady as I can while I try to keep up.

Field note: The unconscious deals not with the forms that we perceive, but with the area between those forms—the formless realm known as relationship. The unconscious is that realm of our awareness that supplies the context of all meaningful perception.

Context! The idea sticks, somehow, inside my brain. Where did it come from, this notion of the unconscious as a matter of context? Something triggered it, I know. What was it?

I can sense myself sort of fishing for a clue in my unconscious as I hike. I can sense something down there, but I can't quite pull it up. Clearly, my unconscious is not under the control of my conscious will at all. I just have to wait until something . . . oh yeah, suddenly it dawns on me: Mr. Nu reading that book upside down! Context and meaningful associations, that's where I got the idea.

It was the image of Nu reading that book upside down, which I barely noticed consciously at the time, that first initiated the notion of meaningful association as a matter of context; and it was the notion of context that "triggered" the image of

Mr. Nu's irreverent prank, by association. Amazing.

"Ah," Jung says, waiting as I catch up to him and falling into stride beside me. He is smiling knowingly at what must have been my obvious little enlightenment. "The tireless unconscious hard at work." And, of course, he is right.

Suddenly, everything tumbles into place for me. We can read, talk to each other, and drive our cars because the unconscious subtly, constantly, and automatically supplies the appropriate *associations* to and between those forms presented by our conscious awareness. We say that we can do these things because we have learned how to do them, but what we mean is that we have come automatically to draw the "correct" associations between the various perceived forms and situations (groups of forms) and to respond accordingly. If we have learned a thing, it means that we can recall to conscious awareness its potential associations in *context.*

I am astounded to realize how unceasingly this subtle, unseen "nonconscious awareness" operates in my own mind, at how quickly I can talk and read, at how effortlessly all the associations arise in their proper contexts with each word, each sentence, each tangential thought. It's like some sort of magic.

"The unconscious never forgets," Jung adds as we enter the first Valley of Nonconscious Awareness together. "It remembers all things, holding them in its formless care, awaiting only the appropriate stimulation. That is why we use free association so much in psychotherapy. Through it, one may recall the most distant of feelings, thoughts, and sensations." He narrows his gaze upon us, each in turn. "Even those once thought too painful to see."[5]

A dense, cold mist seems to reach for us as Dr. Jung speaks these words. The shadowy valley to which we have been headed is now upon us.

Language and Learned Thought Processes: The Social Context

An uneasy restlessness settles over us as we enter the valley between Thinking and Feeling. The trail descends steeply into an impenetrable cloud of fog and shadow, and I feel crowded by vague feelings of dis-ease and dark, half-realized memories. The group begins to bunch up at this point on the trail, having to slow down and struggling to see the way clearly. Everyone is on edge, and we are forced to hold hands in a long line in order to stay on the established path. Suddenly, we are startled by a thin, whiny voice that cuts through the dense fog like a serrated scalpel.

"That is not the right way to walk through the high country," the voice ridicules us through the fog. It sounds like Mr. Nu, but I cannot see where the voice comes from. "You should have worn warmer clothing," the voice calls out again, from another uncertain quarter. "There are standards, you know. You cannot simply dress or act as you please. There are standards!"

The fog is so dense now that it clings to our clothes, weighting us down and inspiring feelings of despair in us all. All of my worst fears begin haunting me, as we move ever deeper into the depression between the two peaks, which we cannot see at all now. My imagination begins to work on me, and I begin to feel small, helpless, and truly lost. I could walk right off a cliff in this soupy cloud, or be attacked by a bear. I even begin to question my confidence in Mr. Nu. How do I know he is not leading us to our deaths?

At one point, I think I hear laughter, like the laughter of children, but bereft of innocence—or am I only imagining I hear it? It is not happy laughter, but taunting, demeaning laughter, and it calls up in me deep, old memories of my earliest days in school, when I was skinny and awkward and shy. When I did not fit in with the established norm.

The laughter tears at my already raw nerves, digging into long-forgotten depths of self-hatred and humiliation. These feelings rise up in me now, so real and so sharp that I begin to suffer with them just as I did in the darkness of my childhood. Are these, after all, only unhappy memories? Or are they actually still a part of who I am? I do not know.

We are quiet, each entombed in our own thoughts as we move cautiously along. I seem to be stuck in memories of my childhood, unpleasant and uncomfortable memories.

I recall all the times I have been ostracized because I thought or talked or looked differently than did the group I was with. Images from my life at the age of eight or nine come tumbling to mind out of nowhere with a force that nearly stops me in my tracks. I try to focus on the path, on the person in front of me—anything to drag my thoughts back to the present. With some difficulty, I regain my "adult" self and begin to analyze my memories.

My thoughts turn to the notion of "group" behavior, and a jumble of associations form: rote learning, shared language, social mores. I begin to see how much of my sense of myself, and my perception of Reality, was formed around my society's collective vision of what is real and true. In the midst of this swirling fog, a light dawns and I perceive the vast impact of socialization upon even my most personal self. The fog seems to lift a bit as I notice how deeply this social context for meaning has influenced my notions of who I really am, what I'm worth, and where I belong in life. It occurs to me that this kind of socialization of the self has probably happened to everyone who ever lived.

I follow this train of thought still further. I can see that, beginning in infancy, our society shapes and informs our ideas of ourselves and of our place in the world. Unconsciously, we each accept those visions as real and true before we even become self-aware enough to realize that we are being taught. Enter, the unconscious social context for meaning.

I begin to see more clearly how even as small children we each may have had to give up large portions of our own immediate experience of being in exchange for our social membership, especially in the form of parental and peer acceptance. Without our even realizing it, we come to believe that the meanings and perceptions we acquired as members of our families and cultures were innately, uniquely, and personally ours. We literally forget, at least to some extent, just who we really are.

Although I realize that our socialization is not essentially an evil thing—it is, I know, essential to our Human survival—I can also see how it automatically demands that we deny parts of our true selves. It standardizes our seeing from such an early age that we may not even know we ever perceived ourselves or our world in ways other than those that we were taught to be true and real. Inevitably, there must be an unknown quantity of the "true self" that gets buried and warped along the way, forgotten.

And yet I recall what Jung told me before we entered this valley. "The unconscious *never* forgets." It dawns on me that there must be some realm of nonconscious awareness where whatever we have forfeited of our true selves is sustained and "remembered." Certainly, the unconscious will find some way to sustain our real life.

With this liberating realization, I let go of the hand of the person in front of me, and I am suddenly on my own again. The fog has lifted even more now, and I watch as the other members of the group let go as well. They string out on the trail before me, each moving more and more freely, according to their individual styles and interests.

Before long, our entire group has made its way out of the Valley of Socialization and around the bend, heading toward yet another "context" of nonconscious awareness. The fog still inhibits our seeing, but now the air itself is heating up. Something new and more vital, more personal, is happening here.

Projection:
The "Forgotten" Self

I hear the tenor of Jung's fatherly voice in the distance. It is a comfort, here in the dusky shadowlands of the unconscious. I am glad to have met him, and to have him as a trusted guide through this realm. He is so unlike Nu Lao Tzu, who seems more interested in playing than in helping us through this tough stretch of terrain. Where is the old no-good, anyway? I wonder. I'd like to give him a piece of my mind for that unnerving prank he pulled when we were blinded by the fog, taunting us with his recriminations and his "standards" while we were lost in the fog and so oppressed by our dark memories. I'd like to tell him what he can do with his standards!

Of course, no sooner do I wonder that when the skinny old trickster appears, smiling contentedly as an old cat. For some reason, his very self-ease annoys me now, and I scowl at him in displeasure. How dare he show up now, after harassing us so in the depths of our painful childhood memories! The more he smiles at me, the more I resent his very presence.

"What are you looking at?" I rail at him, barely able to control my hurt feelings. "You abandoned us when things got tough. You taunted us when we were already scared. Who do you think you are?"

The old man just smiles at me, as though he knows a secret that I, too, ought to know. I feel like smacking him, when he flips out a baseball cap from some back pocket and puts it on. Dangling from the bill is a mirror, facing my way.

"Who do *you* think I am?" he says quietly, the smile now vanished.

The fog has lifted enough so that can I see myself clearly in his little mirror. I see the pain, self-doubt, and fear in my face. I do not want to look at myself, but I cannot avoid it now. The truth about who I am and what I actually feel is right here, right in front of me. As if in an instant, I am struck with a staggering insight: it is I who abandoned myself, years ago, and it is I who must now own that pain.

I crumple, dumbstruck, onto the nearest log. Jung comes over and sits with me. All around there are others in our party having the same type of breakthrough experience: Gazing into Mr. Nu's dangling mirror has shown each of us the anger and fear we are projecting toward others.

Jung tries to explain, using his most professional voice in hopes of calming us down. "If the original associations of an experience are denied or repressed," he begins, speaking softly and slowly, "the unconscious will simply seek out surrogate expressions for its 'forgotten' meanings. The original meaningful experience will be remembered secretly in the faces and imagined motives of the others in our world."

As he speaks, we begin to regain our composure and listen more intently.

"We say, then," Jung continues, "that the originally meaningful experience is 'projected' onto apparently external forms or situations which henceforth stand as unrecognized mirrors for our own perceptions and attitudes. Thus, we do not so much *make* our projections, as *meet* them."[6]

Jung's calm, rational response helps to soothe our distress. His objectivity is just what we need to keep our emotions from overwhelming us. It allows us to regain some sense of reason, and to begin to see what is happening here, in the realm of projection.

Mr. Nu's dramatic mirror trick was more than a lesson in self-awareness. It was an object lesson on the nature of projection itself. Projection is a mirror into which we each might look to find those parts of ourselves that we have buried or repressed—usually out of fear of the suffering those often unattractive truths might bring. Our projections speak to our true but forgotten experiences of being in a sort of secret, coded, metaphoric language.

This sounds right to me. Through the "projective context" for meaning, we unconsciously associate our present-day emotional experiences with unresolved issues and fears from the past. This nonconscious process of association keeps them alive in our awareness even when we cannot or will not accept them into our conscious awareness. Projection is how the unconscious "remembers" the true self that we have forgotten.

This understanding helps me to feel better. It makes both my emotions and the projections they create seem less threatening. I look around at the trees, which are visible now through the lifting mists. I look at my hands, and at those of some of the others in the group who are struggling with their own hard truths. We are separate, yet we are the same.

This paradox brings to mind what we saw this morning, just before Echo Ridge—the image of the entire Universe as an organic and dynamic whole that appears to our eyes as a collection of separate "things," more because of what we *cannot* see than because of what actually *is*.

It occurs to me that, in a sense, we are projecting every time we assume that an object, person, or event is actually the individual "thing" we perceive it to be. We are projecting our own perceptual limits onto whatever we are looking at. We all do this, all the time, as a practical part of our making decisions about what we do and do not like in life. We tend to take the qualities that we perceive as real in and of themselves, even though we can never really see the whole range of qualities for any given object, person, or event.

The kind of projection Jung is talking about is a little bit different. It is a product of our having denied and repressed our own point of view in favor of one that feels less threatening. This is a kind of "compound" projection, in which we project our own point of view onto other people as though that point of view belonged to them. Not only are we projecting our own perceptual biases onto what we are perceiving, we are also projecting *authorship* for those biases so that we believe that this is how the other person sees, feels, thinks, or acts.

This aspect of the projective context always refers to some painful experience that we have rejected out of a fear of suffering and loss. It is empowered by fear and desire. Apparently, then, projection and feeling are natural partners in Human awareness.

With this insight, we have come to the far side of Feeling. The fog has almost burned off, and the late morning sun breaks through the clouds that have obscured our vision. What a relief to see clearly again!

As we move down the path, the brightness and warmth of the sun reenergizes us, and our pace naturally quickens from a shuffle to a full, quick stride. We walk for a long time, as the sun clears the sky of the last morning mists. The forest around us comes alive with the sounds of birds singing, and a slight summer breeze brings the fresh scent of pine to the air, as we round the last bend before finally leaving the realm that was so dominated by feeling. Our senses are filled with the rich mountain air, the warm sun, and the gentle pleasure of walking among the tall trees. I, for one, begin to feel happy just to be here.

The sun has not quite reached its zenith when we finally head into the next valley, at the base of the peak called Sensation. A deep sense of presence overtakes us, and the forest around us seems extraordinarily sharp and alive. We find ourselves slowing down, not from fatigue but because we are feeling so comfortable with where we are. We are in no hurry. We are warm and content. Besides, our bellies are saying it's lunchtime. We start looking for somewhere to relax and enjoy a light snack.

Before long, we happen upon old Nu Lao Tzu, who, as usual, is one step ahead of us. He is sitting cross-legged on the ground in a clearing, with his back to a large square boulder of white granite. He has just washed his hair in a nearby stream, and it lies flattened out atop the boulder against which he leans, long and thin and white. The old man's body is as still as death, his lips just slightly parted, and his brown-tanned face gone smooth and calm as an inland sea.

Some of us settle around the massive rock near him, breaking out a little trail mix or dried fruit to nibble on as we relax. The very image of his elegant tranquillity settles us down, makes us breathe more quietly, and eases us into a sense of stillness.

The Personal Context:
Our Immediate Experience of Being

"Phoo." A weird sound, rather like a sigh, escapes Mr, Nu's dry lips.

I can't tell if he is snoring, if he smells something foul, or what.

"Poo?" I ask.

"No. P'u," says the old man. "The uncarved block."[7]

I still do not get his meaning. I look around to see if I can spot what he is asking for or talking about. The forest is silent and warm, and aromas of warm pitch and earth enrich the air. The trees that surround us stand silent in the rising sun, and nothing else appears within my view except the members of our party and this huge, unpolished rock. This block of granite. The uncarved block?

I get up from my resting place against the granite monolith, to look at it more closely. The flecks of mica in the rock appear to shine with their own inner luminescence as I realize what Nu is speaking to: P'u, the uncarved block—the true self in its purest form.

Every aspect of the Range of Human Awareness has had its effect upon our sense of being. Now we are at the base of pure Sensation, and apparently this valley we have entered is a realm of pure being. Yet it seems to offer none of the mental or emotional manipulations that the other realms exerted upon us—no fog, no vile memories, no voices— just an unadulterated sense of being, of "presence."

Yes, of course, that's it exactly! Like this boulder of Mr. Nu's, there must be some aspect of who we are that does *not* get repressed and "polished" by our social education. Some part that is still true to our original nature and that just naturally expresses itself in how we experience life. There also must be some context of the unconscious that remembers the more primal meaning of the personal self and its perceiving, a personal context for meaning. The notion leaves me feeling luminous, and I stand there, glowing beneath the bright sun.

"Here," says Mr. Nu, approaching me quietly in the warm light. "This is for you."

He hands me an irregular nugget of granite, much like the huge one against which we have been resting.

"You hold onto this, and you remember." He smiles as he clasps the stone between his hand and mine. "There will be times during our trek together when you will almost forget who you are and why you are here. You hold onto this and you remember. P'u, the uncarved block."

I would almost swear that there are tears in the old scoundrel's eyes. Of course, they seem to be watery all the time, but now they seem to emit a feeling of genuine concern, of love, really. At that moment, I feel a deep shame arising in my chest, for all the times I had railed at him earlier. But through the kindness in the old man's eyes, I find within myself a deep compassion, too.

I thank him, lingering a moment in the comfort of his grasp. As Mr. Nu moves on to other members of our group, I put the stone in a side zipper pocket of my pants, where it cannot get lost. If Mr. Nu says that I am going to need it, I trust that I will.

The old man's words lead me to think back to the surprising twists and turns of our journey so far, and I realize how unpredictable the high country can be. We have a long way yet to go, with many unforeseen adventures to come. I don't want to forget a thing of what I've learned so far, and so I get out my journal and make some notes.

Field note: Each aspect of conscious awareness appears to have a partner in the contexts of the unconscious.

Language and learned thought processes help to create an unconscious social context for meaning, where what it means to be a Human being in the Universe is subtly prescribed by our culture's collective ideal of what is real. The fears and feelings that we repress find unconscious expression in a projective context.

The personal context of the unconscious refers to our innate and unique sense of being in the world just "as it is," unaffected by either education or projection.

Question: What then of intuition? Doesn't it have a partner in the contexts of nonconscious awareness, too?

I think for a moment about Mr. Nu, and how much he has taught us so far. I feel a deep gratitude toward the man, and a real affection. His instincts and his authenticity amaze me, and I count myself lucky to have come into contact with a spirit such as him. As I leaf through my journal, I can see his guiding hand on every page.

When I finally look up from my reading, hoping to thank the old man once more for his friendship, however, he is nowhere to be seen. In fact, most of the members of our party have begun packing up. It's time to head on.

Not far up the trail, we find a pathway that apparently leads to the far side of the Range of Human Awareness, where the final peak, called Intuition, stands open and clear against the blue sky. Something inside of us knows that this is the way we need to go, although now none of us is especially anxious to get anywhere in particular. Still, it is as though we are each guided by an innate instinct for life to the next phase of our journey.

The Transpersonal Context:
Life and Human Nature

Although Nu Lao Tzu and Dr. Jung still head up the group, no one seems to be in the role of leader. We now are all, equally, the charges of some larger knowing, of a level of awareness even more subtle and pure than the personal. We all know of this level of being, but it is so universal to our Human existence and so innate to our experience that not many of us recognize it in our daily lives. Up here, however, at the furthest reaches of the Range of Human Awareness, its existence becomes obvious.

As we round the far side of the peak of Intuition, we leave the realm of sensation and of the personal far behind. The valley here is created by the rise of Intuition in relationship to the high country itself, where the central challenge of our Human Nature towers before us, a massive white glacier. The air here is thin and unusually cool, but clean in a way almost foreign to our senses.

The glare from the snow field so far above us makes the

terrain ahead of us difficult to see. The valley floor where we are now is higher and far less protected by trees than any we have visited thus far, and many of us seem to be losing our bearings, perhaps feeling the first effects of the altitude. Mr. Nu notices this, of course, and springs into action, giving us each something present to focus upon. The questions he asks are unanswerable, but they open our eyes to the immediate truth of this realm.

"What is it that moves us as infants to find the nipple and to suck?

"What kind of intelligence is it that leads us from sperm and egg, through cell division, into adolescence, and toward adulthood?

"What force is it that forms Human life into its vital patterns and processes?"

Our intellects, emotions, and even our physical senses are stumped by such questions, which provoke us to something that lies beyond the world of form. Mr. Nu's queries force us to use our intuition, and to accept the "felt sense" of this realm, which the other aspects of our conscious awareness cannot seem to handle.

As we cease to struggle with reason and emotion and our physical senses, settling into the more subtle sense of this place, Dr. Jung takes over, explaining to us as simply and slowly as possible just where we are.

"Beyond the personal," he begins, with a reference to the valley from which we just came, "there exists a transpersonal context for meaningful perception. It refers to our innate relationship to Life as Human beings, and to those meaningful associations that arise unbidden from our deepest psyches to guide and direct both our development and our behavior as members of the human race.

"The natural means by which this realm of Human Nature may reach our conscious awareness is sometimes called instinct. I have referred to intuition as the 'instinctive' function of conscious awareness. Throughout Human culture the transpersonal has always been perceived first and foremost through this function of consciousness, that is, through intuition."[8]

I have to let what Jung is saying sink in before it begins to make sense to me. I am used to thinking of the "transpersonal" as a strictly spiritual realm. Yet I can see, as I sit with what Jung is saying, that our instincts are also transpersonal, in that they emanate from something beyond our personal consciousness. They are, as Jung might say, "archetypal" to our species.

The idea begins to make even more sense to me as I realize that we Humans have all kinds of instincts that guide our behavior: a nursing instinct, a sexual instinct, a social instinct, and a parenting instinct, to name only a few. We may even have a certain complex sort of "nesting" instinct that drives us to want to set up our own places in the world and to try to understand our own relationship to Life and to the Universe in which we live. That is where intuition comes in, as Jung says, in the natural process of our reaching our maturity as real Human beings. From the suckling instinct to our deepest intuitions of the Divine, the transpersonal and intuition appear as dynamic partners in the Human experience of being. Together, they move us through the innate processes of maturing and manifesting our Human potential through the successive stages of our Human development.

I had always had a hunch that there was something guiding me, subtly, from deep inside, but I had never found a name for it that rang as true as this does. I like the notion that this inner guidance is a natural aspect of my own Human Nature, that we all have it, and that it is reliable as a guide for our lives. From this perspective, the transpersonal is not something "out there"—outside of me or reserved for holy institutions. It is just Life, moving through my Human Nature.

Indeed, from our present viewpoint, having explored the entire range of Human consciousness, the dynamic union between conscious and nonconscious awareness as a whole appears as obvious and entirely natural, simply another pair of opposites in union. From this perspective, the unconscious is to conscious awareness as Nothingness is to Being, as space is to objects in the material world, as energy is to matter. It is the subtle process (yin) that sustains the apparent form (yang).

The Tao of the Unconscious

As we move up the trail, continuing to gain altitude, I find my understanding of all that we have encountered to this point expanding with the ever-widening view. I see the unconscious as the atmosphere in which we form our perceptions of the world. It both sustains and influences our experience of being just as do the atmospheric pressure and humidity of the physical environment. There are even a number of different "atmospheric conditions," or different types of contexts, through which the unconscious may operate.

Within the yin of the unconscious, therefore, there is also a yin/yang dynamic. Socialization and projection are the two primary ways in which our Human sense of meaning can be redirected to create new, synthetic visions of our lives. Thus, the social and projective contexts of the unconscious are in a different class of nonconscious awareness than are the more immediate contexts, the personal and the transpersonal.

The social and projective contexts for meaning seem to me much more directive (yang) in nature than the yielding, receptive (yin) personal and transpersonal contexts. Yet even within those two pairs, there is an interplay of yin and yang. The transpersonal is the most subtle of all realms of the unconscious. It stands as yin, relative to its partner, the personal context for meaning. Our social ideals are by far the most directive and obvious of the realms for Human meaning, and so the social context stands as yang to its more subtle counterpart, the realm of projection. This is the internal "tao" of the unconscious.

Once again, as when the Range of Human Awareness first came into full view, I find my mind flooded with the intricate dynamics of the place. The trail rises steeply before us, as we begin our climb toward the high country in earnest. Everyone is moving slowly now, and stopping to rest often, so I might as well take time for one more note before we move up still higher. I will never remember all of this otherwise.

Field note: The dynamic interplay of yin and yang permeates our Human Nature, even to the innermost aspects of our unconscious minds.

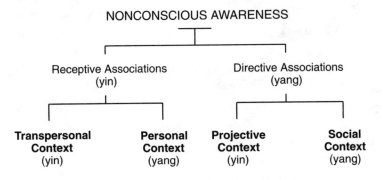

"Very good," says Mr. Nu, as he comes up beside me and takes a quick look at what I've drawn. "You make good charts. Very scientific."

I smile, feeling a real satisfaction at the symmetry my models of the psyche display.

"And very boring," he adds, instantly deflating my ego as he nimbly scampers on up the path. "Come on," he shouts, turning his attention from me and waving the whole group along. "We still have far to travel. We need action! Adventure!"

I am stunned at Nu Lao Tzu's attitude toward my achievement. Have I not just made the first known chart of the internal tao of Human awareness? Have I not just unified the essence of ancient Chinese philosophy with the insights of modern Depth Psychology?

"You have the yin and yang, but not the tao," the old man calls back to me, intuiting my question as usual. He does not stop climbing, but somehow finds the energy to shout at full volume as he continues briskly up the rocky trail. "Yang and yin must unite to create the work of Tao. How do yin and yang unite in your actual awareness? Do you know? No. All you have is some words with lines coming out of them. But you do not know what you are or how you came to be. So how can you know where to go or the true nature of your tao?"

I am amazed that he can keep this pace on such a steep trail and still find the breath to chastise me, but he is not through with me yet. "What is the tao of Human Nature?" he shouts out, as he increases his lead on the rest of us. "You cannot tell what it is from charts and names. You have to go and see it for yourself."

As Mr. Nu completely disappears from view, outstripping everyone in our hiking party, I have to admit that he is probably right. Although I have succeeded in detailing the yin and yang of conscious and nonconscious awareness, I have not even come close to discovering what it actually means to live a meaningful life, or to become a "real" Human being. I may have recorded the basic structures of Human Nature but I have not yet understood its vital Force.

I look up the trail again, and realize that nearly everyone has passed me by while I was pondering the value of my charts. I snap my journal shut and stash it into a side pocket of my pack. It won't help me up this steep grade. There is only one thing for me to do: catch up with the group once again and to try to find out for myself what it means to live a real life.

CHAPTER THREE

. . . .

Ego/Superego:
The Self as Form

The self as form is the virtual self that
the self as process empowers.
It is a persona, a necessary mask, an image we portray
not only to the outside world,
but to our own private eyes as well.
Because its origins are unconscious and therefore unseen,
we tend to take this image of ourselves for the true self.

The sun seems to linger near its zenith as we clamber up the rocky trail that rises sharply from the thick forest through which we had been traveling. The day is warm, and the trail is taxing, as it ascends quickly toward the high glacier known as Mount Persona. The climb is not easy, but we find ourselves moving toward the high country with relative speed.

As we gain elevation, the woods become more sparse; towering, full-bodied fir trees are replaced by increasingly sparse, rugged pines. Small patches of old, gray snow dot the more shadowed spaces we pass. Before long, we begin moving through small subalpine meadows, where our viewpoints on the Range of Human Nature and its surrounding terrain become ever more complete.

The farther we climb, the wider and far-reaching become

our vistas on the land below. With each ascending field the dynamic relationship between conscious and nonconscious awareness becomes more clear. Eventually, we reach a broad alpine field where we can see the entire reach of wilderness through which we have been traveling, and the Range of Human Nature presents itself as one, organic whole.

The view is astounding. In the bright midday sun, we all stop and rest, finding what shade we can under the little pines that still dot the mountainside. As I drink from my canteen and catch my breath, the absolute unity of the vast range below us inspires me to make just one more chart of the terrain.

Field note: Each dynamic aspect of our conscious awareness is perfectly balanced with a corresponding aspect from the realm of nonconscious awareness. Even the internal dynamics of conscious and nonconscious awareness share the exquisite symmetry of yin and yang.

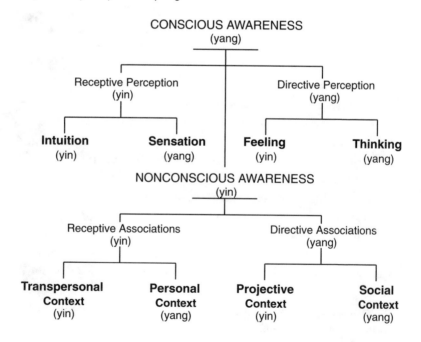

CONSCIOUS AWARENESS
(yang)

Receptive Perception (yin)   Directive Perception (yang)

Intuition (yin)   Sensation (yang)   Feeling (yin)   Thinking (yang)

NONCONSCIOUS AWARENESS
(yin)

Receptive Associations (yin)   Directive Associations (yang)

Transpersonal Context (yin)   Personal Context (yang)   Projective Context (yin)   Social Context (yang)

As I gaze in satisfaction at the new chart, the image of perfect balance it offers brings to mind the state of Perfect Symmetry from which the Universe itself began, where All That Is existed in a perfect state of absolute potential. It occurs to me that the "perfect symmetry" of Human Nature I have charted here also contains the whole range of "pure potential" inherent in our being Human. It includes all of the essential modes and contexts whereby we Humans experience our entire range of being: body, mind, emotion, and even that innate Force that gives us life and guides our growth as perceiving selves, which people often refer to as Spirit.

If my new chart is correct, I have just created a new image of what Jung would call the "Archetypal Self." This notion excites me, and I become intensely absorbed in checking and rechecking my new chart against the actual terrain below. Evidently, this attracts old Mr. Nu's attention, and he wanders over to the rock upon which I have perched, taking a seat beside me.

To my surprise, the little man appears to get excited, too, and whips out his own tattered notebook, into which he feverishly begins to draw. He looks over my shoulder, at my chart, then down toward the range below, then back to his own notebook, where he scribbles some more. His eyes dart back and forth between my chart, the range, and his own drawing. The tip of his tongue pokes out between pursed lips as he continues drawing like this for several minutes.

Before long, Carl Jung, too, comes over for a look. "Ah yes," he says, in immediate recognition. "Images of the Archetypal Self. Very interesting."

Images? Did he says images? Plural?

"Ancient beyond words, this one," he adds, pointing to Mr. Nu's ragged field book.

Once again, as I was the last time Mr. Nu looked at my work, I am crestfallen. I actually believed that Mr. Nu had become so impressed by my latest accomplishment that he was copying my charts. When I look at what he has been drawing, however, I feel both let down and bewildered.

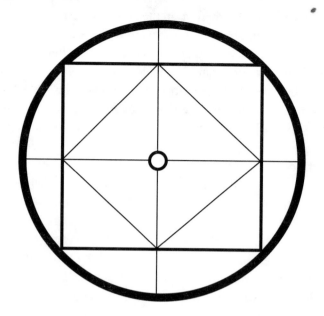

"The Perfect Symmetry of our Human Nature is ageless," Nu Lao Tzu says in his thick Chinese accent, as he smiles at me with a warm twinkle in his eye. "Every Human culture has made its own image of this truth, but everybody—Buddhists, Hindus, Christians, Moslems, even your American Indians—all know what this sign means. This sign means 'Source,' 'Original Nature,' 'Original Self'."

Jung nods, adding a little history lesson of his own. "In Chinese mythology and others, the Great Man would appear at the center of this circle. The four corners of the square often represent the four cardinal directions, which thus speak also to the manifest world, while the circle refers to a nonmanifest Reality beyond the scope of time and space, eternal.

"Psychologically speaking," Dr. Jung continues, explaining the figure in detail, "the roundness of the 'mandala,' as it is known in Sanskrit, represents our natural wholeness, whereas the squares represent the realization of this in consciousness. The mandala represents what I like to think of as the 'nuclear atom' of the psyche.[1] It stands for me as an archetypal image of the Self, the central essence of our Human Nature.[2]

"I got into a lot of trouble when I said that this was a 'Christ' image," Jung adds, somewhat wearily. "People took me literally. They thought I was trying to demean or minimize Jesus. That is not what I meant. I meant only that this image represents the transcendent in Human Nature, the archetypal 'Self.'[3] It is the universal image of our Human Nature in its full, created potential."

Mr. Nu rests his chin on his hand in evident admiration of the image he has created. "The true, original relationship to Life for Human Nature." He adds, with a sigh and smile of intimate satisfaction.

I recall seeing this image, myself, or ones like it in a lot of different settings: in the Rose Cathedral, in Hopi sand paintings, in Tibetan Buddhist art, even in Chinese calligraphy. It always speaks to the same thing: the right relationship between Human beings and their Life source. It really is an inspiring image. My rigid, spindly chart looks like some sort of childish stick figure by comparison, and I am about tear the page out of my journal when Mr. Nu abruptly grabs my hand.

"No! Stop!" he commands. "Every age must establish its own understanding of this universal truth. This image is as good as any. It is a 'scientific' image of the Self, that is all.

"Naturally, there are aspects of our Human Nature that an image like the mandala can suggest and that an image like your chart cannot," the old man offers in determined consolation. "The venerable history of the mandala image lends to it a mystical power that your chart definitely lacks."

Is he teasing again? I pull back, feeling too vulnerable to take another trick. When I look into the old man's eyes, however, I see only sincere honesty, only a man who says hard truths without pretense.

"There is something that your 'scientific' schema can do that this artistic image cannot do as well," he continues, insisting with a sideways tilt of his head that I look at my chart more closely. "Your chart not only shows the balance and the *symmetry* of Human Nature, it also shows the *movement* of the Tao."

It takes a moment for me to see what he is talking about, a moment to get beyond my hurt feelings and really look at the chart I have drawn. When I do look closely, though, I see almost immediately what the old man is saying.

"From the most yin of yin," he continues, pointing to intuition and the transpersonal, "to the most yang of yang— which you call thinking and the social context of the unconscious —this chart of Human Nature indicates an archetypal *process* for becoming fully Human."

"Archetypal processes, huh?" I ponder aloud. The concept does make sense to me, although I am used to thinking of archetypes as mythic images or universal ideas, not as processes; and I make the mistake of saying so. Apparently, Mr. Nu sees what's coming, and scampers away like a squirrel hearing gunshots.

"Archetypes are *not* ideas!" Jung spurts out from behind us, nearly losing his usual dignity. "This, I have said time and time again, although people seem never to listen. Archetypes are not ideas or images. They are the pure potential in our Human Nature. Archetypal ideas and forms spring *from* the archetypes, but the archetypes themselves are without feature."[4]

I knew that, and I am just about to tell Jung so when *bonk*, something hits me on the head. Darn that hurts! It's got to be Mr. Nu. Where is that old mountain goat? Of course, Mr. Nu is nowhere to be seen.

Bonk! Bonk! There it is again! Where is that coming from? Then, *bonk bonk bonk bonk bonk bonk*. A volley of sharp, pointy pinecones comes showering down upon us all from a ledge way up above us. Naturally, there stands Mr. Nu, looking down at our group, and at me in particular, smiling a very happy smile, as though he just brought us the very best of news.

"Tree archetypes!" he calls down to us.

I feel a fleeting irritation with the old man, as I rub my head where the points of the pinecones poked me. Experience has shown, though, that our Mr. Nu does not engage in pranks for his own amusement. He always has a point to make—no pun intended—and by now I know better than to react to his teasing.

I pick up one of the brown cones and take a closer look at it. Clearly, the cone is not an archetypal image of the tree. It has none of the archetypal characteristics of "tree," no branches or roots or needles. As far as anyone knows, a pinecone does not have any ideas, either.

What a pinecone does have, which exists somehow beyond the realm of form, is the pure potential of *tree-ness*. Within that small brown seed cluster, I realize, is all that makes a pine tree a pine tree, including not only how the mature tree will look, but also how the seeds will sprout and take root and grow the first limbs and bark.

I see what Mr. Nu is driving at. The archetypal information in a pinecone determines both how the adult tree that it produces will eventually look and the progression through which it will come into being. A pinecone seed contains the archetypes of both the *form* and the *process* that makes up *pine tree-ness*. That is what archetypes in general are really all about.

The transition of pinecone image to my little chart is easy. As there is with pine trees and all other living things, there is also an archetypal structure to our Human psyche and its innate, natural course of development. Looking at the chart again, I can see this process traced out just as our modern sciences suggest that it unfolds.

As the chart suggests, our Human lives begin with our conception in the womb, where our cells develop toward Human form according to an innate "transpersonal" intelligence. Something beyond our personal intelligence knows how each cell is to divide and differentiate to form all the different tissues needed for our bones, our brains, our lungs, our toenails, and our tongues. Each cell has within it both the potential of our entire Human form and of the instinctual intelligence needed to bring that form to life.

Later on, this same intelligence will move us to seek out

the nipple and to cry in response to discomfort. Indeed, during the first weeks and months of life outside the womb, every Human being is still dependent on this innate and instinctive "knowing" for its survival. This transpersonal intelligence is what leads us to make the right instinctive associations with the world that we perceive, at a time when we cannot yet see with our own individual eyes.

It seems to me, however, that this transpersonal aspect of our being is with us throughout our lives, guiding and directing our responses to Life from a level of awareness far beyond our normal range of conscious perception. It speaks of our innate and primal relationship to Life as Human beings, rather than as any person or separate self. The mode of awareness through which this transpersonal "knowing" first begins to operate is commonly called instinct, although it quickly matures in sophistication during the first months of life into what we eventually know as intuition.

This understanding raises some questions for me about the true nature of what I normally think of as my personal self. How much of who I am is scripted by my genetic heritage? Can there really be any such thing as individuality, given the vast impact of the archetypal design upon our Human Nature? But as I look up from my pinecone pondering, I realize that Mr. Nu and most other members of our party are already moving on, disappearing beyond the ledge upon which the old man had stood.

Quickly, I stick the pinecone in my coat pocket and jot down a note in my journal.

Field note: The transpersonal context for meaning and its function through the "instinctive" mode of conscious awareness known as intuition create our first meaningful awareness of the world.

Question: What, then, determines the nature of our individual personhood?

I have no time to consider the question further, as I find myself once again in the position of having to catch up with everyone else. I have to scramble up the face of the ledge to catch up with our group, finding no established trail to lead me beyond our "archetypal" viewpoint. When I finally crest the ledge, I am a little surprised to find that our group has spread out along the mountainside. We are still together, of course, but everyone seems to have arrived at their own unique viewpoint on the scene before us.

Just a little further up the way, in a semi-sheltered dip in the terrain, I spy both Jung and his friend, Mr. Nu, lingering among one last small stand of pine trees. Somehow these small, sturdy trees have managed to survive despite the difficult conditions at such high elevation, where almost no topsoil at all exists. Indeed, they appear to be growing out of raw rock.

Mr. Nu has become quite taken with a group of younger saplings, and seems actively engaged in a rapt conversation with them about how they like the weather so far this year and what their hopes are for the coming season. He touches them gently, admiring each young branch and stem as though it were a wholly unique treasure, or an accomplishment beyond price or measure.

Person–ality:
"Particles" of Human Nature

At first glance, this behavior seems rather absurd. But as we slow down and step out of our habitual way of looking at the trees, we can see the trees from Mr. Nu's apparent point of view. In all the forest, no tree is exactly the same color, shape, or character as any other, even though they each grew under nearly the same conditions. Each one is an individual miracle, a unique example of how Life expresses itself, through the archetype of pine tree, in an individual form.

"Each of these small trees expresses pine tree in its own way," Mr. Nu explains. "Each one uses yin and yang differently, but it is always pine tree yin and yang. Each one expresses the tao of pine tree through its own individual tao.

"In the language of your modern science, you would say that every pine tree is a 'broken symmetry' from the archetype for pine tree. The perfect archetypal symmetry of pine tree is never expressed in individual forms. Every single tree accents the tao of pine tree differently."

As we look again at our little forest, we see that what Nu Lao Tzu has said makes perfect sense. The attributes that make a pine tree a pine tree are never expressed in totality by any single tree. The coloration varies from limb to limb, the height and girth varies from tree to tree, a certain bark design is characteristic of all pine trees, but identical in none.

We look at each other and see the same thing. Each of us, though we came out of similar backgrounds and may be of similar ages, have our own unique appearance and ways of life. We are the same, except different.

Since Carl Jung is well known for his work in the psychology of individual temperament, I am curious as to what his point of view is on this notion of our having an innate and unique personality, a "true self" that is within us from the womb. I make my way over to where he is standing, alone, writing in his own notebook. He seems a little standoffish, as though maybe my blunder in speaking of the archetypes as universal ideas still has him ruffled. He doesn't seem open to talking to me, but I ask anyway what he thinks about the notion that we each are born with a unique personal "self." He just gives me a cold, verbatim quote from one of his books. He doesn't even look up from his work.

"There is an *a priori* factor in all Human activities," he responds, in a pout, as he sketches, "namely the inborn, preconscious and unconscious individual structure of the psyche. The preconscious psyche—for example, that of a newborn infant—is not an empty vessel into which, under favorable conditions, anything can be poured. On the contrary, it is a tremendously complicated, sharply defined entity which appears indeterminate to us only because we cannot see it directly."

He turns toward me, speaking even more dryly, as though I might be the dullest, most tiresome person he has ever met. "But the moment the first visible manifestations of psychic life begin to appear, one would have to be blind not to recognize their individual character, that is, the unique personality behind them.

"It is hardly possible to suppose that all these details come into being only at the moment in which they appear,"[5] he adds sarcastically, as he turns back to his notes.

It's obvious he's in a mood, so I leave him to his notes. But what he has just said brings a lot of what we've seen to this point into sharp focus for me. I remember his arrangement of personality types, by introvert and extrovert, and by which *mode* of conscious awareness a person innately relies upon most: thinking, feeling, sensation, or intuition. Interestingly, whether a person is introvert or extrovert is determined by whether they rely more on their inner lives or the outside world as their primary *context* for meaning.

It occurs to me that what Jung is saying with his whole temperament scale is that who one most naturally is on a personal level, before any socialization or repression, is a matter of one's unique way of perceiving, of one's own point of view. This insight strikes a chord with what old Mr. Nu said, just as we were leaving Echo Ridge, about our being only our awareness. It starts a tangle of thoughts in my head that I need to straighten. Writing things down always helps me think more clearly, so I make a note.

Field note: Our innate personalities are defined by the unique ways in which we each accent the yang and yin (mode and context) of Human Nature. We, each of us, are particles of Human Nature, "broken symmetries" from the archetypal, perfect symmetry of Self.

Yes. That makes sense to me. We are unique personalities because of the individual ways in which we each perceive and respond to the world around us. Each of us will have a slightly different point of view from every other person in the world. We are sentient beings, whose psychological individuality is made up first and foremost by the unique, innate manner in which we perceive and give meaning to the world.

It also strikes me that our unique, innate personalities create for each of us a personal context for meaning. This context for meaningful perception is not driven by instinct, or by emotion, or by reason, but by our own immediate experience of being. It speaks to our direct experience of reality "as it is" in our own eyes, very much in the style that we saw for the physical senses, back in the Range of Human Awareness.

I turn back a few pages in my journal to give the last chart I drew a quick check against this insight. According to the chart, the personal context for meaningful perception shares a dynamic connection with the conscious realm of physical sensation. In fact, this union stands as the very next stage in the development of the self.

Indeed, it seems to me that this unqualified, immediate experience of being is exactly what infants and toddlers seem to thrive upon, as their psyches respond directly to what their senses tell them. At that stage of development, they have neither learned to suppress their own urges nor to see the world of objects as something "out there." Theirs is a purely personal context for meaningful perception. For them, life just is. Turning forward to the first empty page, I add another note.

Field note: Our pure "person-ality" is the next psychological development after the purely archetypal beginnings of cell division and instinct. It is marked by the creation of a personal context for meaning and a sensory-based "as-it-is" style of consciousness.

During the first years of our lives, we take the world we see just as it is. We do not yet possess the sophisticated feelings and thoughts that will emerge from our psyches in the middle years of childhood and adolescence. We are more or less pure personal beings, taking in the world we see just as it comes to us through the senses, and assigning it meaning within the context of our true personal selves.

This understanding gives me pause. It brings to mind a certain summer day when I was about two years old, my earliest of memories. The sun was shining. Someone must have just mowed their lawn, because I can clearly recall the smell of fresh-cut grass. On the neighbor's radio, a beautiful happy song, called *"Volaré,"* was playing. I don't remember anything else but that. Not what I was thinking or feeling, only this awareness of perfect sensory bliss.

This image of absolute clarity of personal vision immediately brings to mind the look in Mr. Nu's eyes when he gave me that chunk of pure granite. I put my journal away, and pull the stone out of my pocket, letting it rest in my open palm, still and unchanging. P'u, the uncarved block.

As I ponder the glittering stone, I become absorbed in my thoughts. Standing there, I can almost recall that early time of my life, when who I was and how I saw the world had not yet been molded much by fear, sorrow, and the idealized quest for social acceptance. I was a personal self, perceiving the world directly, without qualification, classification, or self–consciousness.

A certain yearning rises in me, and I drift ever further into the image of that pure stone. The granite glitters in my hand, which seems so old and worn now by comparison. A snowflake lands beside the stone, and then another, and another.

I look up, and realize that, as often happens at high elevations, the weather has suddenly shifted. Storm clouds are gathering overhead and the high sun is about to disappear.

Suddenly, I realize also that I am alone. Everyone else has moved on, up the trail, to the next level of our Human development. I have lingered too long in my early childhood. Hurriedly stuffing the small rough stone into one of my pockets, I push on to catch up with the others.

Personally, I would be just as happy to stay right where we were, in that beautiful little dell where life just as it is seemed fine and unsullied, and we could see forever with perfect clarity. Jung is waiting on the trail for me to catch up, and when I do, he notices my reticence. He seems to know what I am feeling. Maybe he feels a little guilty about giving me the cold shoulder earlier. At any rate, he drapes a fatherly arm over my shoulder and consoles me.

"As wonderful as this pure personhood is," he points out,"it guarantees that different people will enjoy different things, and that even the most benign of environments will present us with things that we innately do and do not find pleasant. This process begins with our most basic physical comforts and discomforts, and extends to all areas of our life experience, inward and outward. It is through our desire to have things as we enjoy them that we develop our emotional responses to the world. It is a quite natural progression from the physical sensation 'that feels good' to the emotional evaluation 'I feel good about that.'"[6]

I glance over my shoulder, knowing that he is right and that I cannot live in that idyllic place. I can see, in fact, that the snow is already beginning to cling to the little pine trees below, slowly covering their unique charms with a blanket of pure white. Their pristine, individual character is already disappearing with the changing of the seasons. It makes me a little sad to see their signature beauties becoming obscured. Considering that, I guess I'm glad to be moving on, not wanting to witness these little trees' eventual disappearance.

Ego:
Projection and the Qualified Self

The air has turned cold, even though it is just after midday. One by one, we have each slipped on our all-season parkas. We get out our gloves, as the wind begins swirling the snow about, quickly dropping the temperature to below freezing with the chill factor. Everyone is struggling to deal with the increasingly difficult weather. Despite the turn in the weather, we are determined to follow this path to its goal. Jung calls out encouragement, as we continue the hard climb up the mountain before us.

"Some experiences feel good to us and others do not," he offers, matter of factly, addressing the whole group now as we bunch up again on the slick, steep ascent. "Naturally, we tend to move away from what feels bad and toward what feels good. Before long, we have accumulated enough experience with what feels good and what feels bad so that we qualify certain repeated experiences in the abstract—as good or bad.

"We begin to perceive pleasant experiences, and the events that appear to cause them, as good in and of themselves. We begin to qualify our own experience of being as desirable or undesirable, and to try to avoid aspects of our own lives that we find intrinsically unpleasant. It is through these inevitable rubs with our environment that the sense of the isolated 'I', the ego, develops."

I don't like the way he's talking now. It sounds to me like he is trying to prepare us for the worst. The snow is coming down harder and harder, and my feet are getting wet and cold. I look around at the other members of our party. I can't see their individual faces anymore, except through the small "windows" left by their cinched up parka hoods—just enough of an opening to see through and to breathe.

I look around for old Nu, but he seems to have disappeared again. The snow is coming down steadily. The slick, rock-strewn trail upon which we have been climbing has slowly given way to what looks like perpetual snowpack. A thick, frozen layer of ice and snow covers the mountainside as far as the eye can see. I don't like the look of this place at all. Before long, I stop looking around at the scenery altogether, and just keep my attention centered on trying to stay warm.

As I trudge on, however, this narrowed focus allows me to think more deeply about what Jung has said. I can see how, as soon as we begin to qualify our experiences as pleasant or unpleasant, we begin to take the world that we perceive as something "out there," which needs to be manipulated and controlled. It is only natural, then, that we come to perceive our *selves* as something separate from the world we see.

Once we begin to perceive ourselves as separate from our environment, the evolution of the ego is inevitable. We just naturally begin to think of our "self" as an object in its own right. We develop a self image, and a formal sense of "I." We even start to qualify ourselves according to who we want ourselves to be. We become the objects of our own perception. We begin to think in terms of "I," the ego, the qualified and qualifying self.

The ego, the qualified and qualifying self: the idea sticks in my brain. I ponder this vision of the ego for awhile, and suddenly it dawns on me that what Jung is really talking about is projection. As soon as we begin to evaluate the world that we perceive, we start *projecting* our own point of view onto the world around us. The ego, the sense of "I" as an objective self within the world perceived, is simply a by-product of those projections.

With this insight, I realize that we have moved beyond the timberline of the true self altogether. With the evolution of specific feeling states, we have moved beyond the pristine stand of the personal self, beyond P'u, the uncarved block, into the realm of projection and qualified being.

It is little consolation to me now that this is just what our chart has predicted. The differentiation of pure feeling states will naturally engender a projective context for meaning. Evidently, the ego is just as naturally created when we begin looking at how we feel about ourselves.

With deep melancholy, I reach into my pants pocket, trying to touch, at least, that emblem of the true self that Mr. Nu gave me. I can't find it anywhere. I can't feel anything through these thick gloves, and I cannot afford to lose touch with the group at this point, so I can't stop to look for it. Have I lost the stone? Or is it only temporarily misplaced? I have no way to know and, as deeply as I feel the loss of this most profound of personal artifacts, I cannot afford to grieve for it now, not in this worsening storm. I have to forget about it and move on, or I will lose contact with our group and, perhaps, become permanently lost.

The snow is coming down so thickly that we can hardly see where we are going, when Jung finally leads us to the shelter of a massive rock shelf, which lends protection enough from the storm to allow us at least to lean against the hard cliff and rest. His finding this place in near whiteout conditions proves our confidence in his skill and knowledge as a guide. Even so, some of our party have gotten so tired by this point that they cannot go on. They elect to make camp on the mountainside, right here at the height of the ego's development, and attempt to wait out the storm. Although we may never know whether they will survive that decision or end up a frozen aspect of the glacier itself, the rest of us must move on if we are to have any hope of completing our own quest for real life.

Jung himself seems to hesitate, as though waiting for something or someone to appear. I cannot believe that he would consider ending our journey halfway up the Persona, but I can't imagine why else he is hanging out at this spot. Suddenly, from out of nowhere, however, a loud yelp and a crescendoing *swoosh* breaks upon us, as Mr. Nu comes sliding down the slippery slope, catching air as he clears our overhang, and side-sliding to an abrupt stop in the snow below us like an expert skier.

"There you are," Jung chides Nu Lao Tzu, when the old man slips out of his skis and sidesteps his way up to our resting spot. I can see that Jung is trying to be stern, but cannot hold that attitude. Clearly, he is happy simply to see that Mr. Nu has made it through the storm to what evidently was their prearranged point of rendezvous.

The rest of us are quite astounded, and even overjoyed, to see Mr. Nu again, though he looks very strange wearing his buckskin parka and what appears to be a pair of homemade wooden skis. Where has he been and how can he travel up here with such primitive gear?

"Once you know and understand this landscape," the old man says, with his usual intuitive accuracy, "it is not so bad. Of course, it is always dangerous to stay too long in the land of the

Overjoyed, but I know a few things that make traveling here much more pleasant and safe. Come on. I'll show you."

The old man scampers away, slipping only slightly now and then, at an angle just slightly off to the side of our established trajectory. Jung follows suit, beckoning us along. Obviously, our two leaders have something special in mind. Those of us who have decided to continue jog our packs into place and fall in line.

Before long, we spy masses of steam rising like fast-moving clouds from out of the earth. As we approach the steam cloud, we find a large crater where a geothermal vent has melted a large hole in the snowpack, leaving a clear, warm pool of water to collect in the bedrock below. By the time we get there, moving slowly in the snow beneath the weight of our own packs, Mr. Nu is already at the bottom of the crater, dangling his bare feet in the steaming pool.

How Mr. Nu got down to the small pool is a mystery. For the rest of us, it is enough just to be warmed by the soothing vapors as they rise to the surface, and to see that real earth still exists beneath the glacier's icy facade. We sit around the rim of the crater created by the thermal vent, warmed by the life of the Earth herself, which escapes to the surface in an anomaly here. Evidently, there are places even in the Persona where real life breaks through now and again.

The snow seems to fall a lot lighter here, although I imagine it has something to do with how much warmer the air itself is at the vent. As we look down upon old Mr. Nu, we can see our reflections in the little pool, which is pure and perfectly clear. Only someone as experienced as our Mr. Nu would be able to find this place in a snow storm, so when he begins talking about this place and what it might represent we all listen.

"The world of separate things is a mirage, like the reflection in this kind, warm pool," the old man begins. "At first, when you come here, you see the whole vista: pool, old man, snow field, and sky. But then after a while you start to notice things, especially your reflection in the pool, and all the images of the whole world reflected in it.

"If you look at the water in the pool itself, you see nothing. It is perfectly clear and without form. Even though there could be no reflections for you to see without the water, the water itself is by nature featureless and hard to perceive. That is how Reality itself actually is. The images of separate things are all on the surface, but what gives things their being cannot be so easily perceived.

"When we Humans are young, we always become enamored of our own reflections. We want to make the world as pleasant as we can and not have anything disturb our quiet pool of life. We think that our reflection in the pond is real, and we do all we can do to protect it and make it strong.

"This is as it must be," Mr. Nu continues, smiling, as he splashes his legs noisily out of the pool and starts putting his boots back on. "It is only Human Nature," he adds, with a twinkle in his eye. "You have to have someone to be while you are finding out who you really are."

With that, the old man pulls a small grappling hook from his pack, heaves it over the crater's edge, where it digs snugly into the frozen snow a few feet beyond, and nimbly climbs up to the surface. He offers a quick word of warning before he disappears into the snowstorm, up the mountain, without us.

"Just remember, you are a part of all that you perceive. 'The eye cannot perceive itself.' The world of separate things is an illusion. You say 'projection,' right? Don't forget! Don't forget!" And he is gone, clean out of sight.

From all that we have seen to this point, we know that the old man is right. We know that the appearance of the world of separate forms is an illusion, a product of projection. This has to include the *self* as form, the self-image known as "I."

None of us can see our selves in total, because so much of who we really are is unconscious, and far beyond the range of our conscious perceiving. Evidently, we tend to take the conscious "I" as the true self, simply because it is all the self that we can see. This is natural and unavoidable to our growing up. Still, it is an illusion.

As I ponder this, I turn my attention back to the reflecting pool below. I can see clearly the primal relationship between the facade called the ego and the bedrock of the real self. Barely any snow reaches us at this warm crater, giving me an opportunity to jot a quick note in my journal. It may be my last chance to write anything for quite a while.

Field note: The ego is the qualified self. It is a product of the process of projection. It arises at an early age from our natural desire to avoid pain and pursue what is pleasant. The ego is the center of conscious awareness from which we can deal with the world of form. Still, it is an illusion.

As I write this, it occurs to me that the process of projection is neither a good thing nor a bad thing. It is simply a natural and inevitable aspect of our Human development. It comes into being when we, as toddlers, begin to experience distinct personal feelings about ourselves and the world that we perceive. This is what we have been calling "simple projection," where we take the qualities that we perceive for any given object or event as an innate aspect of that object or event itself.

It seems to me that the ego is largely a creation of simple projection. While it is not the whole, true self, it tends to reflect the personal self and its own unique point of view within the limits of our conscious awareness. It is a sort of partial image of a self that could never be wholly imagined because so much of it is unconscious and in ever-evolving process.

Yet the glacier that makes up Mount Persona, the mountain we must cross to reach the realm of real life, appears so much more complicated than that. It is built not on bedrock, but upon layer after layer of blue ice and frozen debris from countless ages past. As we pack up and continue our quest, following Mr. Nu's lead and Jung's guidance, therefore, the trail becomes ever more difficult and tricky. We come upon crevasses into which we could fall, perhaps never to be seen or heard from again. On top of that, the snowstorm is getting worse the higher we climb.

Superego:
The Ego and the Ideal Self

Eventually, we find ourselves in a complete whiteout, and we have to rope off to each other as a safety precaution. Although it could happen that one person falling into a crevasse could pull everyone he is tied to into the fissure with him, it is still safer to travel as a group in this realm. Considering the conditions, none of us has a choice. We will most certainly die without the security of the group.

As we move on, Jung picks up the theme of his earlier lecture, apparently attempting to keep us from getting too discouraged or from feeling lost. He seems to know the way and we do not, and so we listen, many of us having to repress our true feelings of panic, fatigue, and dread. Curiously, we can hear him clearly despite the wind and snow, tied to his every word as we are. In a sense, he is our real lifeline.

"Almost as soon as the ego develops, it begins assessing its own qualities," he calls through the gale. "Before long, we just naturally begin to suppress some of our own evaluations of the world, in favor of others that offer more pleasurable possibilities. We may literally forfeit some of our own true feelings about things, in favor of those offered by our parents and teachers. This is usually done in order to avoid unpleasant consequences."[7]

As I recall, this is the kind of situation we encountered in the Range of Human Awareness, when we first entered the social context for meaning. It refers to the development of "compound" projection and habitual self-forgetting.

If I remember correctly, it goes something like this: As we are taught how to act and think and speak, we confuse our own evaluations of the world with those of our parents and teachers. The original projection is very *simple* and direct, a product of our personal experience of being. The other is *compounded*, not only with someone else's vision of the world, but also often with the pain and fear associated with our having devalued our own immediate experience of being. The former—simple projection—is a natural by-product of the evolution of our personal perception. The latter—compound projection—is a by-product of that perception being thwarted, diverted, perverted, maimed, or repressed.

We begin learning to limit who we are primarily through the control our parents place on us as infants, toddlers, and young children. During these early years, we tend to acquiesce to their demands simply because they either overpower us or threaten us with unpleasant experiences. By the time we begin actually to understand the reasoning behind the parental restrictions, we have already become thoroughly schooled in those ideals for behavior and belief that will become the foundation of our own inner censor.

Through language and the thought processes that our parents present as acceptable, we receive the guidelines for self-control by which we slowly learn to manipulate our own desires. Eventually, the desires that the ego may safely pursue become restricted, censored, or suppressed according to these learned "ideals" by the new, more social functions of the psyche. Unconsciously, we start censoring ourselves with these learned thought processes, superseding our own wishes in favor of the ideal.

As I consider all this, in the driving snow, now unthinkable miles from my comfortable house down in town, I begin to feel leaden and sad. I can hardly see anything, and what I can see is prescribed by the scope that my hood will allow. I am feeling quite small and unseen.

As we approach the summit of Mount Persona, our blindness becomes complete. We huddle together on the trail, virtually unable to move, freezing to the bone. Even our leader, Carl Jung, is finally affected by the bleak conditions, and he gives the order to "dig in."

Eagerly, we break out our mummy bags and a few of our mountain tents, digging shallow clefts in the snow for protection, and spiking the tents to the ice so as not to be blown away. We climb inside, several of us sharing each tent to help conserve body heat. We get into our bags and settle in, having no choice now but to wait out the storm.

Outside, the wind howls so fiercely that it muddles our thinking. As I listen, I seem to hear voices yelling out, though I cannot be certain it is not a hallucination brought on by fatigue and fear.

"If you don't stop crying right now, I'll give you something to cry about!" the storm seems to roar.

"You're not hurt, so just get up and stop acting like a baby."
"Oh, you don't want that!"

"You go tell that man you're sorry right now! What were you *thinking* when you did that? You're going to get it when your father gets home! Stop that right now!"

"Put that down!"

"Don't touch!"

"BE QUIET!"

As the storm rages on we each find our own demons to deal with, but mine sound so vivid that I can't believe no one else hears them. Of the people who happen to share the tent that I am in, only Carl Jung seems unperturbed. He tries to calm the rest of us down, explaining the nature of this place and its frightening atmosphere.

"Whereas in our early childhood and infancy our desires and behaviors were held in check largely by outside forces," Jung begins, in a calm, rational tone, "before very long we begin to censor *ourselves* according to the learned ideals of our culture. With the development of our thinking ability, we become capable of evaluating ourselves and the world in which we live in terms of abstract ideals, rather than in only the simple terms of pain and pleasure."

He nods toward the storm that is roaring outside. "A voice then comes up in our own psyches that has the power to direct and supersede our own personal ego and its wishes. Freud calls the voice, which is based upon reason and the social ideal, the 'superego.'

"With the advent of the superego, we begin to take on our parent's points of view as though they were our own."

At the same time that Jung is saying this, the storm seems to settle down some. Jung seems satisfied that we have all gained control of ourselves, and snuggles down into his own bag to conserve his energy and get some rest. Before long, the wind abates just enough so that I can let his words sink in. What he has said begins to make sense.

Most of us have experienced countless times, perhaps now forgotten, when our parents rejected our childhood responses to life. This is simply a part of social training in most families. Some of us experienced the loss of parental acceptance as only mild rebuffs aimed at our "bad habits." Others were brutalized or lost a parent altogether through death, divorce, or abandonment. However we experienced it, and however often, the loss of parental acceptance was a powerful force in our young lives. Intended or not, the implied message we received was, "You are not acceptable unless you change your point of view to fit the ideal." Parental shorthand for this message is, "Behave yourself!" These voices of social authority from our youth soon became our own, and the inner critic called the superego became an automatic part of who we saw ourselves to be.

As I lie here, in my restrictive bag, like a caterpillar in a cocoon awaiting spring, I can see in my mind the entire landscape of our Human being as we have traveled it to this point. Everything that has happened to us, and every formation that we have surveyed, has appeared as a natural aspect of our Human Nature. Even the formation of the illusory ego and the restrictive ideals of the superego are essential to our Human survival in the first half of life. We could not be Human without them.

Having sentience guarantees having fears and desires, which lead inexorably to projection and the illusion of the self as a form, separate from all else in the Universe. The ability to form abstract concepts and adjust our behavior accordingly, coupled with the innate Human urge toward socialization, demands the formation of the superego. Everything that brought us to this place, where we are slowly being buried in snow and ice, at the peak of the formation known as Persona, is an aspect of the archetypal Self and its inevitable process of development.

I cannot believe, however, that this is the end. There must be more to our real lives than this eternal facade, this glacier of compound projection. We have followed the true path of our Human Nature to the peak of our social development, yet I know that another terrain lies on the far side of this mountain, and I, for one, intend to get there.

Mount Persona:
The Path of the Virtual Self

There is nothing we can do about our plight at the moment. Although the storm seems to be weakening, there is no point trying to move on until it lets up enough for us to see where we are going. Most of the people in our tent are busy cleaning and repairing their equipment, or making small talk while they wait for the storm to pass.

It occurs to me, however, that we are going to need some sort of a plan of action, some sense of our direction, once we do get going again; so I take this opportunity to look over my notes and review where we've been, in hopes, as Mr. Nu challenged me back at the Range of Human Awareness, of learning something about where we are headed.

As I understand it, the *superego* reflects the self as colored by its relationship to the community of selves known as society. It creates an abstract, ideal image of the self built upon the learned ideas about what "should" be desired and achieved, i.e., upon cultural ideals for defining value and acceptability. Although this ideal self-image comes into being quite naturally through the process of socialization and the development of thinking as a function of personal awareness—just as our chart predicts it should—it is obviously not the true personal self.

The ego, on the other hand (to the extent that it remains

true to the viewpoint of the intrinsic person–ality) stands as an extension of the process of perception that engendered it. Therefore, the ego might be understood as a direct expression of the self in form.

Yet we have also seen that the ego itself is only a function of a larger personal psyche. The personal self in its full range of being far exceeds the limitations established by the self-image and the desires of the formal, ego-oriented "I." The ego, then, is not the real self either.

Person–ality appears to me to be the purest level of existence for the personal self that we have seen thus far. The innate personality represents the self as both perceiver and creator of the personal universe. It reflects the most pure and most immediate appearance of the individual self in its relationships to Life.

It seems to me that the innate personality is sort of a blueprint for the formal self. It is a photographic negative from which the self-image develops. While it may be understood to have definite characteristics and a general typology (temperament or "type"), its essence is the process we call meaningful perception.

I flip through my notes in an effort to see the big picture or some pattern that might tie all of these ideas together. Obviously, the true self far outreaches mere image and conscious awareness. It takes in the whole spectrum of meaningful perception, including the vast, trackless realms of the unconscious. The true self can never be contained in any image, for true self is not a thing; it is an immediate experience of being.

Taken together, the ego and the superego stand as a complex reflection of the true self as limited by form and social training. They create the self-image that we each bring into the adult social realm for the intents and purposes of our pleasure, acceptability, and survival. The ego/superego complex is not the whole, true self, but rather an aspect of the true self's innate, Human development through time.

Therefore, the ego/superego "I" may be understood to constitute only a self in effect—a virtual self!

Yes! That's it. The self as form, the ego/superego "I," is the *virtual self* that the self as process empowers, just as the virtual particle is an illusory form whose reality rests in the "real" particle from which it springs.

Like the virtual particle, the virtual (ego/superego) self is a force that looks like a form. This is definitely worthy of a field note!

Field note: Like the virtual particle in the realm of subatomic physics, the ego/superego "I" appears to stand on its own as real; but, actually, it has no existence at all except as a fleeting extension of the process that spawned it.

Because it is the function through which we choose and evaluate the outer world, this "virtual self" also constitutes the force field through which the personal self manages, affects, and incorporates the outside world.

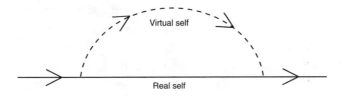

This analogy makes a lot of sense to me, considering what we have seen thus far on our journey into the high country of life and Human Nature. At the peak of the pathway of our Human growing up, the virtual (ego/superego) self creates a collage of illusory images that surround their source like a cloud of virtual particles surrounding a nucleon. The ego/superego "I" actually creates a sort of virtual reality, through the process of projection, in which our personal existence appears as something separate from the Universe in which we live, and from the other Human beings who live with us.

Apparently, this has the practical advantage of allowing us

to work within the world of separate things efficiently, and to refer to ourselves as individuals within the social realm. The disadvantage is, of course, that we tend to lose track of our true selves, of our true immediate experience of being, and of our innate relationship with Life.

Thus, it seems to me that this high mountain trail along which we are traveling toward our true personhood must eventually descend toward the bedrock of our real lives. The natural pathway of our Human being must, like the path of the virtual particle, turn downward, back toward its source. The true and total "I" is not up here, in the thin air of Persona and the "cocoons" that aid our survival. It lingers, instead, in the lower mists of the unconscious, on the other side of our social adulthood.

It is at this point in my contemplations that Carl Jung takes an interest in my work. He shuffles his bag over next to mine and glances over my notes. He seems to find them agreeable. He rolls over onto his back and, staring rather intently at the tent ceiling, offers a few contemplations of his own. Although I had not noticed it, the sound of the storm has quieted to a mere whisper, and Jung now speaks in a soft, contemplative tone.

"As children we are moved through life at others' paces, etched with others' tastes, and earnestly encouraged to participate in life as our cultures and societies have named it," he says, as though remembering his own early life. "What do we know? We are children. We are new to the world and naturally dependent upon other people through the first two decades of our lives.

"We are not even fully developed as perceivers until mid–adolescence, and yet we spend those first fifteen or so years erecting what will be our personal identities. We choose, choose wrongly, and misunderstand due to ignorance, incompetence, or fear. We build our visions of the world the best we can upon the models of our benefactors."

With a sigh, he adds, "At the end of adolescence we are

supposed to be finished and prepared to make our mark upon the world. We are adults. We are all grown-up.

"This is the societal ideal for the completion of the self, and it is a lie, or, rather, it is only half a truth—for the societal ideal is only equipped to deal with those intents, purposes, and events that can be perceived by its members as real and of practical value. The societal ideal knows the self only as an apparent form; it does not know the inner world."[8]

With that statement, I realize that the whole world seems to have grown still. Perhaps the storm has passed more quickly than we had anticipated, or maybe the wind has simply died down. Either way it's nice to have it quiet for a change.

I begin to feel calm and sleepy in the still and silent air of our now cozy tent. Perhaps I need a nap. I roll over, and begin to fall asleep, as all that I have seen and understood slips off the shelf of my conscious awareness into an open abyss.

But the good doctor will have none of it. Before I know it, he is rustling my shoulder in excitement. "No! Don't go to sleep now," he commands me in a hushed tone. "You will never wake up. Don't you hear how deathly quiet it has become?"

I nod, feeling a little groggy and not comprehending why the quietude should bother us. In exasperation, Jung blurts out, "We are buried beneath the snow."

Jung bangs on the ceiling of the tent. It does not move; it's frozen solid. The falling snow has evidently formed a thick, icy shell around our tent, sealing out the sound of the storm and, with it, all access to fresh air. I can't believe I had not noticed how dark it has become in here, and how stale the air has become.

I look at Jung, and then at the faces of our companions. No one says a word. No one has to; the truth is clear enough in our faces. If we cannot dig ourselves of this place, we all are going to die.

PART TWO
. . . .
Yin

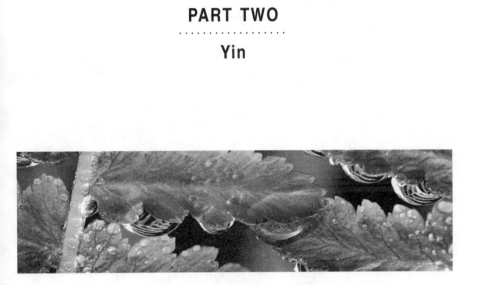

"We stand on the peak of consciousness,
believing in a childish way that the path
leads upward to yet higher peaks beyond.
That is a chimerical rainbow bridge.
In order to reach the next peak we must go down
into the land where the paths begin to divide."

Carl G. Jung
Individual Dream Symbolism
in Relation to Alchemy

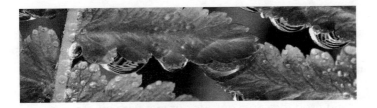

CHAPTER FOUR

· · · · · · · · · · · · · · · · ·

Metaphors
of the Virtual Self

Every important relationship we have now will carry with it
bits of our unresolved conflicts from the forgotten past.
In this way, our present day relationships may act as metaphors
for our unresolved internal conflicts.
These are the metaphors of the virtual (ego / superego) self.
They are both the prime obstacle and the essential pass to
our living our true lives.

Without our knowing it, the structures we have erected to protect us from the storms that rage so often on the heights of the Persona have slowly turned into our potential tombs. Inside these tents of ours, a dim, unnatural glow has subtly replaced the sunlight that had so brightened our beginning. Whatever light reaches us now is filtered through innumerable layers of ice and snow.

Our shovels and pickaxes are of little use here. Every time we try to dig toward the outside world, more snow falls in upon us, and we risk filling even our little air pocket with ice and debris from the storm. We are all wet from the effort to dig ourselves out and, though most of us have climbed back into our bags in search of warmth and comfort, we are cold now and shivering. The air inside our icy tomb is getting thin and stale, and we are becoming increasingly hypoxic.

Of the hikers who happen to share the tent that I am in, only Jung seems to withstand these dire conditions, well-accustomed as he is to situations such as these. He proceeds to jam and prod the snow outside our tent with his archaic walking stick, in an effort at least to make a hole for air. He seems to be making headway with his walking stick where our shovels had proved useless. He isn't going to free us, but at least there may be a trickle of fresh air.

To lend force to his efforts, he chants, with each desperate thrust, the truths of our unhappy circumstance. "We learn most of what we *think* we know about ourselves and our *relationship* to life before we have the real *capacity* to *judge* the information," he grunts in short phrases, thrust after thrust, jamming his walking stick a little further toward the fresh air with each stroke.

"None of us," he says, pausing for breath himself, "not even the most secure and confident of individuals, may consider ourselves exempt from taking a long, hard, inward gaze if we wish to find our life's true meaning.

"In short," he adds, as he breaks through into the light of day with one last, tremendous push, "we do not know what it is that we do not know about ourselves."[1]

We don't know what it is that we don't know about ourselves. We don't know what it is that we don't know about ourselves. The phrase swims around in my befuddled brain. I think it makes sense, but I cannot quite see how.

Despite the little stream of air that now begins to trickle in, I have begun to succumb to the mind-numbing effects of oxygen deprivation. Everything that Jung is saying strikes true somewhere underneath my conscious mind, which cannot seem to quite grasp hold of anything. I try to concentrate on what he is saying, but my whole being is in a whirl.

I can feel myself dying inside and my life begins to pass before my eyes, though not as a personal history. Rather, I see the progression of Human life itself—inflected, no doubt, by the context of what I have witnessed up here, in the high country of Human Nature.

As I begin to lose consciousness, I experience a vision. I see an endless stream of children, rising from out of the earth and moving into the lowlands of the forest. In my vision, my hallucination, they wander, lost, in need of guidance and security. They gather into groups for safety, growing quickly into adolescence, and then into adulthood, at which point they gather other groups of newly born children together, until the whole Earth is covered with groups of people, and groups of groups that turn into cities teeming with people.

Each new group of children quickly ages and takes on the responsibility of forming the next group to come, organizing the new crop of Human beings, quite unconsciously, upon the same essential formats that they, too, were raised. I see the great cities of the Earth, dominating nature, even moving out into the mountains.

As the domination of the realm of nature by the cultures of the world becomes complete, I see an icy pall fall over the Earth. Everyone and everything freezes into whatever pose their social position has assigned them. The Earth is white, and cold, captured in a picture-perfect image of successful civilization.

Then I hear my father's voice, though he has been dead for almost twenty years. "Good work, son. You made it. You deserve a rest."

I shiver and fall into a stupor.

With the gradual influx of fresh air, I eventually regain my conscious awareness enough to realize that I am shivering. Before long, however, the shivering stops. I know from experience that this is not a good sign. It means that I am sinking into hypothermia. My being is succumbing to the cold, and soon I will lose consciousness once again, perhaps forever. I need to get out of here.

Desperate for some consolation, I pull off a glove and attempt to reach into my pocket to touch the stone, that one emblem of true life that Mr. Nu gave me. I can barely move now. My body is numb, and something is restricting my movement, but I can't seem to bring myself quite into consciousness enough to realize what it is—this warm bag, this lifesaver, this comfort I've crawled into to survive. I manage to get one arm worked down into the pant leg pocket where I had first secured the stone. At first, I can't find it, but as I reach all the way down to the bottom, it is there. I can just touch it, but I cannot pull it out. I can't quite get hold of it; but it's definitely there, still within my reach.

Jung has moved from his work on the air hole to trying to bring us around. He pulls my arms out of the sleeping bag and begins rubbing them and my hands, talking to me about everything and anything. As I come back around, I half realize that the vision I had, the hallucination, is what will actually happen to all of us if we stay stuck on the frozen facade of Persona. Somehow, we simply *must* break free of the Persona.

A fleeting part of me wants to be back home, regrets having come on this journey at all; but such cowardice disgusts me, and I push it out of my mind. I know I cannot return to my old life, in the lowlands of Human existence. I *have* to survive and move on.

Yet the temptation to regret my having come on this journey of self-knowledge lingers, tingling just below my conscious mind. After all, if we do survive, there probably will be others of our party who will, indeed, opt to return to the comfort and safety of their accustomed lives. Still, I fight as hard as I can fight against the urge to give up and give in. There is something more to life, on the far side of this deathly place, and I'm going to find it or die trying.

I must be rambling in my inner struggle, in a half-conscious haze, because Jung begins responding to my plight. "There are, indeed, those who will choose to return to the lowlands," he says in a hushed tone, perhaps for only me to hear. "They will choose a route from here known as *regressive restoration of the persona*. For many, this may be the best thing. Some people are not suited for high-country life, and fare better living smaller, less challenging lives.

"For others," and here he puts his face inches from mine, forcing me to look into his eyes, "such a decision would be catastrophic, for their true selves will never be able to live in such conditions. The unconscious will never leave them alone, but will insist in every way possible on revealing the interior truth of their lives."[2]

I can hear him, and I understand what he says, but I am distracted by visual fantasies and odd physical sensations. I try to ignore them, but my struggling against them only makes them more powerful. I try to get up, to get out of here at whatever cost, edging now toward hysteria. Jung pushes me physically back into my place.

"Your symptoms are meaningful," he admonishes. "Do not fight or ignore them. Listen to what they are telling you. They are not literally real, but they are yours and right now they are all that you have."[3]

Perhaps we all are too far gone to understand, or maybe Jung just doesn't know how to get through to us. Somehow, what he is saying about listening to our symptoms sounds like nonsense. I do not want to die here, and I do not want to go back to the habitual life I was living, but I do not know what I can do.

Jung's early efforts have given us fresh air, but we are going to need more than that to come to back to life. We need to break free of this shell. Once more, Jung tries to get us to understand what he wants us to do.

"Listen to what your hallucinations are telling you. What does your body ask you to do? What are you feeling? Pay attention. Pay attention," he pleads.

It would be so much less painful to simply allow my body to fall to sleep and my mind to drift through the hallucinations that seem to be coming on ever stronger. I confuse Jung's voice with the voice of my father. Suddenly, in my mind, I am a young boy again, straining for my father's attention.

I fight to stay conscious, trying to do as Jung wants me

to—driven half by an old need to please and half by the will to survive. The fantasies and the feelings and the physical sensations I am experiencing commingle with my actual reality, leaving me helpless to take any meaningful action at all.

As I lay there, I begin to hear still more voices. I cannot tell for certain whether they are mere hallucinations or whether they are real, but they seem to me to be coming from the outside. I believe that I also hear the sound of digging. Are we about to be saved?

"Watch out for *ulterior meanings*," one of the voices calls, muffled but intelligible through the snow. "A lot of these people are going to be operating from archaic child-oriented or parent-oriented ego states. Things that they say may sound like adult statements, but very often they carry unconscious references to past trauma. If you hear anything like that, don't move them until we establish what game or script they are involved in."

Game? Script? Even in my weakened state, I know this is not your average rescue worker talking.

"It's Eric Berne," Jung assures me with renewed confidence, "the creator of Transactional Analysis.

"Don't worry, he knows this area very well. He has a unique approach to it. He specializes in language and learned thought patterns. He's talking about the inner parent and the inhibited child it creates in the unconscious."[4]

I must be coming around some, because this statement of Jung's hits me like a brick. With a thud, I realize that all the voices I have heard—including my father's voice of just a moment ago, the parental voices I heard when we first reached the Persona, and even the derisive laughter of children that hurt me so much back at the social context in the Range of Human Awareness—all of them are in me, are my own voices, my own being. They are the voices of my *virtual self.* They are the voices of my own unconscious, reminding me of things I do not wish to see.

Suddenly, everything that these "phantoms" have said takes on a new importance, new "ulterior meanings." The voice of my father, which was telling me that I have "made it" by reaching the summit of my social adulthood, is actually a part of me, though perhaps one learned from him, that wants me to settle for what I've achieved in my life as a social adult, and stop here. This is an attitude I despise, but now must accept as my own, learned or not.

As soon as I realize this, other images and visions of my true feelings spring forth on their own from the unconscious. My touching the underlying, *metaphoric* meaning of my father's voice within me seems to have triggered yet more unconscious associations, each of which speaks to other of my unconscious attitudes and fears. It strikes me that all of these thoughts and these words that have bothered me so are actually *metaphors* for something unconscious that I need to see.

With my normal defenses now shattered, I am overwhelmed by a sense of sorrow and loss. Some archaic grief surges upward in me, urgently bursting upward like lava in a volcanic core; but my body clamps down on it, turning solid as rock as the muscles between my shoulder blades go into spasm. I can hardly breathe now, not because of anything in my outer environment, but because of a crisis within me.

One of the rescuers who is digging toward us seems to know that this kind of reaction may well be occurring, what with our having been buried so long in the snow. He calls down to us, in a soothing, smooth baritone voice.

"Everything that has happened to you psychologically is also recorded in your body," he calls. "Don't resist it. Relax into it and listen for what it has to say. Let your body tell you what to do."

"That's right," adds yet another male voice from above us, this time in a thick German accent. At first, I wonder whether it's Sigmund Freud, but I don't think it is. "Just cool it," he advises.

Is he kidding?

"Your entire being is one unified gestalt. Become your body. Imagine you are your body trying to get your attention. What do you say, as your body?"

I look over at Jung, helplessly, incredulously. Am I really supposed to do these "exercises" in the midst of a crisis? Jung nods. "That would be Alex Lowen and Fritz Perls," he says, adjusting his own body and breathing more fully. "They know what they're talking about.

"You have a choice," he adds in dead seriousness. "You can either panic right now and fight everything that your being is trying to tell you, or you can enter into the experience consciously. It's up to you."

Jung closes his eyes and appears to enter meditation. Following his lead, I do the same. I try to pay attention to what my body is trying to do and to go with it, pushing *into* the spasm, rather than fighting against it. I intentionally contract my spasming back even further, until my shoulder blades touch and my back is as arched as it can be. What does this posture say? I ask myself, using my last ounce of courage and strength, letting go to the pain.

"Ah-ah-ah-ah!" The sound erupts from my gut. There are no words for what I suddenly feel in my depths. I try to stay with it. Something raw tears away inside of me, and I begin to sob, still barely holding onto this image that my body has made: a posture of one in unbearable pain.

I am amazed, when my body finally releases me, to feel a tremendous energy and warmth spreading throughout my arms, neck, and chest, as though some circulation that has been restricted for years has just been released. A weeping escapes me that has no thought to it—pure emotional release.

Jung moves closer to me, as we hear our rescuers free the first of our companions in the next tent over. He manages to pull my notebook from my pack, open it to a fresh page, and hand me a pen. "Write," he says. "Write or draw or scribble whatever comes up. No thinking, no censoring, no editing. Just write. Let the unconscious speak for itself."[5]

So, I do, even though in the shadows I can hardly see the page. My hand, once numbed with cold but now invigorated with a new supply of blood and vital energy, moves so quickly as images and realizations flood into my conscious awareness that I cannot write or sketch fast enough to keep up with it.

By the time our rescuers reach our tent, I have five pages worth of unintelligible notes and odd drawings. I can't decipher most of it, but that doesn't matter to me now. Something inside of me has shifted; some internal conduit has opened. These scribblings are only shorthand for something that I already know but have forgotten. They will be enough to help remind me, when the time comes to fully remember.

When our rescuers finally get enough of the snow moved away to pull up our tent flap, a brilliant white sun shoots through the door, blinding me. I had not realized how dark it had become in our tiny ice cavern. I suppose I had simply gotten used to the shadows.

As we are pulled from our snow-packed pit, we are given broad goggles with dark, reflective lenses that limit the light to our eyes. The sun hangs now about halfway to the distant horizon in a blue sky, dotted with cumulus clouds, scud from the last passing storm. I realize, as we are helped into dry clothes and given hot tea from a thermos, that we truly did summit Persona before we were buried.

Indeed, as I look to the west, on the far side of the mountain we've climbed, I can just barely make out the far distant highland plateau toward which we have traveled for so long today. Real life is almost within sight. I sit for a while, warming in the sun, and reflecting on all that I have just been through.

Although it seemed like an eternity that we were trapped there, only a small portion of our day has passed. Still, that was plenty of time for us to lose our ability to tolerate the true light of day, and for me to lose sight of my self in the process. I know that this small breakthrough is only the beginning. We all still have a long way to go.

Everyone is exhausted, and we want to rest, but the thin atmosphere up here is as dangerous as anything we have yet experienced. The weather is clear now, but to linger here is simply to hazard another snowstorm. Besides, we still have some serious hiking to do before sunset, and I am anxious to get moving.

My back is still sore from the shoulder blade spasms, and my psyche feels tender to everything, as though I just had been born; but it feels good to be moving again. Jung seems less deeply affected by our ordeal than the rest of us, and I suspect that he has been through this kind of thing many times before. Still, he, too, has to wear the same eye mask as everyone else, at least until we get down from the summit. It seems snow blindness can happen to anyone, up here.

This thought reminds me that I have not seen Mr. Nu since before the big storm, and I become worried when I realize that he is not with our group. Indeed, as I look around, I realize that several of our members are not making the trip into the heartland of the high country with us. Did they succumb to the cold and the darkness? Did they decide to turn back? Are they lost to the Persona glacier forever? I have no way to know. Up here we each must make our own choices, whether to risk moving onward, to stay as we are, or to return to that which is less challenging. No one can say what the right choice might be for another.

I can't believe that Mr. Nu would turn back, though, and he certainly would not make a home of the Persona. So where is he?

I ask our rescuers as we make our descent.

"Oh, Nu Lao Tzu?" they reply. "He's the one who warned us you were all trapped up here. He saved your lives."

Well, I'll be! But where is he?

"He's waiting for us down at base camp. We'll be there in an hour or so."

"Base camp? You have a camp up here?" I inquire incredulously.

The three mountaineers look at each other in mild surprise, as though I had just asked the obvious.

"We live here," they answer in unison.

"This is our life's work," adds one of them.

"We study the hinterland of Human Nature," adds another,

"and give aid to the travelers who want to surpass the persona."

"We each have a specialty, of course, but essentially we all do the same thing; we just use different metaphors," the third says, and they all nod in agreement.

I find this a little hard to believe: that people would live their whole lives at the base of Mount Persona, exploring its icy terrain day and night, dedicating their lives to its understanding, and to helping the stranded traveler to safety. I look at Jung, and he nods that it's true.

"I, myself, am as much an anthropologist as I am a psychologist, I suppose," he offers. "But there are those who man the aid stations out here, whose sole interest is in exploring the structures of the ego complex, and in finding new routes through it."[6]

Well, I guess that makes sense. At any rate, I'm glad they're here. Without them and their daring work, I might well be dead by now. This, too, makes me think of Mr. Nu.

As we make our way down the icy facade, moving now ever closer to the realm of real life, the ice crystals left by the last snowstorm glitter fiercely in the afternoon sun. They remind me of the sparkling mica in that chip of granite that Mr. Nu gave me, and this leads to me to wonder whether anyone ever mistakes this facade for real life. I ask Jung about it, and he looks at *me* now incredulously. A short pause, then he answers.

"Yes, of course; that is the entire problem, isn't it?"

Evidently, I am weaker than I had realized, and my thinking still is not clear. Obviously, Jung is right. The whole problem is that we take on our learned visions of ourselves long before we are able to judge for ourselves whether that information is accurate. Moreover, our true, immediate experience of being is buried inside the unconscious, which thereafter may only speak of it in metaphor, what we call compound or "neurotic" projection: the metaphors of the virtual self.

Naturally, our projections and self-delusions will appear to us as actual reality. It could not be otherwise, because the whole process is unconscious and begins before we even realize that it is happening.

Yeah, I think to myself, it really is true. We don't know what it is we don't know about ourselves; and we tend, therefore, to live out our lives in illusion.

"No one makes it over this mountain," Jung expounds, as he accompanies me down the snow-covered mountainside, "without falling into some sort of delusion. Inevitably, we all need some assistance in finding our way to real life. That's what all of these helpers are doing up here."[7]

I am exhausted from our ordeal, and I need to stop for a moment to rest and collect myself even though we are only halfway down the mountain. Jung stays with me as some of our group move along, and others, who were worse off than I, begin to catch up. I gaze down the slope, to the base of the glacier, where large jagged rocks poke up out of the ice and a few hardy pine trees offer signs of new life. As I look more closely, I can just make out a few wooden cabins, nestled for protection up against the rocks.

The shelters remind me of aid stations I have come upon before, while skiing in other terrain. These structures, however, are larger than those tiny, seasonal huts. These are more the size of those year-round dwellings you see in Antarctica, where serious scientists dedicate their entire lives to the study of that barren land. I suppose, really, I should not be surprised to find that kind of help out here, in the deep heart of the high country of Life and Human Nature.

I want to get a better look at the buildings below, and at the landscape into which we are now heading, so I take off my goggles, which have fogged up from my perspiration. One of our rescuers insists that I put the masklike appliance on again, and right away. He tells me that even here, at the lower levels of the Persona, the reflective light can be so bright that it can actually burn your eyeballs, causing long-term or even permanent blindness.

"This vast, frozen face cannot be seen well from the surface," Jung counsels as we move along once again. "The

Persona and its internal facades are not something you can understand in the direct light of consciousness. You have to see it from beneath."[8]

I don't understand this last comment, and cast a quizzical glance Jung's way. "You'll see," is all he says.

I'm willing to keep my goggles on, at least until we clear the Persona proper, if they will help save my eyesight; and I'm also willing to wait until later to find out what Jung means about getting "beneath" the Persona. Right now, I just want to get down from this mountainside and into the warmth of one of those cabins. We are not far now from the base of the Persona glacier, and I'm anxious to see our old friend Mr. Nu, to thank him for saving our lives.

So it is, that when we finally reach the main lodge at base camp and old Nu comes sauntering out to greet us, I embrace him as if he were a long-lost father. He hugs me back good-naturedly, evidently amused at my big dark goggles and my childlike show of affection. He pats my back, reassuring me that I'm okay. When he pulls back, however, I'm surprised to see that he has slipped on a strange pair of goggles. They have opaque lenses that he cannot possibly see through, and there is a wire leading from the mask to a single glove, which the old man wears on one hand. Even in such an emotional reunion, the old goat cannot resist teasing me.

"Come on, follow me," he says as he stumbles blindly around on the rock-strewn snowfield, bumping into other travelers and reaching his gloved hand out in an effort to touch a reality that only he sees. Despite our fatigue, or perhaps in part because of it, we all crack up. We can't help it. But the point is well taken and clear.

I get it. Very funny. He's wearing a virtual reality mask, like the ones you plug into computers. He seems to be teasing me, and the others in our group that have made it this far, about our big goggles, and about our recent ordeals on Mount Persona. Of course, he is also teaching a lesson, and his point is not lost on any of us.

We are all familiar with those computer programs that can generate the illusion of three-dimensional space. You plug in your visor, which is actually a small monitor, and a glove, which allows you to manipulate your virtual environment. As your gloved hand moves, it appears on the monitor. As your head moves, corresponding shifts in the computer-generated reality shown in the monitor mask create the illusion that you are actually in a computer-generated space. What that virtual reality will look like depends, of course, upon what has been programmed into the computer.

What Mr. Nu is proposing so graphically, I suppose, is that those "metaphors of the virtual self"—those projections that we each experience as a result of our childhood repressions and unresolved internal conflicts—create a virtual reality, too. In his comical charade, the monitor mask represents the persona, I guess—the mask that we wear both for the outside world and for ourselves, the mask that both hides our actual faces from view and feeds us a preprogrammed version of reality. The computer glove is the ego's compulsion to try to manipulate the world thus perceived. As Mr. Nu demonstrates, such attempts are, of course, bound to meet with failure in the real world because the glove is only powerful within the virtual reality. We are actually blinded by the mask through which we "see." Thus we each tend to go bumbling around in our lives like damned fools when we are under the influence of the ego and its persona—of the virtual self.

It occurs to me, too, that in the realm of the virtual (ego/superego) self, the "computer" has been programmed by a child who has long ago forgotten that he wears a mask at all. The metaphors of the virtual self appear to us as "real life" so long as we leave our masks on, and most of us rarely realize when we have donned them. Naturally, the image of the world created by a frightened, wounded child will not very likely give us a clear image of our lives as they actually are.

As I consider this image, I am struck by how often I have found myself stumbling around in my own life. How often have

I become angry or frustrated at someone or some situation that turned out, in the long run, to be nothing at all like what it seemed to me at the time? How often have I "run into" problems I did not see coming, but that in retrospect appear perfectly obvious, even inevitable? How many times have I watched as people I know and care for make the same mistakes, over and over again, blindly, like some preprogrammed, animated toy that repeatedly bumps into the same wall? You'd think we would learn.

"Our projections are not something we *make*," Jung observes, as Mr. Nu stumbles somehow straight through the doorway of the big lodge before us. "We *meet* them. This is often most difficult for novice travelers to grasp. Our projections are products of the unconscious, and so we are, of course, not conscious of them, even when they are right there, in front of our faces.

"To us, they seem as real as these boulders at the base of this glacier," he adds, as we step up to the doorway of the main building, into which Mr. Nu has just disappeared. "That is why we all need help of some kind in detecting them. They are, by definition, our personal blind spots."[9]

Deciphering the Metaphors:
Removing the Mask

Jung graciously motions for me to enter the lodge before he does. When I do, I am quite surprised at how dark and dismal this place looks inside. Indeed, I can hardly see a thing. It has an interesting design, a round central room framed by four office doors. But the lighting is terrible.

Mr. Nu comes up behind me, taps me on the shoulder, and whispers in my ear. "You can take your visor off now."

Oh. Yeah. I had forgotten I had it on. No wonder everything looks so depressing.

My embarrassment must be obvious, because Eric Berne, a slender, balding man in glasses, whom I recognize from his book covers, approaches me with words of consolation. "Don't worry," he says almost patronizingly, "it happens to everyone."

As I look around the large main room, I notice that each of the four doors that face us is marked with the kind of red cross that usually marks a first-aid station. Beneath the cross on each door is a designation: Thinking, Feeling, Physical Sensation, and Intuition.

"Come on, let's take the tour," Jung says, taking my arm. "You look like you could use a checkup."

I hesitate to follow him, though I ought to know better by now, because I'm leery of "quick fix" psychotherapies. It seems to me that we have come all this way just because we *don't* want to settle for surface responses to our real lives.

Jung notices my hesitation and takes me aside. "You know, no single path through the high country has all the answers," he points out, patiently. "In my day, it was Freud, Adler, Rank, and myself. Each of us had a specific aspect of the psyche for which our approaches were best suited. We disagreed, sure; but the work that each of us did complemented the work of the others, as well.

"Freud knew about sexual repression, Adler did personal power and family dynamics, I ended up working mostly the archetypes of the unconscious, and Rank was most interested in art and neurosis."[10]

Sweeping his arm toward the four doors in the foyer, he adds, "These therapies came later, building on what we had done. Each of these therapies concentrates on one type of neurotic metaphor, according to which function of conscious awareness they find most interesting."

This last comment piques my interest. Somehow, I had been thinking of projection as mostly a matter of ideas and attitudes. It had not occurred to me that the unconscious could speak through my body and my intuition, as well as through my mind and feelings. Now that I think of it, though, that back spasm I had certainly had something to say about my inner life!

"The classic process of projection, where we assign to other people attitudes that we have repressed in ourselves," Jung continues, once again reading the question in my hesitation, "is actually just one of many ways in which the unconscious psyche portrays the true, forgotten self.

"Sometimes the unconscious will convert emotional pain into physical pain as an alternate expression of the unrealized truth about your life. Such a 'conversion reaction' has been known to cause paralysis, fatigue, muscle and joint ache, and general nerve dysfunctions that often mimic or exacerbate other common physical diseases."[11]

This makes perfect sense, of course. The unconscious will attempt to find covert expression for our unresolved internal conflicts and our unexpressed true personalities wherever it can. That is its function, where projection is concerned. It isn't likely to choose only one or two functions of conscious awareness through which to express its secrets. The way we see ourselves and the world around us, the things we say and how we say them, our posture and physical health, and even our dreams and our fantasies—all may act as metaphoric images of our unrealized personhood and our unaddressed wounds. How could it be otherwise?

I look at the four doors again. I have to admit it makes sense. Still, I find myself hesitating. My legs are unwilling to take me where my mind wants to go, and I can feel my heart rate increasing. A familiar queasiness rises in my belly, and I realize, just for a flash, what the real problem is: I hate to go to the doctor.

When I tell Jung the truth, he bursts out laughing, but manages to regain his professional manner right away. I, myself, find my insight fairly amusing. I do not want to go see a doctor about my unconscious fears and conflicts, because I have unconscious fears and conflicts about doctors.

I have to admit that one or more of these approaches might have something, at least, to show me about the deeper realms of the high country. After all, their creators have explored this area pretty extensively. It may be that none of these approaches holds "the cure," if there is such a thing, but they may well have discovered *something* that I ought to know about, as a high-country traveler.

I enter the first office, marked Thinking, and the first thing I see looks a little like an eye chart, or a drawing of a traffic light. According to Jung, who accompanies me here, it's a chart of the structure of the ego/superego complex.

Some other members of our group are already seated in the small room, which looks more like a classroom than a doctor's office. I take a seat, while Jung moves to the back of the room. Dr. Berne is delivering a lecture on his diagnostic method. He reads from a manual that he apparently wrote.

"In technical language, an ego state may be described phenomenologically as a coherent system of feelings, and operationally as a set of coherent behavior patterns," he recites, slowly and carefully. "In more practical terms, it is a system of feelings accompanied by a related set of behavior patterns. Each individual seems to have available a limited number of such ego states, which are not roles but psychological realities. This repertoire can be sorted into the following categories: (1) ego states that resemble those of parental figures, (2) ego states that are autonomously directed toward an objective appraisal of reality, and (3) those that represent archaic relics, still–active ego states that were fixated in early childhood.

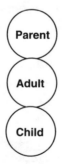

"Technically these are called, respectively, exteropsychic, neopsychic, and archeopsychic ego states. Colloquially their exhibitions are Parent, Adult, and Child, and these simple terms serve for all but the most formal discussions."[12]

He says that he uses this model to determine where people might be projecting their unfinished childhood dramas into their present-day social interactions. He calls these projective transactions "games."

That said, Dr. Berne asks if any of us are experiencing side effects from our time on Mount Persona that might require the type of treatment he is offering. Timidly, I raise my hand.

"Yes," he responds, pointing to me.

"Well, I seem to have discovered a father complex," I offer, already regretting my boldness.

"Okay then, why don't you come up here and we'll discuss it," Berne suggests.

"I would, but I think it's connected with a fear of doctors," I reply.

"Well, then, why don't you sit down and speak with one of my assistants?" he responds.

"I suppose I could, but I doubt that they could help me, considering that I'll be here such a short time," I answer.

By this time, I really am wishing that I hadn't volunteered anything, and I find myself resenting the doctor's discussing so personal an insight with me in public. What I really want is for him to come to me and offer comfort, maybe pay a little personal attention to me.

"Hmm," Dr. Berne says, at last. He picks up a thick book and flips through it. It looks to me like one of those diagnostic manuals most psychologists keep in their offices, only this one is for his own approach, Transactional Analysis.

When he finds the page that he's looking for, he has a member of our group pass the book back to me. "Read that, and see if it makes any sense to you," he says, as he moves on to the next "patient."

The page he has turned to shows a diagram of a particular game, outlining the apparent transaction in solid lines and the ulterior transaction in dotted lines. The title of the game is "Why Don't You-Yes, But."

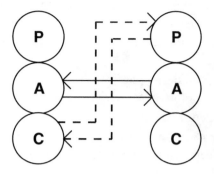

Below the diagram, there is written a short explanation of its meaning in the psychology of Transactional Analysis:

"Why Don't You-Yes But" occupies a special place in game analysis, because it was the original stimulus for the concept of games. The following example will serve to illustrate its main characteristics:

White: "My husband always insists on doing our own repairs, and he never builds anything right."

Black: "Why doesn't he take a course in carpentry?"

White: "Yes, but he doesn't have the time."

Blue: "Why don't you buy him some good tools?"

White: "Yes, but he doesn't know how to use them."

Red: "Why don't you have your building done by a carpenter?"

White: "Yes, but it would cost too much."

Brown: "Why don't you just accept what he does the way he does it?"

White: "Yes, but the whole thing might fall down."

Such an exchange is typically followed by silence....

> Since solutions are, with rare exceptions, rejected, it is
> apparent that this game must serve some ulterior
> purpose. YDYB is not played for its ostensible purpose
> (an Adult quest for information or solutions), but to
> reassure and gratify the Child.[13]

A flash of recognition surges through me like electricity. Although I do not quite know what to do with the insight, I realize that Berne has seen through me. I glance up and catch Dr. Berne's eye. He winks. I smile.

I knew walking into Berne's office that my visit would be a short one, and that we would not have the time for in-depth psychotherapy. So what was I looking for? I did not realize it consciously at the time, but what I really wanted was reassurance, someone in authority to tell me that I was okay and to act as though I mattered. I wanted to be parented.

What I *needed*, however, was to come to my own aid, and recognize the delusion of helplessness under which I had been operating. Berne's redirecting my attention, from the apparent to the ulterior meaning of my interaction with him as a "father" figure, offered me the opportunity to recognize *myself* in my vision of him. I became my own authority, for the moment anyway, and at that moment I was no longer the helpless child in need of some outside authority for my validation.

Of course, this one insight will not cure my innermost insecurities, but I feel somehow seen in a rewarding way and a little relieved, a little clearer about myself. I feel that I also have gained an insight into my own habits of thought and social interaction—that I will be able more quickly to spot my neuroses when they show up in the future. Undoubtedly, this insight will come in handy as I delve ever more deeply into my own Human Nature.

I am amazed at how my feelings of resentment toward Berne have vanished, just by my consciously recognizing the nature of the unconscious game I was playing. Yet something still lingers that has not been resolved. I can feel it. There is something much deeper than just a habitual way of behaving that I can't seem to quite get hold of. Perhaps there will be something in the next room that can help.

I leave Eric Berne's first-aid office and move on to the one next to it, marked Feeling. I can hear laughter coming from the room inside, and a big, booming German voice teasing someone. I walk in, and find that a few members of our party have already made their way here from Berne's office. They are sitting in chairs that are arranged in a circle around one empty chair. Frederick S. Perls, or Fritz as everyone calls him, is a big, burly, frizzy-haired man with a wild beard. He is sitting directly across from the empty chair. Attached to the back of the chair is a piece of paper on which the words "Hot Seat" have been written.

"Ah. Are you our next volunteer for the hot seat?" Perls asks me as I wander haplessly into the room.

I don't know what to say. So I say, "Sure, I guess so," and sit down in the empty chair.

"So, what are we working on today?" he begins, bluntly.[14]

"Father ... ahem." I try to say "father complex," but the words catch in my throat, and I try to clear it.

"Ah yes. The father complex." Perls jumps in before I can speak again.

"Well, where is this father that you are complexed about?" Some of my fellow travelers giggle, but I am not amused.

"He's dead," I manage to say, my ears burning with a self-conscious blush. Perls seems to be purposely trying to make me feel bad.

"Ah, dead. Well then, how can he complex you?" he presses.

"Well, he's in my head. Sort of," I respond feebly.

"Well then, let him out." The whole room fills with nervous laughter.

"Here," adds the doctor, more kindly. "You are feeling something that you do not want to feel, and you sometimes think of your father when you feel it, yes?"

I nod, afraid to venture another word.

"Come and sit over here then," Perls offers, getting up from his seat. I do as I'm told.

"Now you are in my seat and your father is in the hot seat. Direct all your feelings to him. Tell him what you are feeling. Instead of complexing it all over the place, and running away from these unpleasant feelings, enter *into* the projection completely. Project your father into that chair and tell him what you feel."

At first, I am too shy to say anything. But Perls has stirred up so much resentment and anger in me that words spill out as soon as I allow myself to open my mouth. "Where were you when I was growing up?" I begin, feeling suddenly as though I were actually speaking to the disembodied presence of Dad in the chair before me. With that first accusatory question, feelings begin forming themselves into words that I cannot hold back.

"Do you know how much I've suffered because you were too busy to be my dad? How was I supposed to know how to be a father or husband, or even a man in the world? You were supposed to be there for me, but you never were. Why didn't you want me?"

I had thought about all of these things in my adult life, of course. But that is exactly the point: I have *thought* them but never allowed myself to *feel* them. What use was there in dragging up old issues? I had to move on with my life and make do as I could. Yet these feelings and the fictions that they have created in my sense of myself as a man in the world are part of my present world, too, and they push through my frail resistance now like crows through the clouds.

"Why didn't you want me?" I hear myself pleading again, louder. I feel as though I am outside my own body now, existing as a purely emotional being. "What did I *do*?"

There it is. The emotional core of this lifelong suffering I have born in relationship to my absent father. Long ago, though I had never realized it, the little boy I had been had decided that he must have done something terribly wrong so that his father did not love him. From that feeling grew this haunting sense that I am somehow integrally flawed as a person.

So much of what I have done and been in my adult life has been instigated by and directed toward living down that sense of not having been good enough for my father to love. This insight seems to lighten something in me, although it hurts very deeply.

I feel clearer somehow. Yet not really safe, not knowing what to do next. Then Perls says something entirely unexpected. He tells me to trade seats with my "father."

What happens over the next few minutes is hard to describe. I begin speaking from my father's point of view to the "me" that I imagine in the empty seat before me. "What do you want from me?" the first phrase escapes from my mouth. I know this question too well. It sounds like something my father would say, though he never said it in so many words: the sense that I was asking for something he didn't have to give or that I did not deserve. I have gone over this many times in my mind, as well. This time, however, speaking from Dad's point of view, I feel a different inflection and meaning than what I had carried throughout my adult life, since the child I was first got that message and decided it meant I was "bad." It feels like it means something else now. I let my dad speak.

"I never knew my own father, son," the father in me cries. "I didn't know how to talk to you, and I didn't know what you wanted, or even what fathers were supposed to give. I hated myself for it, but I never did figure it out. I just hid in my work."

As I speak from this inner image of my father, I begin to see the same struggles in him that I have had to go through in parenting my own children. An inner sense of unity begins to build, as I speak to myself as the father in me, about my frustrations, my failings as a Human being: my wounds, my anger, and my disappointments, my grief and my weakness.

"It wasn't your fault. It was never you. I'm sorry. I am."

By the time I am finished, there is not a dry eye in the room, save Dr. Perls. A strange sense of peace settles over me, as though something has died and been reborn all in one natural cycle. I experience a sense of aliveness and personal depth that seems foreign to me, yet quite naturally mine at the same time. I somehow feel more real and more solid.

"So, that is it then, yes? Not so complex after all," the doctor says at last. "The father and the son form a single gestalt, a single beingness, yes? Okay." His pronouncement is, I know, my permission to step down, and although I wouldn't have wanted to miss what I have just experienced for anything, I gladly relinquish the seat to the next volunteer.

A seat is offered to me in the circle, as another member of our group takes the hot seat. I watch her take her own journey, not all that different from my own, uncovering the core of her own inner conflicts, which turn out also to be rooted in the misperceptions of a child and the human failings of a long past parent. It occurs to me how universal must be this covert suffering, and how ubiquitous, therefore, must be the virtual realities constructed of our unmet grief.

As our Gestalt session draws to a close, it occurs to me that what we have just done is to give the parent and the child of Berne's model each their own voice, directly. In doing so, I feel that I have somehow resolved a chronic inner tension that no amount of conversation ever could have resolved. Thinking and feeling: both metaphoric styles were working in concert.

As I and the others in our group leave Perls's session, my body is tingling and warm, almost vibrating with new vitality from the emotional release I have experienced. Physical sensing is clearly connected to my emotional life, just as are my thoughts and my feelings. The very nature of the Range of Human Awareness suggested that this would be so: all aspects of conscious awareness functioning in unison.

At the same time, however, I am feeling physically tired, and ready for a rest. Part of me is hoping that the office of "physical sensing" will be a nice spa, with a hot tub and a massage therapist. That would be great!

When I open the door to the office marked Sensing,

High Country

however, I find that some members of our party are already involved in what look like some sort of physical exercises. Just what I need after climbing a mountain. More exercise.

I am about to turn and leave when the leader of the group, a slender man of soft, fair complexion and graying hair, welcomes me. I recognize him as Alexander Lowen, one of the men who helped rescue us. I also know him as the creator of Bioenergetics, the first practical, systematic psychology to study the physical effects of neurosis. He is a well-known pioneer in the field of psychosomatic psychology.

"Try this," he says, arching backward like a limp marionette. "The Chinese call it the Taoist Arch."[15]

Chinese? I look around, and sure enough, there's Nu Lao Tzu, leaning into empty space in a perfect arch. He looks almost like he's floating, he is so relaxed and balanced in his back bend. A few other members of our group are here, but none seem as natural to the pose as Nu. Some almost fall over backward trying this exercise, whereas others can hardly bend at all. Still others seem to enjoy and be invigorated by it. I decide that if it's good enough for Mr. Nu, it's good enough for me. I let my back relax and bend backward, placing my hands at the small of my back as our instructor demonstrates.

My shoulder blades are still sore, and I feel the tension there first. But as I relax into the pose, I notice old, familiar feelings of anxiety in my lower back as well, and what I can only describe as a sense of emptiness, a neediness, up near my diaphragm. Recalling the process of entering into my feelings that I have just been through in my dialogues with "Dad," I allow myself to move into these physical sensations, rather than fighting them as I might normally have done.

Lowen's expert eye catches the physical/emotional experience I am struggling with, and he suggests that I allow my pelvis to tilt forward "into" the tension of my lower torso, and that I allow my knees to become more flexible, distributing my body weight more evenly onto the soles of my feet. As I do what he suggests, I find that I feel instantly more grounded, as though my feet were planted more solidly to the earth. A sense of effortless self-support subtly replaces the experience of helpless anxiety, and I begin to feel physically that same sense of inner unity that I felt emotionally in my work with Fritz Perls. It's a relatively small shift in awareness, but a meaningful one, especially in light of all that I have experienced since the snowstorm on Mount Persona.

Dr. Lowen then directs us through a series of other poses, each designed to amplify whatever our bodies might have to say about our habitual attitudes, feelings, and "postures" in life. By the time he is finished with us, we each have experienced some deepened insight into our habitual, unconscious ways of being in the world. The experience is more subtle than those blazing flashes of enlightenment I experienced with Perls and Berne, but no less valid, and quite possibly more lasting.

"We are the sum total of our personal experiences," Dr. Lowen explains, as we lay on the floor, resting and letting our bodies absorb what we have learned under his direction. "Those experiences are recorded in the structure of both the personality and the body. Discovering the unseen traits in your own inner self is not a journey to be taken quickly, however. Like Chinese Tai Chi, Hindu Yoga, and many other more ancient disciplines, it is a process of finding your point of balance with the Universe. As with those and other *spiritual* disciplines, working with the body with a view toward one's *psychological* healing is a lifelong journey of self-discovery."

This last bit of wisdom strikes home to me, as I get up and prepare to move on. I can see how people could become infatuated with the immediacy of each of these therapeutic techniques—Transactional Analysis, Gestalt Therapy, and Bioenergetics—and thus become enamored of them as quick fixes for their psychological woes. The truth is, however, that each of these only can open the door to our inner realms, but the real work of healing must take place on a deeper level, in our daily lives.

Even so, as I have moved from thinking to feeling to

physical sensing through this succession of therapeutic models, I seem to have uncovered more and more subtle layers of my secret inner self. With the first, I realized that I was unconsciously looking for someone to parent me. Next, I came into direct contact with a core emotional element of that unconscious need for security and validation. Finally, I experienced firsthand that sense of genuine autonomy, that sense of reliable self-support and of belonging in the world for which I have been searching throughout my adult life. Each of these insights has built upon the other, bringing me into ever more direct contact with my innermost self. What could possibly follow?

I am feeling so well centered and complete that I consider skipping the last office, the one marked Intuition, as everyone files out of Lowen's session and on to the next. But I'm wondering where Jung went, and I have a hunch that I might find him in there. I poke my head through the open office door to look inside as the others file in and there he is, sitting at the front of the room. I decide to follow the lead of my fellow travelers, most of whom have already found their seats.

I sense that we are going to be doing some sort of meditation, and that feels just right to me, so I settle in, thankful to relax for a while. The instructor introduces himself as Ira Progoff, the creator of the Progoff Journal Workshop. He introduces Jung as the originator of the methods upon which he has developed his technique; Jung leans forward in his seat with a small, gracious bow.

"We begin by letting ourselves become totally relaxed," Dr. Progoff begins. "Our bodies relax, and so do our minds. Just as we allow our bodies to cease all activity, so we allow our minds to become still also. We are just letting ourselves experience the subtle flow of our own lives."[16]

I find the man easy to listen to, and am immediately at ease in his presence, although his accent and mannerisms seem somehow incongruous to his message. He sounds like a cross between an East Coast psychoanalyst and a Far Eastern guru. I like him right away, though.

Once he has led us into a quiet, meditative state, Progoff suggests that we let our minds do whatever they want, no editing or censorship. As images and thoughts arise spontaneously, we are to make short notes about what we have experienced. Naturally, I recognize this exercise from Jung's suggestions, back on the mountain. The main difference with our using Progoff's approach is that we are not waiting for some life catastrophe to push us to our psychic breaking point before we let go of our conscious awareness enough to allow the unconscious to have its say. Instead, we relax the conscious mind on purpose, allowing the unconscious to have its say.

As the session progresses, Progoff has us enter into what he calls "dialogues" with various aspects of our beings—with our bodies, with people from our past, and even with our dreams and dream images. After each dialogue, we spend some time writing and thinking about what the images and thoughts that came up might mean in relationship to our actual lives. As the session continues, we develop a rhythm between unconscious dialogue and conscious response that, in itself, seems to affect a sense of balance and internal cohesiveness.

Not everything that comes out of these exercises, which Progoff calls "process meditation," is meaningful or even intelligible to me. I find it hard to catch the images that float up from so relaxed a state without coming back to my normal conscious awareness altogether, and thus losing contact with the inner "voice." Sometimes the sentences I hear internally do not make sense at all. But I write them down anyway. No editing. I can see that this approach takes some practice, but it offers the advantage of being more self-directed than the others.

It is in my dialogue with the body that I have my most significant breakthrough. As I relax into the meditative state, centering my awareness gently upon my body, I ask it what it has to tell me. I write both the questions and the responses briefly in my journal.

Me - Hello Body.

Body - Hello.

M - Do you have any questions for me?

B - Why do you treat me so brutally?

M - What do you mean?

B - Am I a second-class citizen to you? Do you think that your mind is what keeps you alive? Am I just a slave, to carry your brain for you?

M - No.

B - Why do you beat me?

M - I don't know. What can I do?

B - Let me in.

M - In where?

B - Into your Human being.

M - How?

B - If you make me carry your brain, let it think of me more often. If you make me feel your feelings, take notice of them. Th e dark ones that you don't want to see are killing me.

M - I'm afraid.

B - So you kill me instead of facing your fear?

M - I'm sorry. I didn't know.

B - I am your being. You knew.

M - (silence) Anything else?

B - I like sugar. Don't take that away.

M - Okay.

B - Okay.

This one dialogue, though it seems almost silly, somehow clicks my entire experience at the aid center into place. Everything—my mind, my feelings, my body, and my intuition—get to speak through it, and I realize with lightning clarity just how much of my life I live inside my thoughts. From this flashing insight a wave of others evolves as I write my response to the dialogue.

I live in my mind a lot of the time, because my body carries too much emotional pain. I think some part of me secretly wants to not be here. Not to die, really, but just not to have to feel everything that I do feel, not be completely present. So I'm not in my body a lot.

Something won't let me in, as though there were some kind of boundary inside me between my thinking mind and my being. I know that I'm not my idea of myself. I know that I am something more. But I can't seem to reach it. What is it?

As I write this last question, something opens up in me, and I feel as though I am staring into a deep black hole, a fathomless abyss of unrealized emptiness, sorrow, and loss. I can feel the void there as a physical, emotional, and intuitive sensation of such clarity that it stops my breathing for a moment. What is it? What is in there? As hard as I try, I cannot seem to get to the actual nature of this inner pit. My mind just goes dead as I approach it, as though some kind of a force field barred the way. Something in me feels divided and half-alive, but when I try to see what it is, there is only this dark, empty well of what feels like "thick" space. It's a very uncomfortable experience.

I usually think of myself as a pretty healthy person—passably intelligent, kind, considerate, and well-adjusted. Yet something inside of me, underneath all of that, is not right, not alive, not "hooked up." Is there something wrong with me that I don't know about? Am I actually not "normal," but sick in some way? Or is this ordeal part of the journey we all have to take?

I have touched something true about myself in my work with Berne, Perls, Lowen, and Progoff. I can see that the child I was is still living in me, carrying with me the fear and the self-doubt that growing up did not erase. I have glimpsed what my real adulthood could be, a sense of natural self-support and trust in my rightful place in the life of the Universe. Yet I have also discovered another level, deeper still, which I cannot contact with my thoughts and feelings at all. I just know that it is there.

The only thing that seems certain to me at this moment is that I feel an aching hunger, a yearning to remedy this inner emptiness. I have seen something central to how I got sidetracked in my life, and I've gotten a taste of how it feels to stand on my own as a whole Human being. But there is something else, something more that I cannot get to "in session." That part of the journey, if it can be accomplished at all, is going to demand something deeper of me. It is something that I think I may have to do on my own.

Apparently, I am not the only one who feels this urgency to move deeper still into the hinterland of our Human Nature. As I leave Progoff's office and step into the main foyer, I find small groups of my fellow travelers donning their packs and speaking quietly, in intimate and intense tones, about their individual revelations and their readiness to do the deeper work to which those visions pull them. Slowly, solemnly, we all trickle out the door and back into the frozen landscape of the vast Persona.

Time seems to have stood still while we were in our "healing" sessions, and I am surprised to find, as we exit the lodge, that we still have daylight to travel by. We grab a quick meal outdoors, taking some time to meet our instructors as people. I am surprised, somehow, to find that they are as human as the rest of us, with their own fears and foibles and their own unique personalities. Something in me wanted to see them as "finished," somehow, healed and whole examples of heroic personal success. Suddenly, I realize how childish that sounds, and one more subtle insight strikes me: Neurosis is normal, everyone has unhealed wounds to bear.

None of us knows what will come next in our journey, but what we have learned from Berne and Perls and the others has opened the way to our further self-exploration. I feel a deep sense of gratitude as our helpers wave and wish us well, and we resume our trek toward real life. I know they have given us important tools that we are going to need on our journey.

Yet for all that we may have discovered about our unknown selves—and I am certain I am not the only one who has been faced with such difficult personal truths—I know also that we have not yet gotten to the core of our delusions. Something within me is pushing me to keep traveling, to descend farther into the realm of the unknown within my own nature. I look around me, at the faces of my fellow travelers who have also chosen to continue on the trek, and know that they, too, are now moved by some force within their Human Nature. Although the true nature of this force is beyond our current understanding, it seems to be an instinct that pulls us and that none of us who remain can ignore.

Our party seems to have grown very small. With what may be the most difficult challenge of the whole journey yet to come, not many are willing to or able to explore the final depths of the unknown within. Frankly, once I see where it is we're heading, I cannot blame anyone who has decided to remain behind. For just beyond the boulders at base camp, almost as soon as we leave the security of those established pathways, the ground opens up into a huge crevasse. On either side of it, an ice field slopes away dramatically toward the lowlands. The only pathway left us leads into this gaping maw of frozen rock and ice, through which we each must pass if we are truly committed to reaching real life.

So this is what Jung meant by getting underneath our neuroses. I have known from the beginning, intellectually at least, that any path toward real life must lead eventually to this: the dark core of our neuroses. Standing here, now, looking down its deadly throat, however, is another matter altogether.

We are committed now, though, and Carl Jung and Mr. Nu take up the lead, allowing us one last pause to adjust our packs and muster our courage. Then, in single file, with some fear and trepidation, we each begin our personal descent into the realm of our unrealized sorrow and loss—into the Ice Caves of Neurosis.

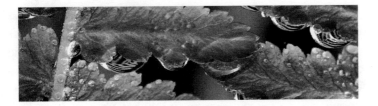

CHAPTER FIVE

. . . .

Sorrow and Loss

Paradoxically, it is the fear of suffering
that keeps us suffering, on and on.

As we enter the unfathomed darkness of the ancient crevasse that serves as a natural pathway to the core of the Persona, a chill breeze blows up the narrow ice canyon toward us. The air is dank and stale, as though it might have been trapped within the gut of the crevasse for ages, stagnated by the sheer mass and depth of the abyss that we are entering now by this slick, slender crack in its facade. The wind plays tricks upon our ears as we descend into the icy maw. It sounds like moaning and crying as it whistles by from unknown depths like a chorus of cold, damp memories from an archaic despair.

On either side of us rise verticals of ancient ice and snow, commingled with the rocks, debris, and broken trees that this enormous glacier has picked up and trapped over the years. Our guides tell us that these formations are sometimes known as the Inner Child and Parent, and we can see in them reflections of our own internal conflicts, both from our literal childhoods and from the long history of inner strife that has secretly followed. They speak to us of the ongoing inner wars between who we are in our own eyes and who we think we should be, between the ego and the superego.

It is amazing how deeply these conflicts extend into our Human Nature. Frozen in time within the icy walls of this crevasse, we can perceive the real fate of every Human being who has ever made it out of childhood. Casting our gaze down the trail to where these massive facades first emerge from the shadows, we can just make out the infant beginnings upon which our formal sense of self is erected, and the suffering that attends the evolution of that self from our first breath.

Here, we see the pain of Human birth, where everyone begins their life by being forced out of a perfect union with the mother and the womb. This traumatic separation from our total at-one-ment with our environment and with the natural flow of Life is so absolutely universal to Human existence that we tend not to think of it as a psychological wound or a source of grief. Yet from our present perspective, it stands out as a primal experience of suffering and loss.

"The birth of a man is the beginning of his sorrow," Mr. Nu recites solemnly, as he heads up our slow, painstaking survey of this ever-darkening passage toward real life. I recall the phrase, or something like it, from the sayings of the Taoist mystic Chuang Tzu. I had always thought it a little overly dramatic. Now, I'm not so certain.

Is it possible, I wonder, that we each have experienced such deep trauma at birth that we are affected for life by a sense of separation and estrangement? The answer seems self-evident as I recall what we have seen of the unconscious and its penchant for sustaining *everything* that we experience in its formless care, even those experiences that come to us before our thinking minds and our emotions have matured. Clearly, even our nonrational, more physical and instinctive experiences will be "remembered" by the unconscious, which tends to seek formal expressions for those subtle memories in our conscious lives. Since even a newborn, who has no well-defined sense of "I," can experience trauma and separation on a physical and instinctual level, there must be, somewhere within each of us, the nonconscious awareness of even that first loss.

As we scan walls that rise up from the trail we are traveling, we can see how the glacier of the "self as form" has been warped, darkened, and even cracked wide open in places by this and innumerable other early sorrows, fears, and losses. The first unanswered cry; the first misunderstood request for comfort, feeding, or rest; the first impatient or misguided parental response to the infant's endless needs: we can see how all of these apparently innocuous events so common to the early days and months of Human life might have torn at the infants that we were with the threat of abandonment, unceasing suffering, and death. Not rationally or even emotionally, perhaps, but certainly on a physical and instinctual level.

Apparently, this sense of separation tends to build from this basic "animal" insecurity, becoming attached to questions of our very worth as we enter our early childhood and begin the natural process of self-image building. Here, every parental "no," no matter how kind or how necessary, was a rejection of our little ego's wish and a threat of slander to the self-image, a potential hint at our unacceptability to the essential "other" in our lives. Just as we lost our primal oneness with our mothers at birth, we lost our unity of consciousness with her at the first "no."

We lost our closeness with our parents more traumatically if we were ever hit, yelled at, humiliated, or ignored by them. Some of us lost our parents brutally, through sexual abuse, which terminates the parent/child relationship with a single act. Yet every one of us—no matter what our early life experience—has lost our inner sense of union with our parents and felt that loss as a genuine grief. Only the level of trauma and suffering will vary.

If what I am seeing reflected in the facades of the Inner Child and Parent are accurate, then everyone who ever lived must have had his or her unconscious blind spots, unrealized fears, and unhealed inner conflicts. I am, in fact, amazed as I slowly parade down the long path into the depths of the Persona at how natural it evidently is for each of us to feel divided from our selves and from the others in our lives. How common—even unavoidable—is the loss of self-esteem, the feeling of abandonment, and the hunger to find some kind of relief from the deep suffering these unhealed wounds can cause. These unrealized threats to our acceptability and worth clearly extend to every aspect of our lives—not only into our parenting, but into all of our adult relationships, deeply affecting the texture and clarity of our marriages, our friendships, our work, and our internal relationships with ourselves.

Indeed, as I prepare to enter the bowels of this scarred glacier, I realize that it is precisely these two experiences of loss—the loss of oneness with the parent or essential "other," and the commensurate loss of self-value—that create the very foundations and structural material of all our neuroses. All of our compulsions toward achievement, our experiences of unbearable loneliness and our fear of being alone in the world, our self-doubt, our obsessive attraction toward our lovers, our addictions, and the innumerable ways that we have forsaken ourselves to gain acceptability to the essential "others" in our lives—all appear to spring from these two unavoidable, traumatic early losses. These two losses truly are universal to the Human race, and their development into neurotic tendencies appears predestined by our innate inability as infants and as children to understand or even name them. Every Human being who ever lived will have had to cope with these two burdens of self-doubt and aloneness.

An eerie melancholy rises in my belly and my chest, the faint body memory of my mother's touch, her hands as they were forty years ago, the lost time of my life that my body still recalls as though it were an instant ago, although my thinking mind cannot seem to quite make it out at all. No words, now, for this longing that I feel, this primitive and ancient wish that I have buried and exhumed again time after time throughout my life, looked for in the touch of others and found only fleetingly, always eventually to be let down and lost again as life, mine and that of the "other" that I loved, moved on. I feel a subtle emptiness, the one I felt first when Mom stopped touching me that way as I grew into boyhood and then adolescence. It seems to seep into me, icy cold and damp and undeniable as it is without remedy, its partner in the absence of my father in my life leaving me with nothing to lean on as I move onward, deeper still into the old despair. I see the way this emptiness has rippled throughout my adult life, expressing itself in my every relationship and personal endeavor.

Obviously, the losses we experience in early life do not simply fade away as we grow older. They hang around within us, frozen in time, obstructing the flow of our lives as they surface again and again in the metaphoric forms of our projections, asking to be called by their true names and healed. The sorrows and losses of our early lives do not go away no matter how old we become. They simply change their apparent expression.

The losses of self-value and of a sense of unconditional acceptance by the "other" are, in fact, apparently the dual roots of all our compulsive projections, and they tend, over time, to become the central focus of our conscious lives. This insight seems to me to be a central landmark on our journey toward real life, and I decide to make a note of it while the vision is still fresh in my mind.[1]

Field note: The loss of oneness with the parent or essential "other" and the loss of self-esteem are the two central sufferings of childhood. Apparently, they tend not to be addressed when they occur because we are too young to name them and because they are so "natural" to Human life. Still, they do not disappear just because we do not recognize them consciously.

The loss of self-esteem and the loss of oneness with the essential other are the yin and yang upon which are founded all of our neuroses. Everyone who ever lived has had to deal with this Human truth.

The rest of the group passes me by while I write this, and they are already disappearing from my view by the time I look up from my notebook. Yet I am not ready to move on. I stand here, mesmerized at the essential simplicity of these virtual facades that make up so much of our complex and difficult lives.

Before long, Carl Jung comes walking up the trail toward me. He says that he has come to retrieve me so that I do not become lost in this dangerous terrain. He stops for a moment by my side, casting a glance at what I've written in my notebook.

"So many things happen to us as we are growing up, and so quickly, that we can never deal with them all," he says, in apparent reference to my newly won insight. "Naturally, we do not simply 'shake this off.' The unconscious receives and sustains for us everything that our conscious awareness takes in. Consciously, we simply remove ourselves from whatever we can not or will not process, but unconsciously these elements of our childhood and infancy remain alive and powerful, affecting any experience that comes into contact with them."[2]

"Neurosis," he adds, moving his eyes across the vast, debris-laden facades on either side of us, "is a product of our inability to meet and to accept our life's legitimate suffering."[3]

Looking at these icy walls through Jung's perspective, I can see how our unhealed early losses multiply in scope and weight as we grow up, tainting our vision of an ever-increasing number of our life events, each of which then becomes nearly impossible to work through as well. The "legitimate" losses that we cannot grieve then tend to pile up, one upon another, building upon our first deluded visions of ourselves and the world around us. All the way into our midlives and beyond, these blind spots grow and even flourish in our lives as long as we do not stop and reexamine the assumptions and unconscious habits upon which our daily way of life has been erected.

I turn to mention this to Jung, but he has already headed down the sloping trail toward the group. I hurry to catch up to him, and we walk single file down the narrow trail. I ask him about the reason for all this delusion that seems to come so naturally to Human life.

"The remnants of our early years that have not been realized for what they are," he answers, "will keep their infantile affects so long as they have not been reunited with our adult minds. That is how they build in later life into neuroses, even though they may not have caused any trouble in our youth. The attitudes of childhood naturally become untenable, because they are not appropriate to adult life. There comes a time, therefore, when these things call out to be dealt with, and present themselves, demanding to be seen for what they actually are.

"It is only when they are appraised with our adult eyes and seen for what they actually are that they lose their power to delude us and disrupt our lives."[4]

Jung's words strike a chord within me. As I move along, following Jung's lead, I understand what he is pointing to as the deeper meaning and purpose of all the chaos and delusion created by the "natural" formation of the universal Human condition called neurosis: Our neuroses—our self-delusion, our addictions, our compulsions, our chronic depressions, our failed relationships, and much of our physical illness—all act to offer opportunities in our later lives to find a resolution for what we could not heal in our early years.

Indeed, I see reflected in these ice facades of compulsion, obsession, and unresolved grief all of the elements of my own unrealized suffering. The increasing darkness of our steep descent into this ice crevasse, the echoes of the footsteps of the others in our party, and the sound of my own breathing seem to entrance me with feelings of my early days, reflected in the difficulties of my later life. Beneath every heartache I have felt and not been able to quite heal, beneath this lingering feeling that I must be missing something, this hunger to feel more alive that seems to keep growing the older I become, the fear of death, and the desire, at the same time, just to numb out and not feel anything at all—all of it now reverberates with the unfinished and unmet sorrows and losses of my early life. I begin to see that my neuroses and the "virtual realities" they create—my self-delusions and the addiction to pleasure at all costs that sometimes overwhelms me—are like scabs formed over my unhealed wounds.

I have to stop again to regain my sense of inner balance. Every sorrow and loss I have not wanted to or been able to address in my entire life presses in upon me now, each one connected with the thread of neurosis to all the others. My recurring sense of failure and inadequacy in my life's work, despite my having done my best; my shame at those times when depression and the search for relief from it have led me into self-degradation and emotional blindness; my recurring bouts of ill temper and anger, which still flair up so unexpectedly even these many years after my having seen how useless and harmful they are—they all crowd down upon me at once as I see them for what they are. They create in me an overwhelming sense of utter futility, and take my breath away.

These are exactly the dark, phantom perceptions that I tend to keep in check, beneath conscious awareness, in order to get through daily life and keep living, and that I manage to keep out of consciousness by staying busy or preoccupied. Individually, no one of them would be sufficient to cause any real problems in my life. The problem is that they are all attached to something much deeper than I can see with my conscious awareness, and so they tend to drag me down whenever one or more of them surfaces in my life. Now, from my present perspective in the gut of the Persona, they surround me like an avalanche of archaic despair, frozen in time. No wonder I do not allow them directly into conscious awareness in daily life. If I felt all of this all of the time, I would not be able to function on even the most basic of levels.

As I stand here, in the face of the entire panorama of my own unresolved suffering, I begin to understand more personally the deep purpose of the persona and its virtual world. If I had felt the full weight of the suffering that I am feeling now when I was a child, or even at the age of twenty-one, it could have easily destroyed me. Even now, I have to look away in order to keep moving on.

As I struggle to regain my composure and continue down the trail, I realize that this overwhelming weight of old debris is not only about me and my own personal suffering. This is about all of us, all Human life, and everyone who seeks and meets the truth about their lives. Our self-delusions, our addictions, our infatuations with the others in our lives to whom we look for surcease for our inner loneliness and insecurity, all of these and so many other of the "unexplained" dis-eases that we face are simply the scabs, the unsightly coverings that keep our unmet suffering alive until a time when we can return with the insight and maturity to heal them. Eventually, they tend to mess up our lives so badly that we simply *have* to stop and take stock of our own perceptions; that, or shrivel up and die, or freeze eventually into some kind of empty social pose. Truly, our personas and the virtual realities they show us are our cocoons: a necessary chrysalis or shell that anyone who wants access to real life must penetrate and then leave behind.

As I turn my gaze from my own inner reflections on down the trail toward my fellow travelers, I can see that they, too, are feeling the inner burden of this place. Some are leaning into the ice walls, turning to their very grief for support. Others are barely standing, crouched and struggling to find a place of balance within themselves; still others seem to have found their footing and are helping their comrades to stand and face the inner night. Clearly, this realm will not be easy for anyone.

Indeed, I realize as I look down the trail that our journey is about to get more difficult by far. I had not realized how far we have traveled into the dark questions of our lives, or how the scenery has changed in the meantime and how dark our trail has become. I turn my attention toward the higher reaches of those towering ice walls that bind the trail we are on, looking for the reason for these deepening shadows, and find, to my surprise, that the two walls have melded high above our heads, creating a thick single arch up near the surface. I can see that this high arch quickly grows much thicker down the trail, creating a small dark tunnel. We are no longer simply in a canyon made of ice. We are, in fact, entering into a passageway of unfathomable darkness, where everything that we have yet to grieve of our entire lives now threatens to surround and even to bury us.

I catch up to the rest of the group at the dim entrance to that cavernous abyss, where the trail disappears into the funnel-like, dark hole created by the merging ice facades. Clearly, the path from here on will offer a deathly challenge to our courage and our confidence in our trusted guides, as the roof of the ice tunnel becomes thicker and thicker, pressing down threateningly upon the frozen path. None of us seems particularly anxious to move into this ominous terrain.

A feeling of dread and depression teases us from the dank cavern ahead, where the path disappears into the endless night. Behind us, there is light, but it invites us only to life as mere personae. If we will have any chance of recovering our real lives, we will have no choice but to enter the realm of shadows that confronts us. Indeed, this journey through the inner darkness appears as an innate and entirely natural, unavoidable aspect of the Human path to real life. We each must enter into it if we are to ever recover the truth about our selves and our right relationship to Life. Of course, that knowledge does not make entering the darkness any easier for anyone. There are no promises of comfort, pleasure, or success in this terrain. Only a predestined date with the unknown.

The Ice Caves of Neurosis:
The Inability to Grieve

Our progression is solemn and quiet, as one by one we leave the light of day and enter into the abyss. Mr. Nu is standing on the trail as we pass, checking our gear and giving us encouragement for the difficult journey ahead.

"This realm has been navigated by many other travelers before you," the old man says, touching us each as though by way of blessing as we enter the vast catacomb. "This is the realm of Mara, which the Buddha himself had to face before he came to understand the true nature of Life. Remember that the darkness and the fear you will experience are natural and part of your own Human Nature. Remember the Buddha, sitting unmoved in the face of Mara's armies.

"Remember," he echoes, as the last of us finally slips away into the cavern's depths. "Remember," he repeats, as he at last falls into line, bringing up the rear.

I do remember Mara from the legend of the Buddha's enlightenment, and the image serves to distract me from my trepidation, temporarily, as I steel my nerves and enter the deep darkness before me. I recall how, after years of wandering the forests and studying with one meditation master and ascetic after another, Gautama Buddha finally sat down under a Bodhi tree, vowing not to move until he became enlightened to the true nature of Reality. Then Mara, the god of death, tempted and attacked the Buddha with every vice and terror known to man, but the Buddha remained unmoved and every "arrow" shot at him fell to the ground at his feet and turned into a flower.[5]

There are no flowers here, I think to myself cynically, as I reach for my flashlight and edge hesitantly into the tunnel. I try to take heart in the old man's last words as I step ever further into the deepening dark.

Before long, we all are deep into the tunnel, which has shrunk to a canal so restrictive that we must crouch and contort our bodies in order to fit through. I can feel the hard, gritty ice rub at my back and my shoulders as I force myself to keep moving into the oppressive, tomblike passageway. The air is so thick that I think I may gag, and the darkness begins playing edgily upon my senses.

We can barely see, although each of us has now dug out our lanterns or flashlights. The lights bring a comfort of sorts, although they are too limited in focus and too weak in intensity to give us a clear view of the realm we are entering. They can show us the pathway, but not the terrain ahead, and their comforting brightness actually blinds us to the greater dark into which we must pass. Still, none of us dares turn them off. They are all we have and, so, seem to me better than nothing.

Being able to see where we are, however, adds little reassurance to our current plight. The low ceiling and the filthy ice that brushes against me on either side as I crawl through the restrictive passageway cue in me an innate, trapped-animal urge to flee. I can't breathe; I want to stand up and cannot. I press up against the ice ceiling in a futile, reactive resistance to all that is stirring in me. I want to cry out or to scream, but do not. Something catches in me at the throat and I swallow my desperation like a lump of thick, wet clay.

As we move along the dark tunnel, these feelings of panic, which I have no way to address, begin to morph into myriad related images, feelings, and physical sensations from my life. Irresistibly and quite automatically, my body recalls the sensation of abject helplessness at being hit, grabbed, shaken, and pushed around in my childhood and youth by my parents, then by my teachers and by the "big kids" at school. Connections I had never seen before arise in me as long "forgotten" sensations and memories. The feeling of utter helplessness surfaces, of being rejected not only by Mom and by Dad but also at times by my friends, and later by lovers and by my own children as they struggled to find their own places within the world—all tied somehow to those first, early losses by one common thread of unbearable suffering that I, nevertheless, had no way to avoid. Now, I feel as though they are all about to come tumbling down onto me, crushing me with their unmanageable weight.

In response to the imminent threat of a painful inner death, I try to summon my courage and my will by bringing to mind all that I have learned about the nature of this place and about its real function in my Human life. I think about my father, and the core truths I have discovered about our relationship or lack thereof. I try to reassure myself that the phantoms that are stirred in me by this endless night, this dark night of the soul, are illusions and mere metaphoric memories of the suffering of days now long gone by. I fight against these impossible feelings with rational thought and the last force of will I can muster.

As I continue walking, however, the dank cold starts to drain the reserves from my flashlight, my courageous conscious will, and even my body. The others in our group appear to falter, too, as they stumble and stop, or cry out now and then, sighing and grunting with the strain of everything that presses in upon them. Yet there is nothing any of us can do but to move on, ever more deeply into the dark night.

Just as I manage to damp down my emotions enough to stay under control, however, the muscles between my shoulder blades clamp down on my spinal column in a horrific spasm. I cry out, and try to straighten up but cannot. Hoping to find some bit of relief, I try to reenact the techniques I found so helpful before, of physically moving into the cramping and allowing my feet to rest more firmly on the ground. But I cannot stand upright beneath the oppressive confinements of the glacier. Nothing seems to relieve my pain. I am desperate to stand straight again. I am confused and overwhelmed with fear, despair, and images of past and future suffering. I need someone to help me. Anyone. But there is no one to talk with. Everyone else in our group is having the same impossible difficulties, and our guides seem to have disappeared into the vast, blank night behind and ahead of us.

I summon the last reserves of my courage as I inch along in the impinging dark, committed now to make it through this place or to die in the effort. I struggle to find inner strength by chanting all the affirmations I can muster, trying in one last desperate effort to bolster my conscious will to action. *I am not my thoughts about myself. I am a capable and worthwhile person. My parents loved me in the best way they knew how. They never wanted me to suffer. I am a capable and worthwhile person.*

But even as I chant these usually fortifying slogans of self-worth, my conscious mind, my body, and my flashlight become ever weaker and less effective against the inner night. This appears, in fact, to be the case with everyone who has ventured here today and, perhaps, ever. No one seems clear as to what to do, and I can hear the sound of desperate effort, the occasional cry of unbearable suffering and unmanageable fear.

Yet there is nothing to do but to keep moving onward. Without our guides, and with our lights failing as they are, we could not leave now if we wanted to. We cannot go back to the way we were before, and we cannot go much farther forward on the strength of our conscious awareness.

As the darkness becomes more and more complete, the tunnel becomes smaller, too, and eventually we all have to stop and give up trying to get anywhere at all. As our lights blink out, one by one, the batteries gone dead, I feel a new panic arise, stronger than any I have ever felt, at the realization that nothing I do now will save me. I feel split open, as though my mind were tearing away from my body, leaving it to die; as though my belly and chest were already caved in by the impending weight of this place and my spirit were leaving with a wrenching rip of the innermost flesh. I flatten out onto the cold, wet ground, exhausted and completely in the dark, without an ounce of will or any notion at all of what I might do to save myself from all that crushes down upon me. Indeed, we all finally give up, lying flat in the icy tube in one last desperate attempt to find the core of our inner truth.

Just then, however, just when we have given up our striving to combat our pain, just as we let go of our willful notions of how this all ought to be and of bulling our way to clarity on the force of our conscious wills, a wail rings out that returns me to my real senses. It sounds like a call, really. Someone has found something and broken free.

One by one, we inch forward, crawling like babies, like wounded animals on our bellies, until suddenly we reach the point where our restrictive ice tomb drops us into a cavern of unfathomable space. I sigh with relief, and I hear others do the same, as I drag myself the last few feet into the cave. At least we can stand upright once again, with the pressure of the Persona literally off our backs.

From somewhere off in the darkness, Jung speaks up. His voice echoes with such reverberation that it suddenly becomes quite clear how vast the inner world we have entered actually is. We are not so much now in a passageway as in another world, an actual underworld of blinding shadows, deep beneath the surface of our daylight lives.

"In the first half of life," Jung says, speaking with a calm clarity that both assures and subtly unnerves me, "it is altogether appropriate that we rely upon the force of our conscious awareness and our wills to cope with the environment in which we find ourselves. It is, in fact, essential that we do so, in order to develop the confidence needed to move beyond our parents and into the world as independent entities.[6]

"Yet there comes a time, after we have reached the peak of our conscious skills and of the established persona, when all of our ideas and our learned abilities will begin to lose their power to affect our real lives.

"At this point," Jung says, as he shows himself at last, turning his own failing light toward his face and, thus, lending it a ghostly visage, "the light of conscious awareness may actually blind us to the deeper possibilities of our lives, just as the light of your flashlights have hindered your own eyes from adjusting to the dark. The deep shadowlands cannot be perceived through conscious awareness directly, and cannot be influenced by the direct force of conscious will, for the simple reason that these shadows are, themselves, unconscious."[7] And, with that, Jung douses his own light and disappears once again from view.

The reality of our present journey begins to sink in, as one by one we realize the absolute futility of our situation. The wind that whistled through the canyon at the start of our foray into this realm is now behind us, a passing product of the transition between the warmth of sunlight and the cool, dank darkness of this underworld. Now, the silence that surrounds us is absolute. We are captive to the vast inner realm of the persona—a realm beyond the light of conscious awareness; a realm dominated by the subterranean force of the unconscious; apparently, a realm of depression, neurotic fantasies, and impending death.

As I sit here in the darkness, wondering how Jung and Mr. Nu will save us from this deadly plight, my body begins to ache with every phantom pain and feeling of dis-ease that I have ever felt. I am filled with the leaden lethargy of chronic depression, and with an excruciating craving for the light of day, for food and drink and comfort. Self-doubt erupts within me, fostered by my inability to satisfy even the most basic of these felt needs, and I begin to question my very ability to make this trek at all. Self-doubt boils into rage at our guides, as I begin to fantasize old Nu and Jung, sitting outside in the sun somewhere in safety, having abandoned us to our darkness like callous cowards after having led us here against our conscious will. Some part of me, of course, knows that this is untrue, but there is a wild, desperate part of me that has no interest in truth or reason now. It just wants out!

I try my flashlight once again, resolved to take matters into my own hands, but it is dead. I try to stumble toward where I think the exit must be, although no hint of its location can be seen. Others do likewise, beginning to panic too. Soon we are all wandering around this vast, dark hinterland in chaos, bumping into one another, bickering, and blaming one another and our leaders, even our parents, for our plight, battling not only our own lostness, but each other and the phantom villains of our individual histories.

This cavern of our inner grief seems a vast, timeless abyss. There is so much we cannot see from our conscious point of view; simply venting our conscious feelings does no good at all. Indeed, the more we push for a release, the more our destructive emotions, addictions, and compulsions push from within us, moving us into all kinds of senseless thoughts, feelings, beliefs, and actions. Clearly, mere catharsis will not remove us from this place.

The darkness of my sorrow and my enslavement to my blackest emotions seem infinite and hopeless, and I find myself falling into a deep despair as I realize the absolute futility of my actions and my anger. I am immobilized from deep within. I sit down on the ground right where I am and give over to my grief. One by one, each member of our group apparently comes to the same conclusion, and the cavern falls into a deathly calm.

Depression absorbs me, seeping into my brain and the cells of my body. As I become immersed in this pure sense of unnamed sorrow, I lose even the desire to move, much less to try to find my way to real life. The dialogue of self-defeat stirs within my mind as I ponder the evident doom of everyone who has made it to this vast, trackless place. Even if we could summon the strength and courage to move on, which way would we go? We do not even know where we are, so how can we be expected to know what to do from here?

I begin to wonder why we came here at all. Maybe this is all just a blind canyon with no exit at all, a figment of our group imagination. Maybe no one ever gets beyond the deepest ice caves of neurosis, and we should all just learn to ignore these "bad" feelings when they come up. Maybe they will simply go away.

But just as the thick, blackened mesh of my despair claims me, a calm, clear, firm, and familiar voice comes echoing toward us from down some unseen corridor, across the way from our place in the darkness of this inner cave.

"In the intensity of your own deepest, dark emotions," Jung's voice breaks through the deep void once more, "is all the energy that you will need to make it through this place.

"Close your eyes. Stop trying to see your way out of your distress, and let the nature of the place itself sink in," he advises, still calm and confident, as though he knew that we would come to this.

I hear a long, deep, even sigh; someone is taking a slow, deep breath in, and an even slower, longer exhale. It is Mr. Nu— his sole comment. Even though he says nothing, I feel better knowing that he, too, is here in the darkness.

Something in me knows that what Jung is saying must be right, and so I do as he suggests, calming down the best I can, letting myself simply be in darkness, eyes closed, not straining to see anything.

As I sit, unmoving and without goal or recourse to my plight, the weight of my internal darkness lifts a little, and I realize how, all my life, I have been struggling to avoid suffering and to achieve some kind of freedom from my own fears and self-doubt. I always found a way to get rid of my pain and my dis-ease, either with caffeine or alcohol or food or sex or some other diversion, some personal achievement, some new drug, some brilliant insight, or some newfound power. None of it lasted. None of it really helped in the long run.

My eyes are still useless and closed in the unmanageable depths of my own inner darkness, but I can see that everything I did to try to avoid my own suffering only added to the toll of my suffering later on. I realize also that I needed to go through what I went through then in order to become as convinced as I am now that all of these attempts to avoid my own suffering are futile. Those delusions, too, are an inevitable part of Human life. Now, I know it's time to stop trying to avoid the painful truths about my life and face them each for what they actually are.

I feel a certain lightening of my grief, as I realize the deeper meanings of the suffering I have endured and have caused to myself and to others in my efforts to avoid the pain I feel. In essence, those deluded acts were unavoidable. Clearly our wits are no match for our own projections and compulsions. Our wits are, in fact, exactly what our unconscious compulsions, addictions, and depressions are designed to thwart. These unworkable, neurotic attitudes are supposed to make us stop and look within for whatever it is that we have not perceived about ourselves.

Finally, I think I get it. The whole purpose of this darkness, this impenetrable depression, and the ultimately futile way of life that goes along with the persona and its attendant neuroses is ultimately to force us to *stop* our conscious minds enough to let a deeper knowing speak. The whole problem, really, is not the suffering itself, but our unwillingness to accept sorrow and loss as legitimate and unavoidable aspects of our Human lives. Within our neuroses is the suffering we could not bear before, and through our neuroses we are reminded of this suffering in the second half of life, when we can finally approach and heal old wounds.

"Suffering itself is not an illness," Jung reminds us, somehow knowing just what to say at this moment. "It is only when we refuse to acknowledge our complexes and our suffering that they become pathological."[8]

Yes. Of course. How could I have missed that? Somewhere in the back of my mind, I believe I knew it all along. It is my fear of facing what I *must* face—that is, my own legitimate life sorrow—that is making this place so devastating and intolerable. I know that even this dense darkness is itself a natural part of my life's journey. Panicking or railing against it is not going to help.

"In order to gain possession of the energy that you will need to make it through this inner darkness," Jung continues, offering more much-needed instruction on dealing with this darkened realm, "you must make the emotional state in which you find yourself just at this moment your starting point."[9]

Start from where you are. Boy, that sounds familiar.

"You must make yourself as conscious as possible of the mood you are in, sinking into it without reserve and noting down on paper all the fantasies and other associations that come up."

I am taken aback at this last instruction. How am I supposed to note anything down on paper when I cannot even see my hands? Yet when I open my eyes, I realize that a weak light is streaming in from some unknown source at the far end of the cavern. It is golden, like the sunlight of late afternoon or early evening.

Between the slight addition of this natural light and the

adjustment to the dark that closing my eyes has accomplished, I find that I can just see my notebook in its compartment on my backpack. I pull it out and, although I cannot really see what I am writing and drawing, I set to work, relaxing as completely as possible into this overwhelming atmosphere and giving free voice to whatever comes up.

"Let your fantasies flow as freely as you can without losing the sense of the emotions that have been overwhelming you," Jung continues. "Know that, whether it makes any sense right now to your rational mind, what is coming out of you is, at present, the fullest possible expression, either concretely or symbolically, of the feelings that could not find voice before. Since the depression and compulsions you have been experiencing are not manufactured by the conscious mind, but are unwelcome intrusions from the unconscious, this free-form fantasying is a good way to get clear about what is really going on, because it lets the unconscious speak for itself. Whatever you could not look at directly gets, in this way, an opportunity to be expressed through metaphor and free association."

As frightening and dangerous as it sounds, this process makes perfect sense in terms of all that we have seen so far in our trek through the high country. The depression that has grabbed us is apparently the product of the efforts of the unconscious to express our forgotten suffering in a meaningful way. Therefore, opening ourselves to the unconscious while immersing ourselves in the depression (or in any other compulsive experience or projection the unconscious might offer) will be, theoretically at least, an excellent technique for moving through this very difficult terrain. I don't imagine it would be wise for the novice to try it, however, without direct supervision from a trusted guide. I get the sense that these deep shadow realms are full of unforeseen pitfalls and blind alleys into which one could, conceivably, disappear forever.

With not a little trepidation, I close my eyes again, allowing myself to immerse into my own deepest fears, sorrows, and neurotic fantasies. My mind wanders all over the place at first;

but slowly, with the assistance of our experienced helpers, I relax my body and my mind until a quiet space opens up within me, just a little. I allow the difficult emotions and compulsions I have been resisting so fiercely into my awareness, letting myself feel everything that they stir up within me. Avoiding my habitual response of either fleeing from my uncomfortable feelings or wallowing in them, I now simply observe what is going on inside of me, as visual images and fantasies arise, along with seemingly random thoughts and intriguing speculations. They come up spontaneously from somewhere beyond my conscious awareness. Many of them seem to make no conscious sense at all—they are dreamlike, odd, even bewildering. I just let them come and write them down.

As I sink into the despair that I am feeling, a softer, clearer emotion arises on its own—sadness, an impenetrable sadness at my lost childhood, and at all the things that could have been and now never will be because my childhood is over. Reflexively, I pull back from these dark feelings and the memories they summon, trying to distance myself from the unbearable weight of this deep sorrow and loss. My whole life is spoiled, I think. It will never be right again.

As I sit with this feeling, letting my awareness soften around it, a darkened image comes into view: a three-dimensional ball of mealworms. They look gross, but I am not repulsed by them, for I have a sense that they are full of life. Certainly, no one would eat them for fun, but they are full of protein and can be eaten and even digested. In fact, the mealworms themselves seem disgusted with me that I won't eat them, and that they are therefore about to go to waste. The sense of the image subtly shifts, and I feel as though I myself am both the mealworms and the sphere that they cover. The feeling is awful. I am covered in worms and trapped within a sealed sphere, but at the same time I am in direct contact with a source of rich if not altogether pleasant nourishment.

Out of habit, I drift automatically toward an abstract, analytical awareness in the face of such a distasteful reality. I recognize the sphere as an archetypal image of the Self. Before long I find myself straying ever further from the relaxed, meditative attitude into an abstract analysis of the meaning of a Self infested with mealworms.

"Critical attention must be eliminated," Jung cautions us, as though he knows exactly what we are likely to be tempted to do just now. "If you see pictures or images, note them in writing or even draw simple line drawings of their basic features. Some of you will hear an inner voice, speaking in thoughts or even audible words and sentences. Everything should be noted down, whether your rational mind thinks them worthwhile or not."

Part of me wants to resist the notion of intentionally absorbing myself in my feelings of sorrow and loss, especially considering how thoroughly in the dark we are about the essentials to our very survival. But as I allow myself to freely experience even this inner resistance, neither denying nor trying to remedy anything, I find that I am, in fact, feeling ever more energized, if no less depressed. Apparently *everything* that comes up in me—even my resistance to letting everything come up in me—brings with it a natural energy that becomes released when I just let it be as it is and express itself freely.

"This inner work by itself can be revitalizing," Jung offers in a pleased and reassuring tone. "It tends to create an entirely new atmosphere in the psyche, thanks to the assistance and cooperation of the conscious mind with the contents of the unconscious."

Taking Jung's encouragement to heart, I allow myself to fall back into the mealworm fantasy. Spontaneously, I find myself picking one of the mealworms off of the sphere and putting it into my mouth. It wriggles as it slides down my throat, and I nearly gag. As soon as the little worm hits my stomach, however, it fills my whole being with light. I look at the sphere, and the place where I removed the worm is now a spot of luminescence, as though some inner light were now allowed to shine through. I look back at the worm in my belly. It seems to be waiting for something. It holds a sign of some sort that I struggle to read, but cannot. The vision fades, and I am left with a sense of melancholy, warm but sad.

As I come back to my normal waking consciousness, I realize that Jung is right. Even though I still do not quite understand the meaning for all of these weird images and feelings that have come up, there is a definite increase in my sense of well-being and aliveness, a stabilization or integration of sorts. Simply put, I do not feel as hopelessly lost as before. I am still pretty much in the dark as to how to get out of this cavern, but my inner pain does not seem quite so vast or unmanageable, although certainly it is still somewhat frightening and uncomfortable. Oddly, I am no longer suffering, even though I can still feel my sorrow and loss.

It occurs to me that this must be exactly how the metaphors of the virtual self lose their power to delude us—by our willing participation in the role of healing for which they are designed; by our allowing them to speak to us directly, in their own language, about the things in us that we have consciously denied or failed to let into our awareness.

I can also see that it is vitally important to go through the sometimes tedious task of writing it all down. Otherwise, what has come up from the unconscious may sink back down into oblivion or be colored by our projections and repressions. By giving the new insight a solid form of some kind, we actually secure it within the world of our conscious awareness, so that it is not likely to come back up and surprise us again as some sort of "projected projection."

A sense of excitement surges through me as I realize in a flash what the whole point of these exercises and of this very trek into our own hinterland has been. It is just this experience of offering the hidden contents of the unconscious a chance for expression in conscious form, of bringing our conscious and nonconscious awareness into dynamic communication and unified partnership. In this, the most important thing seems only that we let the unconscious join with and speak through the voice of the form–making conscious awareness as freely as possible. In essence, as Jung might put it, "the conscious mind puts its media of expression at the disposal of the unconscious.

Passageways:
When Sorrow Finds a Meaning

As each of us enters into the projections and compulsions that we have been trying so hard for so long to overcome, they open up before us into an array of other images, feelings, phrases, and intuitions that somehow seems to bring new light into our inner night. By opening our eyes into the darkness at the right time, and accepting what is actually there (rather than just looking for what we want, expect, or think we should see), we find that we have all the light we need. We begin to see the landmarks of projection all around us, and they help us to define the actual architecture of our neuroses.

As I continue ever deeper into the dark realm of my innermost sorrow and loss, images of my childhood float to the surface of my mind, commingled with images that could have never been: A bloody breaking from my mother's belly, splattering my whole family with red; a sense of flying through my old bedroom, or maybe the room is filled with water and I am swimming there. These are images that I never would have given expression in my normal thoughts, no matter how "honest" I was trying to be with myself about my own suffering. Then come a few cryptic phrases: Summer always is. The sun never goes down. Work on what has been spoiled by the harvest. The water of the life that you are living is not yours, but it belongs to you.

Time and again, as I let myself simply feel my "bad" feelings, an inner pressure builds up, threatening my endurance and my concentration. Yet I know now that it was only my own resistance to the unknown realms of my own being that was causing all this suffering. By simply keeping my eyes open inwardly to whatever comes up, I am gaining an ever-clearer, if nonrational, image of this inner realm; and of the fear, sorrow, loss, and confusion that has kept me in the dark about my life.

Each member of our group is deeply engrossed in his or her own similar processes, and an aura of vitality begins to suffuse the vast, gray cavern where we work. As I turn my attention toward the outside world, I can begin now to make out the boundaries and character of this "endless" realm of darkness, and it occurs to me that it only seemed endless because I had not wholly entered into it. Like any darkened room viewed from a brightly lit hallway, the inner boundaries of the place remained invisible to conscious view, making the darkness and suffering seem endless. The unconscious fears of the lost child inside then became excited into creating all kinds of projective fantasies about its inner suffering.

Little did I know, the light I needed to see my way around this vast inner realm was right inside the very fantasies that I was trying so desperately to suppress and ignore. Once I began to listen to and give shape to those little waking nightmares, everything in me began to lighten up. Now, the fears that I had hid from are actually enlightening my path to real life.

Still, there remains the problem of interpreting the messages that have come up in this way. If we just leave them where they are, we no doubt will trip over them again later. Or, worse, we will end up repressing them all over again because we have not resolved the grief to which they speak or because we have not really understood the message that the unconscious is seeking to express. We must remember that, although things have lightened up a little, we are not out of the dark yet; and we will not be until we have come to see our inner realm with clarity.

When I ask Jung about this, he suggests that a lot can be achieved sometimes just by working in a creative fashion with the images that arise. He says that the very act of conversing with the unconscious—by giving form to whatever comes up, and then responding freely to the new image—can produce a genuine "expansion of consciousness."

This seems to be his invitation for us to move on, and so, one by one, we pick up our packs and our notebooks and move slowly toward the warm golden light that is filtering in still so timidly through some as yet unperceived passageway. As we reach the far end of the "endless" darkness that seemed once to comprise the whole world of our deepest unconscious, we find on the rough rocky walls where the ice ends, myriad ancient-looking cryptographs and etchings, each apparently left here by the innumerable travelers who passed through here before us. Now, we begin to make our marks too, letting our creative inspiration arise from what we have discovered within us.

Soon the cavern is filled with songs, with the scratching of rock on rock, and with chanting, as we each begin to form our raw, spontaneous ramblings and scribbles into actual, finished drawings, poetry, songs, dances, and personal rituals. New images begin to fill the open spaces on the cavern walls, and group members gather together in celebration, singing, weeping, dancing, and chanting with one another in mutual relief from the tremendous weight that was upon us. As I join them, I realize exactly what that weight actually was. It was not the weight of our sorrow and loss, which is as natural to life as breathing. It was our fear of suffering that held us captive to the darkness. Paradoxically, it seems that it is, in fact, only the fear of suffering that keeps us all suffering, on and on.

Clearly, the act of giving the unconscious images a creative formulation—of working with them in an artistic and creative way—yields for each of us a subtle and yet powerful intuitive grasp of our true inner state. What is more, the images that arise take on a certain transcendent appeal, arising apparently not only from our own personal pain, but also from the greater depths of our Human awareness of Life in all its varied guises.

As we finish our individual creations, Jung encourages us to stand back and look at all that has come up—the feelings, the scribblings, and the artful images—and try to come to some kind of critical understanding of how they all fit together in context to our present-day lives. For me, the insights are astounding. I have moved from resentful despair, into abject depression and the ramblings of self-defeat, to an open-ended internal listening that now leads me to a few carefully crafted, deeply personal lines of poetry that seem to both sum up and to validate my entire experience of this particular trip into my inner darkness:

The water in my childhood room had threatened to drown me, shrinking my life to the size of the dot below a question mark. I held my breath as long as I could hold on. Dying, I let go, breathed in the fluid I was fighting, and swam away.

As I write these few lines, which certainly are not great poetry but seem somehow to free something in me, I realize what all of this "recovering the inner child" business is actually about. It's not about the child I was per se, or even about forgiving my parents or reclaiming my self-esteem. Those are all important passageways toward my real life, but they themselves are not the goal of this difficult grief work. The goal, the real prize, the life-restoring experience that letting go into these old fear-based emotions has to offer is simply this: a return to that sense of inner unity, that dynamic union of the conscious mind with the contents of the unconscious that marks our truly personal contexts for a meaningful experience of being.

The change of conscious attitude that allows this inner re-union is simply the willingness to face and to feel deeply my own grief. By breaking through the old taboos against experiencing the suffering of my life, I automatically enter into an unrestricted contact not only with my own true history as a Human being, but also with *everything* that the unconscious has to offer: every creative inspiration, every deep instinct of my Human Nature, every evolving beauty in the ceaseless flow of life. In short, my willingness to experience whatever is in me to experience brings me into a genuine state of unconditioned presence.

No longer so absorbed in my own inner struggles, no longer so fearful of what others might see in me or of what I might find within myself if I relax, I find all the space I need within myself to settle down and just let myself be. As I look into the faces of the others, in the ever-lightening atmosphere of this personal intimacy, I see them as if for the first time, not just as faces or images, but as beings who experience the same sorrows and fears and ecstatic vitalities as I. At this moment, we are one, bathed together in the glow of real life as it filters increasingly through the convoluted passageways of our neuroses, somehow touching each of us enough to let us see each other as the alive beings that we truly are.

The clearer we get about the meaning of the images and insights offered up by the unconscious, the more alive and vital we all become. Soon, we gain the energy and confidence to move beyond our core grief issues, and into their extensions in our larger inner life. Before long, we find ourselves packing up and traveling together, each in our individual styles, along the natural corridors of inner truth, toward the light that now is shining ever more directly into the dark cavern from somewhere beyond this realm.

As we move onward, the ice caves of our neurosis open into vast passageways, filled with cryptic images depicting not only our sorrow, but also our deepest inner being and our true potential as persons within the world of form. What began as a journey into darkness is transformed now into an extended adventure of self-discovery. We find ourselves exploring more and more of this terrain with interest, rather than with trepidation, as we see more and more an archetypal Human quest reflected in our personal journeys.

As we move forward, toward the lighted end to the tunnel, something wholly unexpected begins touching us from the realm beyond frozen facades Neurosis and Persona. We sense it even before we actually get there. A hint of fresh air wafts in on the warmth of a late summer's breeze, thrilling us with both delight and some anxiety. Can this be real? I wonder in near disbelief. Is it possible to move straight from Neurosis into the brilliance of a real life?

The Transcendent Function:
A Conjoining of Opposites

The hint of fresh air and the suggestion that it brings about the nearness of real life excites my mind with myriad speculations. What will real life be like? I know that whatever I may have thought about it in the past must have been tainted by an unknown amount of unconscious projection and idealization. I wanted real life to be a kind of permanent enlightenment, where I would finally get beyond my suffering and foolishness. Now, I can see that this was somewhat infantile and unrealistic. No one knows how much there is that they don't know about themselves. Real life cannot be about perfect conscious awareness. By definition, real life must include the infinite potential of the unconscious as well.

"Rather than waiting to 'meet with' our projections in a way that seems so often to create crises and conflict in our lives," Jung reflects as we move down the passageway that, we hope, will lead us to the daylight realm once more, "we can invite the unconscious to speak to us directly. When we do meet with projections of our unclaimed emotions—or with the compulsive feelings and desires that so often accompany our unresolved internal conflicts—we can enter into them productively and let them show us what it is that we do not know about ourselves."

As I listen to what Jung is saying, walking with my newly perceived friends, I begin to realize how the creative processes with which we have escaped the deadly grips of our core neuroses speak not only to some kind of crisis intervention, but also to a productive way of living daily life. Becoming as wholly conscious as we possibly can of our depressions when they arrive—or of whatever might be bugging us—we can simply watch in a receptive frame of mind for what comes up from the unconscious. The thoughts, images, and feelings that arise into consciousness will be direct and amplified expressions of those very same projections that have been giving us such a hard time for so long. Only now we can work *with* them, rather than expending so much time and energy trying to fight and avoid them. Then all the energy that was trapped by the projection, and that the conscious mind was using to deny the truth, becomes available to the true self. It literally infuses us with real life.

As I look at this process more closely in the growing light of day, I begin to see an old familiar pattern in its workings. Once the unconscious has fulfilled its nature, the power and the responsibility reverts to the conscious awareness, which then uses its new information in context with what it already has seen to create a new situation. After a while, the new situation will inevitably build into new creative frictions and new nonconscious awarenesses, which will incite the unconscious to speak again. Again, the conscious mind can respond, creating an ever more complete (though ever-changing) spontaneous expression of the true self, as it emerges from the dynamic union between those two opposites that make up our experience of being. It's an ongoing, ever-widening, self-perpetuating, and creative cycle of personal growth and evolution.

"Yang reverts to yin when it gets as yang as it can get," Mr. Nu proclaims, popping up from behind me as I hike toward the light in my usual contemplative absorption. "Yin reverts to yang when it has exhausted its yin-ness. This is the principle of reversion at work in Human Nature. It is the same Force that gives the planets their oblong orbits and the sea its crashing waves. To say yes to this inner flow is to say yes to Life as it flows through your Human Nature."

What natural magic this is! I think to myself, as I ponder the obvious veracity of what the old man has said. The illusory projection turns into a clarifying image; it reverts to opposite at the union of our Human yin and yang. It just naturally transcends its original form, and becomes something else. In the process, it moves us directly from neurotic delusion toward real life, from existence as mere personae directly into our true, immediate experience of being.

"The free interplay between our conscious awareness and the unconscious triggers an innate 'transcendent function' in our psyches,"[10] Jung adds from his place at the front of the line as we march briskly through the last of the long, winding corridors that lead toward the high plateau ahead.

"Through the union of the opposites within us," he explains, "we are able to discover our true selves beyond what our conscious awareness alone could ever make of us. We actually become intuitively aware of ourselves as something more than what our conscious mind perceives. Through the conscientious union of the opposites within us, the true self emerges spontaneously into the conscious light of day; the conscious, ego–based "I" is literally transcended, and in its place arises a real, self-renewing, living being."[11]

With this final insight, our pathway breaks through into the full sunlight and we find ourselves standing directly above the plateau toward which we have been striving throughout this arduous trek. The warmth of the sun invites us to sit down and rest a bit before our last descent toward our cherished goal. We gather, one by one, as each emerges from the cave, and we sit together as a true community of travelers, contemplating all that we have seen in our harrowing journey toward real life.

Below us spreads a broad, rocky moraine, a vast, natural field of debris left by the glacier called Persona as it recedes from our real lives. There are no trails here, and no easy route down the long landslide left by our neuroses. Clearly, we will each still have a lot to meet and understand before we reach the lush highlands below.

Whereas we might have found this prospect daunting in the past, we now have learned a thing or two about meeting obstacles in the high country of Life and Human Nature, and we are not afraid. The dynamic union of our conscious and nonconscious awareness demands that we allow the unconscious to speak its truth without condition, and in return it yields a constantly refreshed vitality and ever-widening perspective. This means that sometimes we will have to face things that we find unpleasant and even frightening, not just in therapy or in times of crisis, but in our everyday lives as well. We know that the willingness to face whatever might come up from the unconscious will free us to our own immediate (unmediated) experience of being.

It is, in fact, exactly this response to the unknown within ourselves that opens the way to real life.

CHAPTER SIX

. . . .

Real Life

In order to reclaim our real lives, we must be willing to accept
our projections and the virtual realities that they create
as valuable and meaningul aspects of who and what we are.
In essence, this new attitude is just that unconditional
acceptance we originally wanted from our parents.
Now, Life calls us to give it to ourselves.

As we rest and scan the vast horizon where, for the first
time in our journey, the entire inner realm of Human Nature
spreads out clearly visible before us, it occurs to me how absolute
is the power of Life to shape our Human experience of being.
I can see how, one way or another—either through the
metaphoric images of our neuroses or through our willingness
to face our inner truth directly—the conscious and unconscious
aspects of our Human psyches will find their way to a reunion
with each other. This dynamic expresses an essential law not
only of our Human Nature, but of Nature as a whole. The
unity of opposites is Universal.

Clearly, there is a Force within each of us that is moving us
toward our wholeness, toward our completion as aware, unique
beings. At its essence is the exact same Force that motivates the
entire Universe. It is that unity of opposites that engendered
the creation of the Universe itself: the vital Essence of All That

Is. It is, quite simply, Life moving through our Human Nature.

If we acquiesce to this innate movement within us, taking time to listen to the voice of the unconscious whenever it nudges us with compulsive emotions or addictive appetites, we move immediately toward a state of real presence in our lives. We come into our own immediate experience of being.

Otherwise, if we insist on ignoring the prompting of the unconscious, we tend to fall further and further into delusion, since the unconscious must then find its inevitable union with conscious awareness through projection and metaphor. Wherever we find ourselves unable either to accept or to resolve the sorrows and the losses of our Human lives, there we will find the metaphors of the virtual self, attempting to present an external solution to our internal dilemma. The very structure of our own psyches—in response to the inevitable flow of Life—keeps bringing us into contact with that within ourselves that we have yet to recognize within real life.

This insight really sinks in as I look honestly at how I tend to live my daily life. Often, the suffering and dis-ease with which I tend to grapple endlessly cannot find their own resolution simply because they are not what they appear to be. Often, their true natures are hidden from view by my own erroneous assumptions and habitual way of life or, what is more likely, by my own shame at my failings and my insistence upon protecting my tender self-image.

As I scan the extensive moraine of broken rock and splintered wood that lies between us and the verdant plains of real life below, I am struck by how extensive must be the damage I have caused in my life and relationships through years of unconscious behavior and unrecognized projection. Thus, the vast and treacherous field of shifting rock and earth that now stands between me and my real life appears to me to represent the untested shakiness of my relationships with everyone I know, and with my own body and spirit. Its depth, like that of my virtual self and my delusions, is unknown and cannot be ascertained by thought or sight or feeling. The only way to ascertain the nature of this place is to enter in and then attempt, as best I can, to "go with the flow," knowing that as soon as I step onto its shifting slope of debris from my neurotic existence, this "Moraine of Pain" that lingers in the wake of the passing persona, I may well trigger a landslide of feeling and action that will forever change the landscape of my life.

Wherever I come upon an obstacle that I cannot surmount directly, I will be challenged to expand my awareness, look beyond the apparent, and see what might come up. Some of what I see when I get "stuck" like that will be related to old issues of abandonment and worth. Whatever I discover probably will not be pretty or pleasing to me. Yet every time I get beyond those issues, I know that a new, more vital and truer sense of myself will begin to emerge.

This new sense of self is bound to set in motion other changes in my life. It will tend to challenge my habitual ways of living. I may begin to find that I cannot continue my old relationships with certain people, or my old way of making a living, or even my old lifestyle in general. Naturally, these kinds of changes are bound to bring up even more unresolved issues of insecurity, which will also need to be processed and moved through. The whole terrain is built upon shifting sands.

This will be true for each of us who aspires to a real life. The emergence of the true self whom we have so fiercely sought will unearth unforeseen unconscious fears and resistances that we will have to deal with; and with each of these emerging inner truths will come an opportunity to enter more deeply into our real lives.

Thus, as we each move beyond our core neuroses, we are bound to find our true selves emerging alongside our unconscious, neurotic ways of being. In order to continue moving toward real life, we will have to accept both of these parts of who we are as valuable and meaningful in their own rights. Paradoxically, in order to attain our real lives, we have to accept ourselves first just as we actually are, right here, right now, today and every individual day of our lives.

The Moraine of Pain:
The Ambiguity of the Actual Self

Looking across the top of the Moraine of Pain, I can see clearly a number of access points, where other passages out of the Ice Caves of Neurosis open onto this long, thin ridge above the landslide. Without actually realizing what I am doing or thinking, I begin to scan the ridge and the far side of the moraine for some route other than the one right in front of me; perhaps a cleared trail, where I might avoid having to deal with any more suffering and uncertainty. A subtle dust cloud of half-formed resistances stirs up as I scoot closer to the edge of the moraine in search of a more advantageous vantage point. After all I've suffered through, isn't it enough? After all I've learned about myself, why shouldn't I be able to see my way through these latent contents of my own unconscious without getting all dirty and scraped up? It couldn't be that hard for someone like me who has explored himself so throughly and deeply. Could it?

Yet everywhere I look, the state of affairs appears to be the same. There are no trails, no clear-cut paths, just lots of rock, dirt, and debris.

As I step closer to the edge of the moraine, trying to make absolutely certain that there is no other way, a landslide of questions starts to rumble through my mind: What will my friends and my family think when I stop playing the social roles that I have always played? What will I find myself obligated to when I start looking deeply into how I really live my daily life? Will I lose the life that I have come, for better or for worse, to hold as my identity and place within the world? And if I do, who will I be? If I let go the solid ground of my accustomed self and the persona that tends so reliably to keep me feeling solid in the outside world, what will happen to my life, my loves, my sense of who I am?

Then again, if I do not let go, what will become of me?

This last question brings me to my senses, and I realize that I have already begun unconsciously, neurotically battling myself in the face of my first fearful encounter with my real life. I feel ashamed at my cowardice and the neurotic temptation to avoid the painful truth about my life, whatever it turns out to be. I look around to see if anyone has noticed my reticence, hoping to save face.

Just then, however, I realize that Carl Jung has begun his own descent into the shifting slope of unrealized neurosis.

I had not considered the fact that even he will have to travel down this slippery slope of undiscovered inner truths if he wants to arrive at his real life. This recognition finally convinces me: There really is no way around it; this mine field left over from our inner wars is simply part of every Human life.

"Whenever people first discover the existence of their own unconscious drives and motivations," Jung says, preparing us for the terrain into which he will lead us next, "they tend to turn their newfound insights to the service of their neurosis."[1]

I blush.

"They often act as though they might be able to know perfectly well the meaning of everything that comes out of the unconscious," he adds as he cinches his pack and tests a first step onto the moraine, "raising their new wisdom to an idealized level far beyond reason. That, or they tend to fall apart completely, shrinking back from all the wonderful things that the unconscious might offer.

"Both attitudes," he notes, as he sidesteps still further down the slope, "spring from the still unresolved aspects of their neurosis. This uncomfortable situation cannot be helped, since no one rids themselves of a neurosis overnight, and everyone has some complex or other of which they are not quite conscious.

"The point," he says, breathing a little harder with the effort as he slides almost beyond our range of hearing, "is to remain alert to the potential of new material as it arises, and to respond to it in good time without getting caught up in your own debris."

As I watch Jung make his way carefully down the long,

broad moraine, it dawns on me that what he is describing is actually a sort of "area of ambiguity" between the neurotic and the real self. This notion reminds me of something that I once read in a book called *Neurosis and Human Growth*, by Karen Horney. It pointed out that there are three essential aspects of the Human self: the ideal self, which we grow up believing we *should* be; the real self, which is our pure innate potential and central source of real growth; and the actual self, which is who we are at any given moment in our actual lives. The actual self, says Horney, is that fluid combination of the neurotic and the real that we are in daily existence. It's what we mean when we say that we want to know ourselves.[2] It occurs to me that that's where we are right now, at the very edge of the *area of ambiguity* between the ideal and the real known as the actual self. That's what this Moraine of Pain actually is.

From this perspective, "actual self" is the one whom we must allow into being in order to see our neurotic compulsions for what they are, and thus to discover our true being. It is just this self that we mean when we say that we want to remain unconditionally present and open to the unseen truth about ourselves. What we are actually saying is that we recognize the importance of accepting ourselves, in all our ambiguity, neurosis and all.

As we have seen, to fear, hate, and deny our own fear, hatred, and denial is the essence of neurosis, and so will get us nowhere in the effort to reclaim our real lives. Only the willingness to name our actual feelings and then to feel them (regardless of whether we think that they are good, pleasant, or healthy feelings) will enable us to live our real lives. Indeed, our acceptance of our actual selves, neurosis and all, is exactly what has opened the way to our recovering our real lives in the first place.

As I consider this new insight, it occurs to me that what recovering our true selves really means in practice is adopting an attitude of unconditional compassion toward ourselves, neurosis and all. This understanding seems to shift something in me, so that the moraine before me seems somehow less threatening and "bad." In fact, it begins to look like a meaningful and even attractive challenge to my skills as a high-country traveler.

This new perspective feels as though it might be very important to my making it down the long, rocky slope before me in one piece, without getting carried away by some landslide of unforeseen debris. As Jung makes his way very slowly down that slope before us, I take the opportunity to nab my journal and jot down a quick, short note.

Field note: Paradoxically, in order to reclaim our real lives, we must be willing to accept our projections and the virtual realities that they create as valuable and meaningful aspects of who and what we are. In essence, this new attitude is just that unconditional acceptance we originally wanted from our parents. Now, Life is evidently calling us to give it to ourselves.

As I finish up and tuck my notebook away, I look up just in time to see Jung take a nasty spill and slide several feet into a pile of jagged rocks. He gets up, waves to us to let us know that he is not seriously injured, and tries to brush himself off without falling down again.

"Although, with insight and good will, the shadow can to some extent be assimilated into the conscious personality, experience shows that there are certain features that offer the most obstinate resistance to moral control and prove almost impossible to influence," Jung calls out, smiling sheepishly as he gently mocks himself by quoting from one of his own lectures.

"While some traits peculiar to the shadow can be recognized without too much difficulty as one's own personal qualities, in this case both insight and good will are unavailing because the cause of the emotion appears to lie, beyond all doubt, in the other person."[3]

That is exactly as I suspected. This Moraine of Pain is evidently full of unrecognized depressions, missteps, failings, and unrealized facades. I must admit that, although I realize the necessity of addressing these issues, I do not relish the thought of exploring the terrain myself. Still, as Jung nears the lower reaches of the mammoth rockslide left behind by our shared neuroses, the time comes when another of us can safely start their own descent into the unknown pitfalls of his or her own unseen shadows. I decide it may as well be me.

I get up from my resting place, adjust my pack, and run through my checklist of indicators for neurosis, things to watch out for as I attempt the slippery slope from glacial facade to vibrant, organic life: Unexplained depression, check; compulsive outburst of negative emotion (self-pity, resentment, anger, etc.), check; imagining that I know what another's thoughts, feelings, or motivations are, check; foggy overgeneralizations, check; mysterious physical illness or unexplained fatigue, check; obsessive envy or infatuation, check.

I know that I will need to keep these things in mind because, as Jung has just reminded us, I am not likely to recognize when I am falling to some projection of my own internal shadowlands. Knowing these indicators may be all that stops me from taking a painful headlong plunge into some latent neurosis. I rehearse them in my mind as I begin my approach to the rocky field.

By the time I first set foot on the moraine proper, Jung has nearly made it to the bottom, which is so far away from where I stand that he looks like a small toy figure in the field far below. Because there is always the danger of landslides started by another wreaking havoc in the journeys of those who might innocently find themselves in the near vicinity, I wait a minute longer before starting my descent. *Don't want to take any chances*, I tell myself in secret.

As I stand there, one foot on the moraine and the other on the bluff, however, trying to be polite and to make sure I do this "right," a small thin blur streaks past me and onto the rocky slide below.

"Wahoo!" the little figure whoops, as he steps nimbly from one rock to another, alighting just long enough on each stone to let it slip downward a little, carrying him along toward the next available sliver of shale or wood. I slip and I begin to fall, distracted and unbalanced by the unexpected action, as Nu Lao Tzu leaps from a large rock onto a long, thick piece of old fir bark and rides it like a surfboard down the rocky slope. As I fall, I have only the presence of mind to land on my butt, and soon find myself sliding very painfully on it, over innumerable sharp rocks.

"Damn it, Nu!" I shout, riled to instant rage by his precipitous hijinks. A rush of semiconscious feelings and thoughts streams though me as I bump along, trying at least to stay sitting upright. *Damn it! He always does this kind of stuff to me! Always trying to "teach me a lesson," and never really caring about what happens to me! Damn!*

Fortunately, I catch myself almost immediately and dig my heels in, grinding to a dusty halt several yards down the hillside. When I stop sliding, I just sit for a moment, checking in with myself and trying to get my bearings: self-pity, check; overgeneralization of another's attitude or character, check; fantasies that I know what someone else is thinking or intending, check; resulting pain and embarrassment, check. Projection. Check.

Yet one particularly painful object is still poking into my upper thigh. It almost seems to be inside my pants. Still sitting down, I shake the leg that's getting poked, but nothing comes out. Then I reach into the pants pocket to see if something got in there by accident. I find something small and rough and pull it out: the sparkling chip of granite that old Nu gave me at our journey's beginning.

I hold the gleaming stone up to the light, and then look all around me, still sitting in the rocky dirt where I have landed. In a flash, I get what this landslide is really all about. All of this, even the dirt and the debris and the unsightly shale, all of it, is part of who I actually am. My real self is here, in everything, even in this painful landslide of latent neurosis. It could never have been any other way.

At length, I manage to pull myself upright and dust off

without another spill, slipping the precious relic of my inner journey back into its place, deep in my pocket. I look downhill, and find that Mr. Nu is still standing on his "surfboard," although it is stopped not far from where I last saw him as I was falling. He is looking up at me.

"Are you alright?" he calls up to me. "That was a nasty spill you took.

"I forgot to tell you," he calls as he spies out his next stepping stone. "The most important rule in real life is to always be ready to move on.

"The Tao moves through the Universe without ceasing. If you hesitate to enter your real life, it just might run you over!

"What do you modern-day people say? Oh yeah, 'Go with the flow.'"

I wave a half-hearted high sign to let him know that I hear him and am okay, as he skips off down the hillside, now hopping rock to rock. I teeter a bit as I listen to the man, edging toward another bout of self-pity and righteous indignation. I manage to keep my balance, however, by letting myself feel and listen to *everything* that stirs in me when he speaks. As I stand still and quiet for a moment, I can see the faintest hint of an unconscious knowing settling into my awareness like gritty dust.

Okay, so I was hesitating out of fear, not just out of kind consideration for Carl Jung, who I knew was way too far down the moraine for me to nail with a landslide. And Nu did nothing to me at all, except attack the rough slope ahead with more skill, courage, and enthusiasm than I. Indeed, what really threw me off balance was my own nonawareness of the situation and my fearful hesitation in the face of life, followed by a spike of envy and then anger, resentment, and self-pity. Hmm.

Looking down the slope again, I see the old man skipping and sliding over the endless array of potential tripups like a child using stepping stones to cross a shallow creek. Suddenly, however, he appears to lose his balance as he tries to turn too sharply to avoid a hidden boulder in his path. One leg in the air and the other somehow still supporting him on a flat, sliding rock, the old man careens down the slope on the apparent verge of sheer disaster.

"Woah!" he hollers so loudly that everyone can hear, as we all cringe in expectation of a bloody, dirty crash. But Mr. Nu does something that I never would have thought to do and that surprises everyone. He pirouettes on his one useful leg and, falling, launches himself uphill *into* the Moraine of Pain. Miraculously, this stops the whole disaster in its tracks, leaving the loose debris that threatened to undo him to rattle harmlessly on down the slope.

Nu looks up at us, shrugs his bony shoulders, and sets to work shaking the dirt out of his boots. I cannot tell by looking at him whether his spill was really a mistake, or a performance intended for our benefit. He seems, in fact, entirely unfazed by the fiasco, and soon is skimming his way across the vast moraine, apparently for fun, as though nothing had happened. Soon, he disappears completely from my view into some evidently uncharted domain of the plateau that they call Real Life, far away from where the rest of us now struggle with our fossilized neuroses.

Intentional or not, I get the message: When you find yourself off balance, caught up in a landslide of projections, fall *into* the pain. When the dust settles, acknowledge your mistake with what grace, humor, and practical attention to such remedies you can muster. Then, move on the best you can. Slipups happen to everyone; they are a normal, unavoidable aspect of Human life.

Of course, following this advice is much more difficult than recognizing it, but I do find that it helps as I move onward. I know that there will be an unforeseen number of falls like the one Nu almost had as I move on. But I also know how to learn from each one and to carry on. Indeed, as I continue my treacherous desent into real life, I find that I can recognize potential pitfalls as I approach them. It takes me a very long time to get down to more level ground. Now and then, I fall to an unforeseen depression. When that first happens, I start to feel bad about myself for falling down, but before long the true nature of those "bad" feelings shows itself in context with the journey I am on, and I find my footing once again. Depression, I soon realize, simply means that I need to slow down enough see my real pain.

By the time I reach the bottom of the tricky slope, I am a bit the worse for wear with cuts, bruises, and a dirty face; but I also feel a deepened sense of who I really am in the wide world, and a confidence in my ability to cope with whatever life may bring to me. I realize, too, as I look around at the natural plain that leads off into forests at the edge of the moraine, that real life is not as flat and easy or as green as it looked from far away. There are boulders here, too, and earthy depressions and, I'm certain, unseen pitfalls.

The real difference here is not in the actual terrain, but in myself and in who I have become in getting here.

Self–Realization:
The Highlands of Human Nature

As I stand at the base of the moraine, in the grassy field on the edge of the plateau called Real Life, I watch the other members of our group make their way haltingly down the hillside and I begin to understand more clearly what the realm of real life is all about. Watching each member stumble, fall, complain, weep, laugh, and then move on, I find myself stirred to genuine feelings of love and admiration. One by one, they reach the grassy field where I stand witness to their trials. I can see in their faces the children they once were, and the marks of suffering, courage, joy, and love that tell me I am not alone in my rich, difficult experience of being simply Human. Clearly, we're all in this together.

This experience itself broadens my understanding of the process through which we each discover our true selves in the realm of real life. I can see that the ability and willingness to meaningfully experience our sorrow and loss stands not only as a practical life skill, but also as highly moral attitude. It requires that we adopt a compassionate regard not only for ourselves, but for the others in our sphere, to whom we can no longer assign the masks of villain or savior in the stories of our lives. Now, the compassion that we show toward ourselves automatically echoes in our feelings about everybody else.

It seems obvious to me that depression, compulsion, avarice, envy, addiction, and self-ignorance are unavoidable aspects of Human Nature. The challenge is not to rid ourselves or others of these frailties by force, but to treat these "negative" aspects of our being as the intrinsically meaningful experiences they actually are. Once we step out of the "safety" of denial and repression into the landslide of our actual existence, it may be all that anyone can do to keep from tumbling downhill, over and over. We all will need to stop and get our bearings now and then. Sometimes we are bound to find ourselves carried off by the force of our old debris, helplessly slipping and falling to our own unfinished growth and hidden pain. The only way through this for anyone—short of giving up—is to get up again, brush yourself off, and stand still long enough to let the dust settle so that you can find your place in the flow of things again.

In this way, the difficulties in our lives can actually become the stepping stones we need to approach a truly meaningful experience of being, just as Mr. Nu's hillside ballet has shown. As we gain a dynamic sense of balance in our lives, our relationships with others begin to take on a dynamic quality not often found in early life. A genuine compassion—both for ourselves and those around us—naturally arises from our life experience with sorrow, loss, joy, fear, and all the other Human attributes we share with each other. We become less afraid to be our real selves—partly because we know now ever better who that true self is, and partly because we have also come to understand the underlying nature and meaning of the "negative" emotions that others in our lives might express toward us. Thus, the world becomes a far less frightening and dangerous place in our awareness.

Gradually, the landslide of our early lives becomes a mere

trickle of occasional stumbling blocks and fossilized resistance. There will be old relationships that need to be repaired through an honest retraction of our own projected failings, and there will be others that must simply be let go. There will be new relationships built more on honesty and intimate compassion. Slowly, as our lives begin to clear of the old obstacles to being our true selves, we begin to catch the sweet, fecund aroma of real life.

Naturally, the unconscious will continue to have surprises for us, painful and pleasing, magnificent and small, as we move through our lives. We can never come to know for certain just what it might be that we still do not know about ourselves. Depressions are bound to open up before us now and then, and we may still occasionally stumble over some unforeseen remnant of our unresolved grief. But in the realm of Real Life, these things are simply taken as part of the path, interesting features of normal Human being.

It becomes clear to me, therefore, as I watch the last of my companions negotiate the landslide of their secret pain, that this moraine is, itself, an integral aspect of the high plateau toward which we each have so arduously strived. Clearly, the two cannot be separated, although they are not exactly the same. Real life is not simply an ongoing landslide of pain, yet neither is it a utopia of infantile bliss. Real life includes everything that being Human means in all its mystery and imperfection; Real Life is that level of Human being where who we really are is allowed into existence, where the true self can be fed by the flow of Life and grow into what it was born to be—strengths, weaknesses, and all.

With this understanding, we come into a new and more dynamic view of the term "self-acceptance." In real life, self-acceptance implies the confidence that the true self will emerge from whatever we may face and that the value of our lives lies in the living. Here, the unconscious becomes free to divulge its innermost secrets, beyond issues of pleasure, pain, or perfection, and in spite of our basic Human fear of the unknown. In short, the unconscious becomes an open conduit to Life itself.

Thus, as we gather at the base of the moraine of our unmet pain, ready to take on whatever may lie before us, prepared by our willingness to face whatever we must face to enter into the great inner depths of Real Life, a forest of lush greens and endless, live variety opens before us. Fed by pristine streams of glacial melt, by the life-giving vitality that flows forth from the dissolving Persona, it beckons us onward, although we each are worn and battered from our journey. Somehow, the "aliveness" of this place is, itself, a balm to our sore bodies and our tired minds.

A warm breeze rustles through the trees, and a calm, comforting fatigue sets in as we rest quietly together in the green subalpine meadow that borders the forest plain. The sky above us has begun to take on the soft, variegated hues of early evening, as the sun expresses ever more succinctly all the various prismatic tones and shades that live within its normal daytime light.

Only Mr. Nu has failed to join us, as we reconnoiter for the final leg of our fantastic journey. Perhaps he has returned to his cabin near the Spirit of the Valley or maybe he just feels like exploring on his own. Either way, as I sit leaning back onto my pack and gazing at the multicolored sky, I wish him well with a heartfelt gratitude at having known him.

Just as I am about to doze off, however, I hear footsteps on the forest path ahead. Immediately on the alert to new sounds in this unfamiliar wilderness, I sit upright, my attention riveted on the source of the sounds. To my amazement, I spy two men, aged about sixty or older, one of whom is carrying a big thermos jug and a plastic bag of what look like bagels.

"Ah, Carl! Abraham! So good to see you!" Jung calls out as they appear. "I was wondering whether you would have noticed us making our way down the moraine.

"And snacks, too! Excellent!"

I suspect immediately who these two men might be, but I find it so hard to believe that I almost reject the possibility out of hand. Could these two really be the original pioneers of this terrain, Carl Rogers and Abraham Maslow? Really?

I never would have thought that we would see them up here, although, of course, this is their territory. They must have spotted us when we emerged from the ice caves, at the bluff so high above the forest.

"Well, it's our job, isn't it?" the two men answer almost in unison.

Then the more outgoing of the two, the one I think is probably Maslow, explains, "We saw you making your way through your latent neuroses, and we headed out right away to meet you.

"Welcome to Real Life. Will you be following the path of self-actualization, or are you going to rest here for a while?"

Without hesitation, we all vote in favor of pursuing our self-actualization, although I have to admit that I would not have picked these two unlikely characters as guides to that terrain. The men are not wearing backpacks or parkas, or even hiking boots. Instead, each sports a sweater and cotton shirt, casual slacks, and a clean pair of sneakers. They look like they're out for a Sunday stroll.

They do not look at all like the pioneers whom I would expect to meet out here, at the farther reaches of Human Nature. Indeed, they make for a rather comical duo. Jung finally introduces them to us. Carl Rogers sports a pair of plastic-rimmed glasses, the kind with the wire showing inside of the frames. He has a long, clean-shaven, soft-featured face and is almost entirely bald. His smile is kind, warm, and comforting, if a little nerdish. The other, Abraham Maslow, is almost an exact opposite phenotype to Rogers. He has a round ruddy face, thick bushy hair, a bristly mustache, and the big, robust grin of a brewmaster or somebody's eccentric uncle. Neither visage inspires much confidence.

Apparently, my reticence to accept the two new travelers as genuine pioneers is something Rogers can read on my face. He sidles over toward me, where I sit in a rather resistant posture, munching my bagel and swigging the tea they have brought to us in relative isolation from the group.

"The true self is something that we each discover just naturally in our everyday experience of being, not something imposed upon it,"[4] he says to me. I understand his implication. There is no particular way that a self-realized person *should* look. Indeed, the whole notion of masks and standardized appearances is, I know, specifically anathema to the entire notion of a true self. Apparently I still have many preconceptions and projections that I need to recognize and name for what they are. My self-recrimination at these old attitudes must show, because Rogers shifts his position again, taking a seat on the ground right in front of me and making eye contact with a gentle air.

"Here," he says, sweeping his arm toward the entire plateau, "the individual drops one after another of the defensive masks with which he has faced life; he experiences fully the hidden aspects of himself; he discovers in these experiences the stranger who has been living behind these masks, the stranger who is himself.

"The person who emerges," he adds, touching my knee to let me know that he means me, "is developing a trust in his own organism as an instrument for sensitive living . . . learning to live his life as a participant in a fluid, ongoing process, in which he is continually discovering new aspects of himself in the flow of his experience."[5]

Although these are all ideas that I have thought before and even experienced just recently in my trek to this high plateau, there is something in the way that this kind, gentle man speaks them that makes these ideas sink in more deeply than ever before. There is a kind of force behind his words, perhaps created by his living his own life by exactly these principles. Perhaps the power comes in simply hearing someone say the words. Whatever the cause, tears begin to form in my eyes as he speaks, piercing to a tender inner realm where thought and even feeling cannot reach. Suddenly, inexplicably, I feel as though I have finally arrived, and been welcomed and accepted into my own real life.

"The self, at this moment, *is* this feeling," says Rogers softly. "This is being in the moment," he points out, as he rises and leaves me to my inner experience.

I understand. This is what the whole journey to this point has been about. My willingness to feel just what I feel, and to think what I think without grasping or pushing away, is exactly what leads me, again and again, to that state of real presence known as the true self. There is nothing to do, change, or fix about myself. At the point where I let myself experience whatever I may be truly experiencing, even if it is judgmental and "wrong," I come into my real experience of being.

I sit, almost stupefied by the impact of this direct experience of what we have been thinking about and intentionally working toward in our journey and our psychospiritual explorations. The feeling of presence is tangible. I can sense it as solidly as I do the ground where I sit. A subtle joy and vitality stirs in me, but having nothing against which to push, no resistance or fear, this excitement feels simply like my normal state of being, only clearer, somehow, more alive.

I remain seated in silence, unwilling to move for fear of disturbing the fine equilibrium I have discovered within me, as the rest of the group prepares to move along on our tour of real life. This is what I came here to feel. I don't want to let go of it. Of course, as soon as I begin to think that way, fearful of what might come next and clinging to the pleasurable sensations I am experiencing, my whole inner balance shifts, and I begin to feel a little depressed, even ashamed at my inability to hold onto my true sense of self.

Apparently, my situation is obvious to Carl Rogers. He strolls back to where I am sitting as everyone else dons their packs to move on. He extends his hand with a knowing smile, inviting me to my feet.

"Consciousness," he says, as he helps me up and then into my pack, "instead of being the watchman over a dangerous and unpredictable lot of impulses, of which a few can be permitted to see the light of day, becomes the comfortable inhabitant of a society of impulses and feelings and thoughts, which are discovered to be satisfactorily self–governing when not fearfully guarded."[6]

Clearly, this real life stuff will take a lot of practice. It's a lifelong process, I suppose. I shrug, jogging my pack into place, and fall into line as our group trundles off toward the woods, Abraham Maslow leading. Dr. Rogers simply gives me a wink as I sigh and move on.

The sun, now quite low in the sky, seems to lend a soft pastel aura to the trail as we enter the open, green forest of Real Life. As soon as we move from the base of the Moraine of Pain into this vital glen, the trail splits off into many side paths and directions, weaving, serpentine, braiding away from and then back into the main path at random. Some of our group follow Rogers, some Jung, some Maslow, as we weave our way through the warm, enchanted woods, each leader spontaneously choosing now this path, now that. No matter which path we choose, we seem always to enter the main trail again, so that even though there are innumerable new variations to our real life journeys, they all seem to head toward one and the same destination.

As we walk, we pass dwellings of all types—yurts, tree houses, log cabins, tepees, and tents; A-frames, earth-houses, and open camps. Some of the people we pass wave and call out greetings, whereas others appear deeply engrossed in projects, from writing to knitting to just cleaning up, and seem not to take notice of us at all. So many different types of people, all sharing one Human asset in common: They are all living their real lives.

Somehow, though, it surprises me that these people all live so simply. Somehow it's not what I would have imagined for people who, in some sense at least, must be considered the most successful of Humans. Really, you would not be able to tell that they were great successes from the size of their houses or number of their possessions.

When I hook up with Maslow's group, I ask him about the apparent lack of the normal trappings of a successful life. How can these people tolerate as unpredictable a life as living in this high-country wilderness must offer? Don't they get tired or scared?

"The motivation of ordinary men is striving for the basic need gratification, which they lack," Maslow answers, thoughtfully. "Self-actualizing people lack none of these gratifications; and yet they have impulses. For them, motivation is just character-growth, character-expression, maturation, and development: in a word, self-actualization.[7]

"They live more in the 'real' world of nature than in the man–made set of concepts, expectations, beliefs, and stereotypes which most people confuse with the world.[8]

"These people are uniformly unthreatened and unfrightened by the unknown. They accept it and are comfortable with it, and are often more attracted to it than to the known. They can tolerate the ambiguous."[9]

This last remark throws my mind back to the lip of the cup that Mr. Nu talked about at the beginning of our journey, and to our recent experience with the Moraine of Pain. I feel inspired to know that there really are people living productive, real lives in acceptance of the ambiguity not only of their actual selves, but of Reality and the world at large: people whose goals are not attached to security and wealth, yet who find life rich and rewarding enough to commit their whole selves to it.

"They can accept their own Human Nature with all its shortcomings," Maslow adds, "with all its discrepancies from the ideal image, without feeling real concern."[10]

Of course, this attitude of self-acceptance and unconditional presence is as we might have expected to find in the realm of Real Life. Still, seeing that self-actualization actually can be and is being practiced in everyday life gives me a feeling of encouragement and excitement. I could do this, I think to myself. In fact, maybe I am doing it right here and now.

As I look more closely at the dwellings we pass, no longer

distracted by my expectations of what a successful life ought to look like, I begin to realize that what these dwellings express, rather than opulence, is a simple yet compelling creativeness. Indeed, art and ingenuity appear as a way of life, from the unusual colors and designs of the homes to the music that wafts through the air on unusual, meandering melody lines.

Although I had not thought of it before, it occurs to me that real life itself must be, by definition, a truly creative endeavor. What else can we expect, after all, if everyone who lives their real life is living out a genuine expression of the unique person-ality that they were born to be?

The further we proceed into the realm of Real Life, the more the entire realm takes on an air of living art. Everything seems to be done here with an attitude of creativity, from hanging out the laundry to how people pass their idle time. I can't help but remark on it, as all the disparate trails we've been traveling combine once more into one broad, bright path; one symphonic community of real lives.

"Self-actualizing people have the wonderful capacity to appreciate again and again, freshly and naively, the basic goods in life—with awe, pleasure, wonder, and even ecstasy, however stale such experiences may have become to others," Maslow answers, almost glowing in the vibrancy of the terrain. "They derive ecstasy, inspiration, and strength from the basic experiences of life.[11]

"The creativeness of the self-actualized man seems rather akin to the creativeness of unspoiled children," he adds, as the sunset becomes more intense and the air fills with the mysterious aromas of evening in the deep high country.

"It is as if this special type of creativeness, being an expression of healthy personality, is projected out upon the world or touches whatever activity the person is engaged in. Whatever one does can be done with a certain attitude, a certain spirit which arises out of the nature of the character of the person performing the act."[12]

"It seems to be a more fundamental characteristic of

common Human Nature—potentially given to all Human beings at birth."[13]

Here the trail broadens even more, as it leads beyond the realm of self-actualization, directly toward the vast and fiery palette of the setting sun. The forested plain seems to virtually breathe with life, as the continually shifting colors of the sky penetrate the opening wood, and we move ever closer to a broad, clear view of the late summer's far horizon.

"The mainspring of creativity," adds Carl Rogers, who stands now side by side with Maslow and Jung as we all bask in the warm light of real life which now surrounds us, "appears to be the same tendency which we discover so deeply as a curative force in psychotherapy — man's tendency to actualize himself, and to become his potentialities."[14]

"As a matter of fact," Carl Jung agrees softly, as we all fall under the spell of the woods and the brilliant twilight, "this process follows the natural course of life—a life in which the individual becomes what he always was."[15]

Yes. That seems exactly right. Self-realization: a natural process of becoming what we really are.

As I stand with these time-honored guides, entranced by the setting sun, this understanding cues up an astounding insight as to just what the "mainspring" of our creativity and personal growth actually is. A phrase of Mr. Nu's runs through my mind: Life moving through our Human Nature. This "creativeness," which Maslow speaks of as the central unifying condition of self-actualization and which Rogers sees as the innate movement in every Human being *toward* self-actualization, this force, in fact, that has been driving me and each of us toward our real lives in the face of insurmountable suffering and insecurity, appears to be exactly that same Force that brought the Universe itself into being and that sustains its ongoing Creation to this day. It is Life flowing through Human Nature.

My normal sense of myself disappears for a moment, as this sense of Life flowing through me, through these woods, and through the world as one overwhelms me. The entire

Universe, the people standing next to me, and my own inner being meld together like currents in a cosmic sea. No words or expression of any kind can encompass the feeling. It is simply, to resort to a term Freud and Maslow have used, "oceanic."

I can see that there must be a Reality that surpasses even self-realization, to which self-realization leads and of which it is an inexorable part. There is something out there, on the far horizon, to which I could never have attained without opening to my true self, yet that exceeds my personal self in the same sense as the sea exceeds a raindrop that falls into it.

Something altogether natural is happening here, which nevertheless exceeds my normal sense of "self" as separate from the rest of life. As I stand in the evening glow, and others around me begin to move once more, some toward the far horizon, some to make camp on the high plateau itself, I find myself enmeshed in thought and rising inspirations. *It's real!* I say to myself. *The unity of All That Is is real!*

And with this realization, our entire trek falls into place for me as a natural process. Life becoming aware of itself. Life moving through my Human Nature. The immensity of the vision overpowers me. I need to sit with it and let the images that the epiphany is conjuring in me find voice before I can continue any further.

The Arc of the Virtual Self :
Life, Human Nature, and the Personal Self

I find a carved bench at the trailside on which I can sit and contemplate what is happening in me. I am no longer a seeker in search of some destination, some "other realm." Life is moving through me, and it is enough.

Clearly, there is within every Human being an innate creative Force that demands that the real self be shown, either unconsciously in metaphor or through the direct union between conscious and nonconscious awareness. When activated willingly and skillfully, this reunion of conscious and nonconscious awareness creates what Jung has called the Transcendent

Function. It elevates our being to a level far above the realm of self-image and conscious will.

The potential to this kind of self-realization appears innate to the structure of our Human psyches. It is empowered by the same Life Force that gives us life in the first place. Self-realization simply stands as an advanced stage of a growth process that begins at our very conception and that is predestined to reunite us with the world at large.

This final expression of our true personal maturation is the work of that same Force that quickened the egg within our mother's womb, moved the mouth to nipple at our birth, pushed us toward our formal being in the outer world, and recalls us to our true selves with the metaphoric fictions of neurosis: Life, expressing itself through Human Nature. It begins at the union of opposites called male and female, sperm and egg. From this nebulous point of instinct and the transpersonal, we evolve into our individual senses and, so, into a more personal context of experience. Then comes the organic development of wanting and choosing, and of projecting our experience of being onto the world we perceive. Eventually, we each inevitably find ourselves defined by the projections of a social persona, which strives always to attain its learned ideal.

With the existence of our conscious awareness, there arises the necessity of its exact opposite, nonconscious awareness. From this union of opposites come all the forms of meaningful perception available to Human life. The entire process occurs as an organic unfolding from within, as though imprinted on some psychic gene. It happens whether we want it to or not, and even the most careful planning, by the most talented of people, cannot resist its influence. One way or another, either directly or through the metaphors of the virtual self, the true nature of the self will show.

The formal, conscious "I" we tend to think ourselves to be through the first half of life is an illusion built on all the self-forgetting that we had to do in order to accommodate the outer world of form while we were young and immature. If we insist on taking this persona as the real and whole self, we will find ourselves caught up in an ever more intricate maze of self-deception, neurosis, and fear, all built to give the true self covert life wherever consciousness denies it. Thus, in later life, our neuroses can turn us inward, inciting a genuine quest for real life.

This turnaround requires first that we become willing to change the way we *think* about ourselves, and to reexamine our basic assumptions to see whether they are actually reasonable. This self-analysis becomes possible only after we have matured fully in our ability to reason, and lived long enough to establish a way of life that can be reconsidered. Thus, our coming to maturity as reasonable beings marks both the high point and the turning point of our Human development.

At the pinnacle of our social adulthood, where the ideal is our guiding light and where pleasure and perfection are our desires, we find ourselves inexorably turned toward our inner pain and powerlessness by the unconscious disruption of our dreams, relationships, bodies, and minds. On close examination, the idealized "facts" of our lives turn into metaphoric fictions, offering us uncanny images of our forgotten fear, sorrow, and loss that, if we are willing to just *feel* and listen inwardly, will tell us deeper truths about ourselves than thoughts alone could know. As a result, our compulsive anger, hatred, envy, jealousy, avarice, shame, and self-pity begin to disappear. In their place comes a new, quite different attitude, called compassion, in which sorrow and loss are experienced as wholly Human challenges, not just something that is happening to the separate ego "I."

Truth becomes fiction, and those fictions show a deeper truth, married to feelings of sorrow, which open up the world of secret joy. Fear then resolves itself into compassion, and we find ourselves moving with and for, rather than against and away from, life and its challenges.

Thinking resolves into feeling, which resolves into pure being, so that everything that grows organically from the process of our seeking the truth about ourselves appears as a refinement of opposites in union: nothing is ever wasted or in vain—truth and fiction, sorrow and joy, fear and love, all in a slightly imperfect symmetry of forms in process.

Indeed, the path of our Human becoming appears to follow a perfect arc—just like that of the virtual particle we saw back at the very beginning of our journey into the high country. We move from a prenatal at–one–ness with Life and with the archetypal forms of Human Nature, into the projection of the self as ego, through the idealization of the self as social persona, and then back through that idealized self, retracting the projections and naturally reentering the realm of our true being.

This image is so compelling to me that I have to grab my notebook and record some basic notes.

Field note: In the first half of our life journey, we begin as virtual selves, developing our perceptual modes and contexts in an orderly and preordained sequence, only to reverse the order, at the height of our development, in a return process of refining our tainted perceptions of the real.

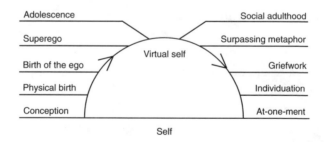

The whole process of our growing up appears as a natural product of the Principle of Reversion: a union of two opposing movements that conjoin to make a whole. The first half of life is outward moving, "yang," and oriented to the placement in the self as form within the formal world of Human culture and achievement, whereas the second half of life demands an introspective, reflective, and receptive, more "yin" attitude. The process of our truly growing is, therefore, one of a return to our true being and to Source.

This return to our original being appears to me as an actual trial by fire, a highly frictional reentry into the atmosphere of our real lives, which welds together the opposites innate to our Human Nature—truth melds with fiction through the metaphors of the virtual self; sorrow finds joy in the end of real grieving; fear turns to love with the acceptance of real life; and individual personhood embraces the Life Force, which unites it with All That Is. Through it all, the unconscious finds its way into our conscious lives; and we become increasingly more real, whole, and complete Human persons just through that inevitable union of the opposites that make up our true nature.

At–one–ment:
The Transcendent "Yes"

As I record this process of self-realization and let it sink in, I find myself urged further still along the path of Life and Human Nature. Some of our party have elected to make camp here, on the plateau of Real Life, but something within me is calling me onward. I have glimpsed Life at its Essence, and I want to see more.

I can see the silhouettes of a few others who have evidently heard the call as well, and I pick up my backpack and follow. I do not know exactly where we are going, but I know that I must take this trail to its end.

Clearly, the process of our Human growing up is one designed upon the same dynamic principles as all else in the Universe of which we are a part. The Life Force that aligns the planets and holds all the countless stars in their suspended interplay of gravity and fission is the same Life Force that guides us toward our self-realization. Saying "yes" to our own lives and to our true selves is, thus, also saying "yes" to Life, to that Transcendent, animating Force behind the life of the whole Universe.

With this understanding, we move beyond mere

individuation as a state of personal fulfillment into a recognition of our membership in something that transcends the personal altogether. Indeed, in order to reach our own individuation we will have had to bend our own personal wills to the directives of our Human Nature, and to the realities of Life as it arranges things throughout the material world. For it was only our willingness to let go of our search for perfection and eternal pleasure that allowed us to move onward in our journey toward true adulthood in the first place. We had to say yes to our own archetypal Human Nature, and we had to say yes to that Life Force that gives us and All That Is our essential vitality.

Our willingness to accept ourselves and our individual lives just as they are brings us into direct union with the dynamic flow of Life itself. When we accept our fears and compulsions, our weaknesses and failures, and our successes and victories as meaningful in their own right, we are saying yes to Life, just as it is. In essence, we are aligning our personal perceptions with the Way of Nature; we are approaching an at–one–ment with what Nu Lao Tzu has called the Tao.

It occurs to me that every journey toward real life and true personhood is as much a spiritual quest as it is a psychological one. The journey demands a process of psychological purification that leads inevitably to the expression and validation of the essence of the Human spirit. In this, the quest for our real lives also demands that we access, express, and validate the Life Force or "Spirit" that enlivens and sustains all of Creation.

This kind of "spirituality" cannot be accomplished by a force of will. It cannot be achieved by subscribing to some set of beliefs, actions, or rituals. It exists as an instinct of sorts within every Human being and is preordained by our Human relationship with Life. In acquiescing to this internal movement, we not only accept our rightful places in our own real lives, but also in the lineage of travelers and adepts from the entire history of Human spiritual endeavor.

Thus, as we move through the further reaches of our self-realization, we come upon a vast, enlightened realm that has throughout the history of Human evolution been recognized as sacred land. There seem to be many pathways to this place, all of which demand essentially the same surpassing of the ego and its fixation on pleasure and perfection. We are entering the realm of the Transpersonal, where the union between Life and Human Nature has been revered in innumerable stories from tongues immemorial. They all speak of the same Tao, of the same Universal Essence as it echoes through the ages of our infant Human time.

CHAPTER SEVEN

. . . .

The True Self
and the Lineage of Spirit

Each of us who undertakes the challenge
to find a profound, resounding "yes" to Life
is also saying yes to the fulfillment of the species
and to the evolution of our race into its full at—one—ment
with the Universe at large

At the furthermost reaches of our Human Nature, at the
outer boundaries of the realm of Real Life, a vast canyon not
unlike the one we saw at Echo Ridge opens up the earth as far
as our eyes can see. Unlike the trail at Echo Ridge, however,
there is no path around the ancient depths of Human Nature
that this canyon seems to represent.

A vast reservoir of crystalline water stretches down the
canyon far below. The cliffside border between us and this
unfathomable lake stretches left and right all the way to the
horizon. It is as though we have come to the edge of the natural
world, to the edge of Human life itself, to the edge of Human
time. All we can do is stand in silent awe and marvel at the vast
expanse of space before us.

"The formless is the great ancestor of beings; the soundless
is the great source of species," a familiar voice recites from
somewhere near yet unseen, breaking the sacred silence with

an ancient Taoist refrain. "Real people communicate with the spiritual directorate; those who participate in evolution as Human beings hold mystic virtue in their hearts and employ it creatively like a spirit."[1]

I recognize the voice as Mr. Nu's, but still cannot quite see where it is coming from, until the old man casually emerges from another path some distance from our own. How did he get here without going through self-actualization? I put this question to him, knowing I am probably letting myself in for some teasing, but intent on understanding the true nature of this place and its terrain. Somehow, saving face and avoiding appearing foolish no longer seem like big issues for me, especially in context to the sacred ground on which we stand.

"What?" he says with a kind, chiding smile. "You think that your psychology 'discovered' Real Life?"

The question makes me blush. Of course I could not consciously believe that modern Depth Psychology is the only true path to the true self. I guess I just had never thought about it. I cast a glance in Carl Jung's direction, but he just shrugs his shoulders and sits down, apparently amused at my predicament.

"Well, is that what you think?" the old man says again, as though expecting a real answer.

I have none.

"Have you already forgotten the Buddha? Very clever fella, you know. He figured out that sorrow and loss only become suffering when you fight them. You ever hear that one?" Of course, we have. It is exactly that story and the concept it exemplifies that helped us muster the courage to enter our neuroses in the first place. I feel a little embarrassed that Nu has to mention the connection, considering how ancient this terrain obviously is.

"Yes," the old man continues, sitting down on the cliff's edge and dangling his feet in the warm, rising air, "all Buddha did was sit down and let everything around him and inside of him come into his awareness, and BOOM! Enlightenment. Yes, I think very clever."

He folds his arms across his chest and touches his right index finger to his chin in an exaggerated pose of contemplation, eyes pointing upward through a frown. "Hmm. I think the Buddha should have been a Taoist," he says. "He and that other fellow. You know, the one you guys like so much? The one who told you not to worry so much about what to wear or how much stuff you have. Now what did he say? Hmm. Oh yes, 'The kingdom of heaven is within you.' Yeah, that guy. I think he should have been a Taoist, too.

"Yes, then we could all just use the same path and not have to worry about all the different visions of our original nature." Old Nu ends with an air of great seriousness, rising to his feet and sliding up beside me, slinging a skinny arm over my shoulder. "Who needs so many different pathways through Real Life? Right?"

Of course, I know as well as Nu Lao Tzu that is not right. Everyone who makes it to their real life adds something unique and important to the Human vision of real Human being in its right relationship to Life. It is, in fact, one of the definitions of Real Life itself that it will be perceived somewhat differently by different people, because they are different from each other, and their real lives are based on just that personal authenticity.

Clearly, if the journey to real life is something innate and natural to Human Nature, then every culture in all of the ages past must also have erected their own pathways here. But why so many different pathways? Why was Depth Psychology not founded centuries ago, perhaps by Buddha? I ask Mr. Nu about it.

"Listen," he replies, "in my culture and in Buddha's culture, we are not so interested in the individual as we are in the whole flow of Life. You in the West prefer to foster individual life. Perhaps one is not better than the other. Probably, we need both: yin and yang.

"Eastern pathways through Real Life follow the call of Life first, Human Nature second. We get here by disintegrating the ego so that all that is left is Life, as it runs through our Human Nature. Everybody expresses this in their individual ways, of course, but we do not accent those differences.

"You in the West have always been more interested in the force of Human Nature. Instead of destroying the ego, you try to purify it by aligning your own personal awareness with the Tao that is in you. Now you have a new pathway you call 'psychology'; but I think that it has the same Tao as old Lao Tzu, or the Buddha, or the Christ, or maybe even Socrates or Plato or Einstein.

"Maybe those teachers are not really equals, but I think that they all follow the same Tao."

With that, the old man falls into silence. Could it be, I wonder, that our psychology is really an extension of the spiritual journeys of the past? Indeed, if the force through which we heal our wounded psyches is, as we have seen, a universal Force in Human life, how could it not be?

Yet this new perspective calls all of my old cultural ideals about spirituality into question. It implies that our true Human maturation is essentially a psychospiritual endeavor, and that a spiritual way of life is simply the natural outcome of our saying "yes" to the Life that flows through our Human Nature, just as it actually is. Of course, on deeper reflection, it occurs to me that the courageous acceptance of whatever life might bring is not far from accepting the "will of God" or of Allah, or of aligning one's will with the Tao, or of accepting life in its Buddhist "Suchness." Really, these "spiritual" mandates all speak to the same challenge. Only the language and the routes by which they arrive at their shared vista differ.

I look out into the vast openness before me, and down at the unfathomable natural reservoir, dark and fluid as the primeval depths of Human Nature. As I gaze across the silent deep, I can make out towering figures from the history of Human spirituality, carved from the columnar basalt that forms the canyon wall. These are different from the etchings and engravings that we saw at Echo Ridge, where the nature of Human reality was only hinted at in metaphoric symbols. These are the actual records of individual Humans and of Human cultures who have made the arduous trek to Real Life themselves, and left behind some permanent impression of their journey to this place, at the far edge of Human time. Each of the pylons of volcanic black rock that lines the water's edge stands for a vision of the Spirit that has come forth from the bedrock of our Human being to withstand the test of time.

In the waters of this reservoir of Human understanding there are reflected the visions of the Buddha, of the Christ, of Lao Tzu and the Tao, of the Prophet Mohammed, of the Talmud, and of the great Goddess of the East. It ripples with the legends of the Torah, of King Arthur's Holy Grail, and of the Hindu Bhagavad Gita. And in its secret depths there lies the history of the whole Human race, as well as its hope for a future.

Apparently, there is a single stream of consciousness that feeds these ancient waters of Humankind's quest for oneness with the flow of Life, an underground river of unknown origins. Its undercurrent has directed the development of Human thought since before recorded time, and is now clearly apparent in the form and content of our modern psychology. At root, each age and its successful religions seem to have at least this much in common: Each one stands as a unified and willing Human "yes" to Life.

"Come on," Mr. Nu beckons, "there is more depth to Human Nature than what we can see from even our individual self-realization. There is the Self, the realization of Humanity itself, of which we each become a part whenever we say yes to Life as we each have by now."

"Come on," he calls again as he descends a nearby trail that winds narrowly down the cliffside toward the water. "We have an appointment to keep."

An appointment? Does he mean to say that this is where the old man has been leading us all the time? Is it this, and not our individual liberation, to which this whole journey has been directed?

There is no time to ask questions. The sun is sinking low

on the horizon. It is, in fact, only the vast, open expanse of sky created by the canyon before us that keeps the sun in view at all. Thus, one by one, we single file after the small, nimble man, down the steep canyon wall.

The trail descends sharply, as we approach the great depths of Human being. We are leaving the realm of ordinary time, entering the open spaces of the eternal in Humankind. We are moving beyond even real life, and into the essential union between Life and Human Nature that appears to have sustained the very quest for real life itself over the entire history of our Human race. We are entering a vast "openness" filled only with the formlessness of space and light, held and surrounded by the metaphoric images of that Spirit that both sustains and transcends the entire world of form, and that we have been referring to as simply "Life."

Every now and then along the trail we find, etched into the trailside walls, artifacts and inscriptions from the history of travelers who have been this way before us. The deeper we move into the canyon, the more ancient the artifacts appear to be.

At one point, not far into our journey down the canyon path, Mr. Nu points out an inscription written in Chinese from the eighteenth century A.D. It is from the *Hui Ming Ching*, or *Book of Consciousness and Life*.

"The subtlest secret of the Tao is Human Nature and life," Mr. Nu reads aloud as we gather around his find. "There is no better way of cultivating Human Nature and life than to bring both back to unity."[2]

We gaze in amazement at each other, and then back at the inscription. Life and Human Nature: Could this archaic Chinese text be talking about what it sounds like it is talking about? Or is it perhaps a matter of semantics or some "mystical" incantation. Mr. Nu seems convinced that this text speaks to exactly that quest upon which we have been embarked in our modern trek through the high country, except that it speaks from a very different cultural point of view. In fact, to support his claim, he pulls from out of his back pocket a tattered copy of *The Secret of the Golden Flower*, a well-known modern commentary on the *Hui Ming Ching*, reading it to us like a guidebook to ancient ruins.

"The text combines Buddhist and Taoist directions for meditation," he reads with an air of seriousness, casting a sideways glance at we unbelievers. "The basic view is that at birth the two spheres of the psyche, consciousness and the unconscious, become separated.

"Consciousness is the element marking what is separated off, in a person, and the unconscious is the element that unites him with the cosmos. The unification of the two elements via meditation is the principle upon which the work is based. The unconscious must be inseminated by consciousness being immersed in it. In this way the unconscious is activated and thus, together with an enriched consciousness, enters upon a supra–personal mental level in the form of a spiritual rebirth."[3]

As I listen to what Mr. Nu is reading I am amazed at how much of its ancient symbolism suggests the same goal as that of modern Depth Psychology. It describes the outward-moving nature of the development of the personal self, and the necessity of redirecting the "vital energy" inward if one is to achieve the height of Human potential. This process is understood as a refining and purification of consciousness by means of contemplation and by restricting the flow of thought that would normally go to the outside world.

It occurs to me that the whole of modern Depth Psychology is dedicated to facilitating just such a process. Recovering the inner child, accessing repressed memories, healing depression, and "curing" neurosis all depend upon the rectification of our conscious attitudes with the contents of the unconscious. The height of such healing—that is, individuation or self–realization—really only means that we have healed the split between our conscious awareness and the life of the unconscious. It means aligning our personal lives with the movement of Life itself, through a willing immersion in the innate flow of becoming that has sustained and enlivened us since our very conception.

Yet this little treatise is by no means the sole replica of earlier safaris into Real Life. One by one, as we go further along the trail and, thus, into the recesses of our Human Nature, we come upon more and more ancient reflections of the essential Human quest for its real relationship with Life. With each switchback, as we zigzag our way into the depths of Human time, we come upon another startling artifact from the Human journey of the Spirit. Each one appears as a trail marker of sorts, calling to mind the very journey that we each have undertaken to this sacred realm by following the modern path of Depth Psychology.

As we move deeper into Human time, nearing the first few centuries of the Common Era, we find an intricately painted bowl left by some intrepid traveler from, apparently, around 300 A.D. A lot of the imagery is vague and hard to recognize, it being from so distant a culture. It's interesting, but I really would like to move on before nightfall, so I'm surprised when Mr. Nu stops here, sort of milling around.

Jung appears to find the bowl and the area around it particularly intriguing, possibly because the bowl is an artifact of early Western mythology. He too seems somewhat distracted, however. He hands the bowl to Nu, who examines it, looks around a bit, and hands it back to Jung, who sets it back into its niche. Neither man says anything. They seem to be waiting for someone or something, and they are both as startled as the rest of us when an authoritative voice booms toward us from the switchback below us.

"You break it, you buy it," the apparent intruder calls out in mock irritation. We spin around to find a tall, gray-haired man in his eighties sauntering up the trail. I recognize him in an instant: it's Joseph Campbell.

The whole group is stunned into silence, although by now we probably should not be amazed at anything that we encounter along our path. So this is our mysterious "appointment." Joseph Campbell, the master mythologist. We can scarcely believe our good fortune.

"Aha! There you are!" calls out Mr. Nu, as he scuttles down to the much larger man and gives his hand a hearty shake. "I am so happy that you could make it."

"Not at all, not at all," answers Campbell graciously, as he walks with his escort toward us. As he and Nu reach our little group, Campbell and Jung embrace like the old comrades of the high country they are. Then the master mythologist turns to the artifact that we have been admiring.

"Ah yes, the trials of Orpheus. An excellent choice," Campbell remarks as he reaches the group, which is still gathered round the artfully painted bowl.

Jung picks up the bowl and hands it to Joseph Campbell with a knowing smile. Campbell examines the bowl with admiration and an air of familiarity. Clearly, this artifact is not new to him.

"Have you explained this fine artifact to your fellow travelers yet, Carl?" he asks, turning the bowl delicately in the evening light.

"No, the honor is all yours," Jung answers. "Show them everything. They ought to know. They have earned the right to be shown in whose footsteps they follow."

Campbell nods, looking directly at each of the few who are left on this journey. He speaks to us as someone telling a story. A story that, as it unfolds, becomes eerily familiar to me.

He tells us that this is a sacramental bowl depicting the mythic descent of Orpheus, the fisherman, into the watery abyss of the netherworld, much as we descended into the shadowlands of the unconscious. He seems intent on drawing particular parallels between this earthenware ritual artifact and our recent quest for real life. We listen.

Campbell begins by pointing out that there are sixteen figures stationed around the perimeter of the bowl, and that each station provides an important insight along the journey to Real Life.[4] Stations 1 through 4, he explains, depict Orpheus the fisherman descending into the underworld, where he is guided by the feminine into the realm of the goddess of darkness, Demeter, and her daughter, prize of the underworld, Persephone, at stations 5 and 6, respectively.

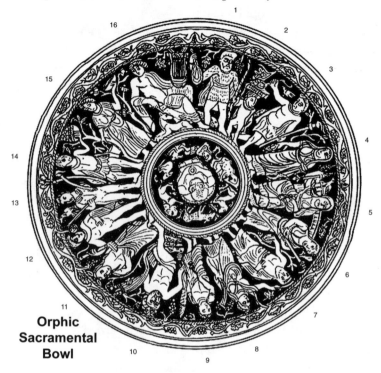

**Orphic
Sacramental
Bowl**

Surrounded by the mysteries of Death, but touched by good fortune (8 is Tyche, the goddess of Fortune, and 9 is Aathodaeman, god of good fortune), Orpheus is introduced to the ruler of the abyss (station 10). Here, the traveler is confronted with the realization that, as Campbell puts it, "all the gods and demons, heavens and hells, are discovered and displayed within us—and this ground of being, which is both giver and taker of the forms that appear and disappear in space and time, though dark indeed, cannot be termed evil unless the world itself be so termed."

The 11th station shows Orpheus fully initiated into the world of Human being as a somewhat androgynous figure. "His hair is long," Campbell points out, "and his right hand, on his belly, suggests a woman who has conceived," all of which speaks to his having attained a union between feminine and masculine forms of awareness, thereby generating a new life within. "Above the crown of the head," Campbell continues with his characteristic enthusiasm for such mythic imagery, "symbolic of the center of realization, is a pair of spiritual wings. The initiate is now fit to return to the world of normal day."

Campbell tells us that the next two stages are thought by some to represent scourging, and it occurs to me as he says this that such has been, in fact, the fate of many who bring special knowledge of the shadowlands into the common light of day, where it is not always so welcomed by the norm.

Campbell, however, sees the figures at stages 12 and 13 as the mythic twins, Pollux and Castor, one of whom was mortal and the other immortal. As such, these two figures represent a movement beyond the opposites even of being and non–being, of living in the everyday mortal, Human world while maintaining contact with the Eternal, the Transcendent.

Orpheus passes through this stage as well, as Campbell points out, accompanied by the porteress who first introduced him to the dark side, but who now sports vines and fruit, symbolic of fulfillment. She leads him toward Apollo, here the very personification of the Transcendent (station 16), where the cycle ends and, perhaps, eternally begins again.

Clearly, this sacramental bowl portrays a pathway along the high country of Human Nature very much like that through which we have just passed. It was the "feminine," the unconscious "yin" aspect of our being that both called and led us through the darkened underworld of our own Human Nature, especially during our own trek through the Ice Caves of Neurosis. There, we, too, were faced with our own extinction (as ego–selves, that is), and were challenged to enter what seemed from the outside to be a bottomless abyss of suffering and fear. In essence, it was the death of the virtual self that we had to grieve before we could ever find our way to real life.

As we now know, this is the kind of journey anyone who

wants a real life will have to make in one sense or another. Perhaps the Orphic initiate was called to tread a path that challenged his or her most basic fears and insecurities through ritual rites of passage and intense religious study. For us, the path was more literal, as we were called more directly to meet our own personal depressions, addictions, and compulsions as agents of our unnamed fear. Either way, the truth remains, eternally perhaps, that the pathway to true Humanness lies in our willingness to face our own dark side.

The successful journey through our inner night results in a reunion of the opposites within us, which were only kept apart by our fear of suffering and annihilation. This union of the opposites within us brings forth a new life: not just a stronger ego "I," but a truly new creation—a new, more authentic and creative expression of the true self, which is discovered daily in the process of our living our true lives.

I can see how this process of inner union has made each of us both more fully Human in the personal sense and more fully alive as aspects of Creation. It seems naturally to yield both psychological health and wholeness, and spiritual awakening. Through the process of accepting our innermost selves and our innate places in the world, we come into a new relationship with Life as a reliable and known Force that transcends our individual wills, and to which we find we can safely lend our willing "yes."

As the circular arrangement of the Orpheus myth suggests, this is a process that, it seems to me, we each will need to undergo over and over as we lead our real lives. Time and again we will be faced with aspects of our unknown sorrow, our undiscovered potential, and our self–ignorance. Accepting each new challenge Life offers will demand once more that we enter into the unknown within us, accept what we find there as potentially worthwhile and meaningful, unite the divided self within us, and emerge once more into the Human realm, saying a more true and meaningful, more profound "yes" to ourselves and to Life than we have done before.

Apparently, the essence of the trek to true Human being is one shared by Humans of a great many epochs throughout our Human past, although the actual route each traveled must have varied greatly. The path of Depth Psychology that has led us here now, at the turn of the twenty-first century, appears to be simply the latest incarnation in a lineage of avenues to real life that stretches, unbroken, as far as Human eyes can see. Like all the other paths that have come before, it is simply a creation of that Spirit that moves all else in the Universe: Life, expressing itself through our Human Nature.

Mirror Lake:
The Well of Tao

Carefully returning the Orphic bowl to its niche in the wall by the side of the trail, Campbell motions us to follow him, as he descends the last several meters toward the water's edge, deep in the canyon beyond time. I dub the dark reservoir Mirror Lake, for its panoramic reflections of the vast history of Human psychospiritual evolution. The vision is, for lack of a better word, breathtaking.

Campbell tells us this is his favorite stomping grounds. A well-known authority on this terrain, he has spent much of his life exploring these cliffs. He offers us a guided tour of the reservoir, which he will narrate with excerpts from his four-volume *Masks of God*. Of course, we all immediately accept. He begins the tour with a few short introductory lectures, all centered on the understanding that there is both a biological and a spiritual continuum within the history of Humankind.

"There is a unity of the race of man, not only in its biology but also in its spiritual history, which has everywhere unfolded in the manner of a single symphony," he explains with a sweeping gesture toward the warm canyon walls, "with its themes announced, developed, amplified and turned about, distorted, reasserted, and, today, in a grand fortissimo of all sections sounding together, irresistibly advancing to some kind of mighty climax, out of which the next great movement will emerge."[5]

Campbell notes that this symphony, which seems to issue forth from some clear, pristine Human need to sing with life in its own voice, has been gaining momentum and maturity for at least two hundred thousand years. From this point of view, it appears as though Human Nature itself were in the process of evolving into its own complete union with Life, just as the individual self matures into its own real experience of being. If this is so, then what we are perceiving here must be the spiritual evolution of the essential Human Self.

Apparently, the beginnings of this evolution remain unknown. Those beginnings fade into the depths below the water line of the dark reservoir, just here, at the headwaters of the reservoir of Human understanding. With a twinkle of impish joy and mystery, Campbell quotes for us from Thomas Mann's *Joseph and His Brothers*, as we gather round him at the water's edge. "Very deep, is the well of the past. Should it not be called bottomless? The deeper we sound, the farther down into the lower world of the past we probe and press, the more do we find that the earliest foundations of Humanity, its history and culture, reveal themselves unfathomable."[6]

I look more closely at the water as our new guide speaks, and notice, to my surprise, it is not still after all, but moving very slowly on some deep and unseen current—an unfathomable river on the flow of Human time. Its appearance as a placid reservoir apparently is caused by the great depth and breadth of our Human history, as it appears from the vantage point of an individual lifetime. But Campbell is inviting us to look at the history of our religions and mythologies from quite another angle; he wants to show us what they look like from their own level, as aspects of our Human psychospiritual evolution. He leads us along a shoreline trail, toward the furthermost recesses of the reservoir of Human understanding, where our tour will begin. There, we find a large, sturdy boat, moored to an ancient rock outcropping. As Campbell helps us into the craft he points out the first signs of Human spiritual endeavor, right there at the headwaters of Human time.

We can clearly perceive the crudely hewn niches in the sheer stone cliffs to which he is referring. The manmade clefts continue down the cliffside far into the obscure depths below us, disappearing at what Campbell estimates to be about 200,000 B.C. Some of them hold the enormous skulls of prehistoric cave bears—each with a leg, jawbone, or circle of stones arranged ceremoniously in or around it—while others appear to be ritual burial sites for the Neanderthal dead.

Our craft begins slowly to drift along the cavern wall. The vessel has no motor, only two long oars and a rudder by which Campbell steers our attention as we drift along, moved by some unseen current from below. We are drifting through the birth of Human Nature in the endless flow of Life.

Campbell points out that "Neanderthal Man* reveals in Central Europe the earliest dependable evidence found anywhere of an establishment of myth and rite: ceremonial burials with grave gear, and bear–skull sanctuaries in high mountain peaks."

These are the earliest known primeval stirrings of our Human being, and of the whisper that said yes to Life, sorrow and all. It seems to me, as we drift so near these artifacts, that they reflect the very *conception* of our species as a psychospiritual entity, very much as our own individual conception sparked our individual lives from out of an unfathomable pool of potential Human being.

This appears to have been an era when *Homo erectus* was only a burgeoning potential, when Human Nature was as yet unformed, and hominids lived more or less as appendages of nature. They killed woolly mammoths and giant bears with hammers and spears, and ate the meat raw. They gathered other food where they could find it. They were attached to Mother Earth as fetuses, undifferentiated either in individual expression or in general existence from Nature herself. Indeed, the mind of Humankind appears to have been in gestation. It was slowly

*c. 200,000-75,000/25,000 B.C.

evolving toward something more autonomous and new, which would someday find its own way into the world at large.

Indeed, as we drift onward with the flow of Human time, we can see Human beings very much like ourselves coming to life on Earth and finding their place in the flow of All That Is. By the beginning of the Paleolithic Era, around 30,000 B.C., the Neanderthal has disappeared, been replaced by another hominid line called *Homo sapiens sapiens*, our direct ancestors.

As we survey this period of our past, we see that Humans are roasting their game rather than just taking it as it comes to them. They are sculpting figures of the female form, which suggests the worship of some goddess prototype and of woman's life-giving power. These and the cave paintings of that era appear to represent the primordial beginnings of Human myth and religion, of Humankind's innate wish to find a union with the flow of Life.

Campbell tells us how stone images of the naked goddess appear in painted temple caves quite clearly different from the little ritual sites of cave-bear magic. It is as though Humankind were entering a more and more conscious relationship with Life as an entity in its own right. For, whereas the cave-bear rituals appear to have reenacted some central drama in the daily life of the Neanderthal for his survival, with the goddess statues we see the first glimmers of a conscious effort to relate to the Life Source itself.

Campbell gently steers the boat as he describes the caves themselves, with their painted chambers and vaults, and how they seem to reflect a deepened sense of spiritual existence, of Humankind's growing awareness of its extension beyond the known. He points to a series of caves in the distance, whose openings we can just make out. As we drift past these markers from about 10,000 B.C., the creative response of these early Humans to Life gains ever greater intricacy, organization, depth, and power. We must agree with Campbell, as we look at these, the first temples ever made by Human hands, that their creators were not "mere primitive magicians, conjuring animals. They were mystagogues, conjuring the minds of men."[8]

Campbell speaks now with awe and obvious excitement. "What a coincidence of nature and the mind these caves reveal! And what an evocation it must have been that drew forth these images! Apparently the cave, as literal fact, evoked, in the way of a sign stimulus, the latent energies of that other cave, the unfathomed Human heart, and what poured forth was the first creation of a temple in the history of the world."[9]

These caves appear to me as cosmic wombs, images of our Human emergence as a sentient species into the realm of physical being. The whole ambiance reminds me of the yin from which we each emerge at our physical birth. Only here it is the birth of Human Nature itself that we witness, and the Life Force that moves it toward its completion moves in millennia instead of months or years.

The similarity to individual Human growth really strikes home, however, as we drift through the eighth, seventh, sixth, and fifth millennia B.C. Here, Neolithic images of domestic life arise, images of a kind that never existed before in the history of Humankind. During the Neolithic period, Campbell tells us, animals were raised and kept for food rather than being tracked and hunted, and food was harvested instead of gathered. Here, in the Age of the Early Planters, Humankind was learning to manipulate the earth for its own intents and purposes, and to develop an image of itself as an entity separate from Mother Nature.

Clearly, the Human race was learning to say "I"; it was developing, essentially, an ego.

As we continue our tour, Campbell points out how, relatively rapidly, the primitive concept of the goddess as Source of the life-giving power transformed into an image of the protector of the hearth and field. Here, Human culture appears to have become ever more the focus of religious thought, and we can see a conscious organization in the Human way of life that speaks of a real self-awareness. Goddess worship was directed more and more toward the furthering of specifically Human aims—as opposed to a simple worship of Nature—and societies were organized, for the first time ever, by rank according to one's skill. More ego building!

Campbell uses an oar to keep us close to shore, as we drift farther still down the canyon, past a collection of pottery shards and whole pots that date, he tells us, from around 4500 B.C. They are gorgeous, still retaining their original color and their intricate geometric designs. The lesson that they hold is clear: people were beginning to conceive of Life in abstract terms. A thousand years later, by 3500 B.C., Campbell says, Humans suddenly learn to write, keep a calendar, do math, and follow social rules set down by designated priests and kings. "The whole city now, and not simply the temple compound, is conceived of as an imitation on earth of the cosmic order, while a highly differentiated, complexly organized society of specialists, comprising priestly, warrior, merchant, and peasant classes, is found governing all its secular as well as specifically religious affairs according to an astronomically inspired mathematical conception of a sort of magical consonance uniting in perfect harmony the Universe (macrocosm), society (mesocosm), and the individual (microcosm)."[10]

The goddess image is also getting to look more and more like an abstract rational concept, the closer we get to the high Neolithic age, about 2500 B.C. or so. This abstraction of religious icons is significant for Campbell, for it seems to have prefigured an explosion of diverse Human points of view that would eventually determine the nature of the world's great cultures and beliefs. It was the beginning of a new age in Human psychospiritual development, in which the cultural Ideal, not Nature herself, would be the guiding light and source of Human life. Humanity, apparently, was entering its tumultuous adolescence.

Our tour guide elaborates on his point. "Now in the Neolithic village stage of this development and dispersal," he remarks, "the focal figure of all mythology and worship was the bountiful goddess Earth, as the mother and nourisher of life and receiver of the dead for rebirth. In the earliest period of her cult,** such a mother–goddess may have been thought of only as a local patroness of fertility, as many anthropologists suppose. However, in the temples even of the first higher civilizations,*** the Great Goddess of highest concern was certainly much more than that. She was already, as she is now in the Orient, a metaphysical symbol: the arch personification of the power of Space, Time, and Matter, within whose bounds all beings arise and die: the substance of their bodies, configuration of their lives and thoughts and receiver of their dead. And everything having form or name—including God personified as good and evil, merciful or wrathful—was her child, within her womb."[11]

Until this point in Human history, we have been passing through essentially just one broad channel, with little divergence between the evolving responses to Life by Human Nature. But now the walls of the canyon begin to differentiate, diverting the flow of Human life into alternative directions East and West. With this divergence there comes a definite split in the consciousness of Human culture.

This split is just as yin and yang as the split between conscious and unconscious that we saw with the development of the superego in the realm of individual psychology. Indeed, it seems that this is exactly what was happening in Human Nature as a whole, as humanity entered the age of the Great Diffusion at about 2000 B.C. The sentient, formal "I" that first emerged in Sumer around 3200 B.C. took on an ever-widening variety of cultural appearances and faces, as the Human "superego" differentiated to East and West.

The whole world seems to have split into two divergent styles of being as the abstract concept of the existence of a Divine ideal for Human life spread out from Sumer (in what is now largely the country of Iraq). Not only did the Goddess herself fare far better in the East than in the West, her whole

---

**Perhaps around 7500–3500 B.C. in the Levant
***Sumer 3500-2500 B.C.

feminine, nature-affirming, process-oriented "yin" style of existence flourished there as well. And not only did the Father win the West (as did also the Son, of course), but the whole rational, heroic, individualistic, yang-styled Ideal thrived there, too.

As Campbell points out, this is what we might expect for normal Human psychology. "Psychologically and sociologically," he says, "the problem is of enormous interest; for as all schools of psychology agree, the image of the mother and the female affects the psyche differently from that of the father and the male. Sentiments of identity are associated most immediately with the mother; those of dissociation, with the father. Hence, where the mother image preponderates, even the dualism of life and death dissolves in the rapture of her solace; the worlds of nature and spirit are not separated; the plastic arts flourish eloquently of themselves, without need for discursive elucidation, allegory, or moral tag; and there prevails an implicit confidence in the spontaneity of nature, both in its negative, killing, sacrificial aspect...and in its productive and reproductive.[12]

"In India the power of the goddess—mother finally prevailed to such a degree that the principle of masculine ego initiative was suppressed, even to the point of dissolving the will to individual life; whereas in Greece the masculine will and ego not only held their own, but prospered in a manner that at the time was unique in all the world..."[13]

Campbell rows us through the maze of channels that develops here, at what he calls the Age of Heroes. As we drift and push through each divergent conduit, we can clearly see how each of the world's burgeoning cultures developed visions of the ideal union between Life and Human Nature as reflected in the lives and actions of specific legendary Human beings, and of gods with specifically Human characteristics. Between 1500 and 500 B.C., we see the birth of Zeus in Greece, the trials of Moses and his chosen of God in the Levant, the moral agony of Arjuna as he converses with Krishna in the Bhagavad Gita in India, and the recording of the Gathas of Zoroaster in Persia. The Human persona is on the rise.

We see this process reach its final culmination and plateau within the age that follows, in which the way to union with the Divine was no longer shown only in magical adventures of a mythic few, but offered to the masses through the grace and wisdom of enlightened masters of the unassailable Divine "Truth." This Age of the Great Classics (500 B.C. – 500 A.D.) displayed the enlightenment and mystical transformation of the Buddha; and the birth, death, and resurrection of Jesus Christ. It was ushered in by the emerging Tao of Lao Tzu and crowned by the Divine vision of the Prophet Mohammed.

We can see in each of these perfect personifications of the Divine in man a reflection of his culture and its inherited beliefs. Each assumed the trappings of his society, while at the same time rising above it to offer a vision of the Real that came to him directly through Divine or Sublime inspiration. From the words and actions of these few then came the final great age of their cultures, in which each society made its vision of the Real a function of its cultural identity as never before in the history of Humankind.

Clearly, Humankind was ascending to the peak of its social adulthood during this epoch, crowned by these diverse icons of the societal ideal for moral and religious perfection. From the legendary teachings of the Masters of this era—from Buddha, Lao Tzu, Moses, Jesus Christ, and Mohammed— appeared a lineage of the world's great religious doctrines and beliefs by which the cultural borders of the ever-expanding Human world were determined. This ushered in an age of Great Beliefs (500–1500 A.D.), in which the classics of the penultimate spiritual personae of each culture evolved into unassailable truths by which each member of a given culture was expected to judge and conduct himself. Thus, finally, the Human search for a meaningful vision of its place in the cosmos seems to have reached its peak as an assumed and regimented social norm.

As we drift onward, farther still in Human time, we witness

the establishment of the world's great systems of belief—
primarily Hinduism, Judaism, Buddhism, Christianity, and
Islam—under which the great masses of the world's Human
population came into an organized, systematized relationship
with Life. Around these great beliefs, great nations evolved;
and the people of the Earth settled into normalized ways of
living that were sustained and justified for scores of generations
by the learned visions of their given cultures.

Yet as Campbell steers us through the tenth century, the
scene begins to shift once more. In China, we can see the icons
of the Buddha crumbling fast, destroyed by China's rulers in a
perverted attempt to use Taoist mysticism to their own will.
Neither Taoism nor Buddhism ever recovered their central
places in the culture, but fled instead, as Chan Buddhism,
to Japan where they survive as Zen. By the early 1200s, a
Neo–Confucianism had taken over Chinese culture, removing
it from its original relation to the fertile Void, and replacing
that with the abstract ideals of filial piety, social virtue, and
service to the state.

Meanwhile, the Persians had been raiding India since 986
A.D., and by the year 1200, the last glimmer of Buddhism had
been extinguished by the servants of Allah. In 1565, the last
remaining Hindu capital had collapsed at Vijayanagar, and the
whole of India's religious empire had perished forever.

At the same time, in Europe, the Catholic Church had fallen
into decay and decadence after having become the supreme
power in all the Western world. In fact, as Campbell now points
out, "After a moment of high victory in the reign of Innocent
III (1198-1215 A.D.), the authority of this priestly organization
was challenged and substantially overthrown. It was immediately
thereafter that a new mythology—quite new—neither of animal
nor of plant divinities, nor of the cosmic order and its God,
but of man, gradually came (and is still coming) into
the fore..."[14]

Campbell falls silent as we drift through this latter-day epoch
in our Human history. The canyon walls that have been towering

above us East and West, offering giant reliefs of the great ages of Humankind, enter an astounding decline. The diverse channels through which Human life has flowed now seem to rush into a more shallow and turbulent flow of time, and the whole canyon seems to crumble nearly to the waterline. Boulders of debris from the far walls erupt at random here and there out of the water, making navigation tricky. At last we have to head for shore as we near our own time at the turn of the twenty-first century.

I can see in Campbell's eyes, as he deftly maneuvers his craft into a calm eddy from which we can disembark, a certain melancholy at the current state of our Human evolution as makers of myth and ritual. Clearly, he knows this canyon well, and loves the stories that it has to tell. How could he not be a bit discouraged at the fall of the great mythic ages past into this tumble of unformed potential that makes up our present age?

Yet Campbell also seems to know something that is not so apparent from the terrain where we stand now as we pull our gear up and heft it onto our backs. There appears to be no trail from here except the riverbed, which lays flat and rocky before us. I don't know where we go from here. Somehow, this uncertainty feels okay.

"Whereas formerly," says Campbell as the last of our party exits his boat, "life so held to established norms that the lifetime of a deity could be reckoned in millennia, today all norms are in flux, so that the individual is thrown willy-nilly, back upon himself, into the inward sphere of his own becoming, his forest adventure without way or path, to come through his own integrity in experience to his own intelligible Castle of the Grail."

He nods farewell to us, warmly embracing Mr. Nu and Carl Jung before he pushes off into the turbulent river, rowing expertly back to his favorite haunts. I can see that he knows these waters very well indeed. Clearly, rowing against the current is not new to him.

He calls out one last salute of encouragement to us as he maneuvers past the river rocks into the calmer waters, his image growing smaller by the minute as he rows.

"There are, today, no horizons, no mythogenetic zones. Or rather," he adds, shouting to be heard above the rapids' rush and touching an oar handle to his chest, "the mythogenetic zone is the individual heart."[15]

And with that, he all but disappears from view into the ancient canyon beyond time.

The Arc of the Absolute Self

Looking back up the canyon of Human time, watching the great scholar of the history of myth melt into the great depths of Human time, we can easily imagine the whole unfolding of our Human history, opening up from one dark underwater cave, far in the nameless past. Above and beyond that cave stretches the land of daylight, the shadowlands, Mount Persona, and the whole range of Human perception. From our standpoint in the present, here at the new headwaters of Human evolution, we can see the shape of Human Nature and of its past evolution, all in one vast, panoramic vista.

As Campbell and his boat disappear amid the gathering dusk, we turn downstream, following our guides, Carl Jung and Mr. Nu, who have already begun picking their way briskly down the riverside. As I walk, I recite to myself the chronology of all that we have seen from Campbell's vantage point in his sturdy old craft. I want to remember all of it the best I can.

At the far end of the reservoir of Human time was the cave art of the Neanderthal and the apparent conception of Human Nature. Something vaguely Human seemed to whisper to me from that cavern at the far reaches of Human time, but its voice was quiet and primitive. All I could see for certain was that Human Nature had found a conception and was gestating within the womb of Mother Earth.

By 30,000 B.C., Humankind was finally born into a physical relationship with life as something capable of its own movements and gaining awareness of its own singular being. Human sentience had experienced a physical birth into the material world. Like an infant, it was examining its own hands, trying out different tastes, and learning how to adore Mother as an entity in her own right.

Soon, by evolutionary standards, Humankind began to say "I" and to enforce its little will upon the land and animals as it chose. With the advent of the Early Planters came the beginnings of organized culture and of a truly Human way of life. This was the birth of our first concrete self-image as a species, the birth of the Human ego.

Ever more quickly, Humanity gained an abstract appreciation of its place in nature, such that, by 2500 B.C., Human life had reached a new plateau of sophistication based upon language and learned thought process. There, the abstract Ideal, which started as a simple reverence for the Goddess as the Source of our existence, took on more and more diverse shapes as Human thought spread East and West from Sumer. Human Nature was exploring the potentials of ideal and persona, just as do we individual humans with the advent of the superego.

Following this "Great Diffusion" of culture toward the East and West, I saw a worldwide Human adolescence in the Age of Heroes, in which these ideals became personified within the legendary lives of individuals who found themselves in one way or another blessed by direct contact with the Divine. Then, finally, Humankind found its true social adulthood in the Universe in the epitome of Human maturation: the Divine Man incarnate in personae such as Buddha, Jesus Christ, and Mohammed. There, Human Nature had, at last, achieved at least the appearance of an independent union with the Life Force in its many guises, and proceeded to build its homes on the foundations of the great ensuing systems of belief.

Yet, as I look back on this awesome evolution of Human awareness, something still seems to be missing. Rather than being the ideal life that its beliefs portrayed, the Human world was then, as it is today, still full of strife. The great beliefs warred with each other, and warred within their own ranks as well. The Divine vision that once inspired them became buried under layer after layer of deceit, avarice, envy, hatred, and fear, until the whole of the world's Great Beliefs began to crumble beneath the weight of their own claims to glory and perfection.

From our vantage point in the present, it seems clear to me that the whole evolution of our Human being and civilization, both East and West, originated with a single, innate, and essential Human quest for a true vision of the right relationship between Life and Human Nature. From the cave-bear rites to the rise of the Goddess, to the Vedas and the Torah; through the evolution of the teachings of Buddha, Christ, and Mohammed from local beliefs into the world's enduring belief structures; all the way to our modern science and its new vision of Human life and its true place in the Universe—every new epoch of Human mythology marks a new evolution of the age-old quest of Human Nature to find its right relationship with Life. Indeed, there seems to be an innate drive in Humanity as a whole toward a conscious at–one–ment with the Life Force that sustains both it and Universe of which it is a part.

This insight gives me pause, and I feel compelled to stop one last time for a final look back up the canyon. Our group is moving very slowly now anyway, as everyone seems to have been affected by the weight of Human time.

Looking back upon the development of Human mythology from our current perspective, with the whole terrain of individuation as a background, all the world's great myths and religions appear to me simply as metaphors for this true Self in its ineffable march toward a conscious at–one–ment with the flow of Life. Every single one of those competing "unassailable" truths that made up the dogmas of the world's great religions grew originally out of one and the same vision, whose roots lay in the innate Human drive toward a reunion with the Life Force that sustains us. The face or persona that each assumed seems to have depended more upon the culture in which it arose than on anything else; remove the mask and you find just one, quintessential Human vision of the innate, archetypal relationship between Life and Human Nature.

Just as the metaphors of the virtual self hold our unspoken personal truths for us until the time when we are ready to reveal them to ourselves, these myths and legendary figures all seem to me to reflect something that cannot be spoken of directly. That "something" is the Essence, the Tao, the Divine in Human Nature; and it must be spoken of in metaphor not because it has been repressed, but because it exceeds all form by definition.

If this is so, it seems to me that every age and culture will have needed its own style of metaphor to match its level of evolution and its cultural contexts for meaning, just as all Human beings have their own unique personal "mythology" for remembering their true, original relationship with their own life and all the other persons in it. No one image of the Divine could possibly be meaningful to all the diverse cultures and ages of Humankind. As all later religions everywhere reveal, God speaks to the heart, and knows all the languages of Humankind.

Clearly, we Humans have arrived at a point of our history when the mythologies that make up these "Metaphors of the Absolute Self" have all but lost their power to guide and to instruct us. Ours is the age of World Culture, as the historian Frobenius calls it, in which the mythologies that supported the diverse cultures of the world are crumbling beneath our feet. Indeed, the cultures of the world themselves, as well as the very realm of nature that supports us, are also falling radically into decline, and we seem to be headed exactly for that final, abysmal apocalypse of which so many of our myths have spoken.

From where I now stand, all of our religious images and stories appear to have lost their viability and their power to direct us as a culture toward our right relationship with Life, just as the metaphors of the virtual self lose their power to inform us of our real lives. That is, by our mistaking them for literal truths of unquestionable validity in and of themselves, which we must then defend vehemently against all others, these metaphors and the unexamined ideals they represent have come to mark the meter of our personal value and power in the world.

High Country

As we have seen, once these ideals and images are accepted as unassailable truths, we have no choice but to hold both ourselves and the whole world to their abstract tenets for behavior and belief, even if it leads to the absurdity of our annihilating one another in the name of Life, of berating each other in the name of Love, and of condemning one another in the name of the one true God. These truths are transformed from pathways leading to our individual communion with the Universal Essence of Life, into political agendas and dialectic credos that divide us from each other, from nature, and from ourselves; in short, they become our cultural neuroses.

Just as our personal neuroses become compulsive regimens for living in the tyranny of should and the search for personal perfection in ourselves and others, our spiritual beliefs seem to become hardened into artificial stances full of fear, anger, resentment, jealousy, and shame whenever they are removed from their original contexts within the union between all of Life and all of Human Nature. Then we are challenged either to surpass these metaphors for a more direct look at Life and Human Nature or to fall to our own mass delusions. That is, in fact, apparently the challenge of our present age.

This panoramic vision of our Human Nature in its vast relationship to Life is too much for me to hold in my head at once. It's too much to consider in one trip. I need to make a map of the terrain for later reference and to help me think about this all in depth as time goes by. I pull out my journal and make some notes.

Field note: Human Nature appears to be evolving psychospiritually along exactly the same lines as do individual Human beings. This is as might be expected, since the Archetypal Self that is evolving in this way is that same Self from which the archetypal processes of our personal growth arise.

Each of us who says yes to our individual process, therefore, evidently also furthers the spiritual evolution of our species..

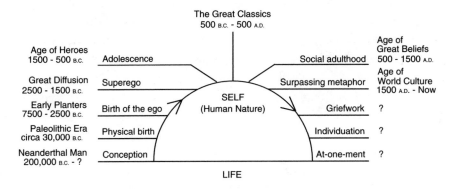

The Age of World Culture:
Metaphors of the Absolute Self

As I look up from my journal, I realize that daylight has nearly faded, and that the rest of my party has almost moved beyond my sight. I stuff my notebook into its compartment and hurry down the riverbank toward them. Even in the deepening twilight, though, I see evidence all around me that the chart that I have created might well be true to life.

It occurs to me as I gain on the group that this very chart and the whole present journey through the high country of Human Nature that it represents are both products of just this Age of World Culture. Here, the path of modern Depth Psychology by which we have been exploring the whole realm of Human Nature appears to have come into being as an aspect of the evolution of the Human Self through time. Indeed, it seems to stand as an emerging vision of our Human place in Life, ideally suited for deciphering the underlying meanings of the myths and legends that have come before.

The lay of the terrain itself suggests to me that such a path is needed and might naturally arise right about here, around the twentieth century, where, indeed, we come upon the diverse interpretations of the world of myth within the works of Carl Jung and Joseph Campbell. As I finally catch up with my companions and fall into step with them, I am reminded of the many other intrepid sojourners to this realm from our modern times whom we have not met on our current journey through the high country: consciousness researcher Jean Houston, cross–cultural psychologist Jack Kornfield, religious historian Mircea Eliade, archeologist Alexander Marshack, psychotheorist Ken Wilber, and social scientist Jurgen Habermas, to name a few.

Each will have approached this land from his or her own unique point of view, and will have come up with his or her own vision of the realm of Human myth. Here, we find Carl Jung's exhaustive study of the prescience of alchemy as a vast metaphor for the psychological process of transforming the "lead" of inert ego matter into "gold," the precious metal of the true self. Here, too, is Campbell's *The Hero with a Thousand Faces*, where the growth process described in psychoanalysis is found reflected metaphorically in the hero myths of all the ages; Jean Houston's revival of the ancient "mystery" schools of Greece as viable templates for the development of a sacred psychology for *The Possible Human*; Kornfield's vital synthesis of Buddhist tenets and Depth Psychology into *A Path with Heart*; and Eliade's many works on the effectiveness of myth in Human Nature, such as his *Myths, Dreams, and Mysteries*, wherein mythologies are seen as common and essential aspects of our modern times, now hidden and unconscious, lacking the proper images for release. Of course, the perspectives offered in this journey that we have just taken together also suggest a certain lasting value to our myths as metaphors for Human growth.

Ken Wilber, on the other hand, uses a different sort of "template" by which to gauge and decipher the realm of myth, one erected a century or so ago by psychologist Jean Piaget to describe the growth process of the Human self as ego. Just as we have done, Wilber explores the possibility that Humanity, in general, is evolving psychospiritually along the same path as do individual Humans; except that in Wilber's view, the ego is the only personal self there is. Using Piaget's vision of ego development as an essential aspect of his map for the emergence of the Human self, Wilber finds many valuable parallels, placing myth (as did Piaget) as an early, isolated stage in Human growth. This is a natural and appropriate vision of our Human myth, from the viewpoint of the ego as sole personal self. It also stands, therefore, as a viable interpretation of the realm of Human myth, depending upon your point of view.[16]

Yet whether we agree that the myths and religions of Human history are viable reflections of the path to Spirit or whether we accept them as some infantile relics of the past, we each are called upon now, in this Age of World Culture, to decipher some kind of underlying meaning for those myths in order to move on and to make sense of our Human place in Life.

There are those who feel that resurrecting one or another of the old myths or religions and revamping it to fit our modern times may be the key to our salvation. Others feel that our doom is sealed, either by Divine decree or by right of our own relentless folly. Only time will tell which of these views is true. But one way or another we are faced now, in our modern age, with the dire need to decipher our myths in some meaningful way, or else give up completely and allow ourselves to fall to the encroachment of a global neurosis.

Either way, perhaps we all may agree that we are headed toward an age of tough griefwork, in which the ignorant and neurotic management of our spirits and our Earth will likely grind the virtual wheels of "progress" to a halt: either through a radical depletion of our natural resources and our common Human decency, or through an enlightened transformation that brings the masses of Humanity into a global realization of our folly and delusion. One way or another (or maybe both), Life is moving on, and we must somehow learn to live and to let go or else die.

Yet, as we have seen in our own journey through the high country, sorrow and loss are not the same as suffering. We only suffer when we fight the flow of Life. Otherwise, sorrow simply comes and goes like any other noncompulsive feeling, leaving us with something else completely: our real lives and rightful sense of being in the world. If it is thus for each of us, it is very likely thus for Humanity.

It seems to me that the question for our age, then, must be whether we will step up to the ancient challenge of the Spirit with our best foot forward, honoring the pathways of the past and etching our own mark into the reservoir of Human understanding. Each of us who undertakes the challenge to find a profound, resounding "yes" to Life is also saying yes to the fulfillment of the species and to the evolution of our race into its full at–one–ment with the Universe at large. Each of us who seeks out his or her real life, who willingly descends into the caverns of personal suffering and fear in service of the true self, is therefore also participating in the spiritual evolution of Humanity itself.

From this perspective, our individual movement toward personal wholeness, which we encountered as the alive self on the plateau of individuation, appears as an articulate reflection of the dynamic nature of the archetypal Self—a virtual, particle/ wave photon arcing out of and back into Absolute Self, and mimicking its nature in our own.

Thus, the personal self and the archetypal Self must be understood as yet another pair of opposites in union, and the area of ambiguity that defines and unites them might be called simply the soul. Even Carl Jung seems to have been unable to delineate the enigmatic relationship between the two, self and Self. Yet from the perspectives offered on the path that we have chosen in our current journey through the high country of Human Nature, the presence of a Life Force and of a dynamic archetype for Human growth appears as undeniable as the presence of real Human selves: they are separate but inseparable, dynamic opposites in union.

Both the archetypal Self (the innate guiding Force of Human being) and the personal self (the innate and unique personal expression of that Force) are evidently with us from before birth. Both unfold in an orderly manner, creating the illusion of a world of separate forms and of separate formal beings, then calling for a return to Source. Together, they create yet one more bipolar aspect of the enigmatic Tao. On the personal level of existence, we are our experience of being, nothing more and nothing less. If we follow the insistence of the Life that is within us, we will live our real lives and become true Human beings. Otherwise, we will live out an illusion of our own unconscious making.

Yet there is a meaning to our lives that transcends even the most profound experience of personal existence, which nevertheless may be experienced only by people who have claimed their true personal selves. For following the true life we were given aligns us with the tao of being Human, that is, with the soul of Humanity, the Self. Everyone who follows the innate course of his personal evolution to its finish is, therefore, also assisting all Humanity in its ongoing journey toward an at–one–ment with Life that, from our present point of view, we can hardly imagine.

Like the individual Human being, the archetypal Human Self appears simply as an aspect of the flow of Life from which it has emerged. Like everything else in the Universe, it is not a static object, but a form in process whose development must follow the same natural laws as all else that is, according to the dictates of its own unique nature. Through it all there runs the recurrent dynamic of the opposites in union, of which even this discussion and the paper on which it is printed must also be a part.

To the extent that we discover our true personhood, we are literally becoming self–aware aspects of Life. We are the Universe awakening to its own nature. We are, as psychiatrist Erich Fromm has said, "life being aware of itself."[17]

With this understanding, we find ourselves approaching journey's end, at the seashore, beside the Ocean of Our Remembering. This is the sea of Human potential, whose expanse is vast and whose depths have yet to be fathomed. It represents the vital essence of what we are as Human beings in relationship to Life.

We each might well perceive our individual selves as waves upon that sea. We arise from the Formless for a few moments to gain a unique apparent form of our own in the world, only to fall with sound and fury back into the boundless flow of Life. The sea of Self is what we all are made of. Yet the shape each of us takes will be unique and meaningful, according to our place in space and time. Our being true to form is what gives the Ocean its vitality, and our individual lives their own creative force.

On a personal level, the meaning of life will differ with each individual person. We find it by saying a wholehearted "yes" to the unique self we were born to be, and then living a life in which that true self may find real, creative expression. On a transpersonal level, the meaning of life is beyond formal expression. It is to be found in the experience of oneness with the Spirit—with the Tao, the will of God—as it speaks to us through our Human Nature.

Here, our journey ends and it begins. The route through the high country that we have just surveyed is, after all, only the pathway of a real Human life. There could never really be a goal to it, for as with any really interesting hike, the whole point is in being there, not getting somewhere else.

In that sense, there is no journey here at all. For the entire high country of Human Nature rests within each of our hearts and minds, and only waits for us to find our way to where we really are.

Someone has built a fire on the beach and, as the sun sinks to its temporary rest beneath the far horizon, those of us who have become that close community of travelers that find their way to real life and then beyond it, stand together, arm in arm, leaders and followers now equal in the Way, as we tell tales of the day, and sing songs of the far distant past that now lives on in each of us. And the ocean rolls the rhythm, and the wind relays the tale, and the sands beneath our feet count out the numbers of the travelers who have been this way before, are here with us now, and who will find their way to real life some day. Someday.

AFTERWORD

. . . .

The High Country in Daily Life

At the end of any trip into the high country, there is always a journey home and a return to normal life in the lowlands of everyday culture. This can often be a letdown and a wake-up call to the soul. Traveling through the cities and towns that spread from the foothills into the lowlands of common society, with visions of Real Life and of the mystical terrain that we have traveled through still fresh in our awareness, we may be struck by the absence of clear reminders that there even *is* a higher ground upon which people can live.

The vista of tall square buildings, bustling traffic, and billboards encourages us not to settle down and check in with ourselves, but to stay busy, make money, worry, fear, and resist our old age and death for as long as possible. With the exception of the rare cathedral or random work of art, there are no images or signs recalling us to Spirit, nothing that urges us to settle down and listen inwardly, no billboards that remind us to accept and cherish our legitimate suffering as a genuine gift from the unconscious. For the most part, what we see as we return to our daily lives is designed to encourage us to go with the flow of traffic, not of Life or of our own Human Nature.

Not long after my first trip to the high country, many years ago, I realized while looking at this state of affairs in my culture that I would need to create a place in my daily life for all the things that I had seen from higher points of view. I knew from experience how difficult it is to keep from getting caught up in the overpowering momentum of one's job, of one's culture, and of relationships with people who do not know about real life. I knew that I needed to create a space where real life can exist on its own, and where I can go to reconnect with the true self that is trying to come into being from deep within me.

Even knowing all of this, however, I found myself becoming distracted from settling down and looking inwardly within a week or two of my return to everyday life. Unless some crisis demanded my specific attention, I tended to get swept up in my daily waking life. I suspect that, in part, this was so easy to do because there were often uncomfortable, lonely, or downright painful feelings that are niggling around the edges of my consciousness that I would have to face and feel if I slowed down. It was so easy to find chores that needed to be done, or to "take a break" by watching television or going out or playing at some hobby rather than to take an hour to check in with myself. In fact, I found that the more I was in need of checking in—that is, the more neurotically and habitually I was living—the harder it was to get myself to slow down and take a closer look within myself.

It occurred to me that what I needed was a space in my own home where real life was available at all times; a place where I could go and sit and be immersed in the high-country atmosphere without having to re-create it at a point when I was least able even to imagine any other point of view than the neurotic, compulsive one I happened to be caught up in. I needed a sanctuary.

When this insight first occurred to me, I was living in a very small house with people who did not know much about high-country living, so I had to keep it simple. I found an old wool blanket that felt firm and friendly, a blanket that I could sit on like a cushion and never use for anything else. I kept it folded up on the floor in the corner my bedroom along with a candle, a notebook, and a special sweater, which I put on only when I was going to leave the outside world behind. Pulling out the blanket, putting on the sweater, and lighting the candle became the "sacred" ritual that I performed before meditation. I felt as though that space in the corner of my bedroom became sacred every time I performed this preparation ritual. Just sitting down there had a calming, quieting effect upon me, and I began to have high-country experiences right there, in my plain old bedroom, without going anywhere at all.

Before long, I came to realize that all I had to do in order to make contact with the high country within me on a regular basis was to get myself onto that blanket. I didn't have to force myself to slow down or to meditate, and I didn't have to wait until a crisis came up before paying attention to how I was feeling. All I had to do was to make an appointment with myself to contentiously go through my setting-up ritual, to sit there in my sacred space for twenty minutes, and before I knew it something in me had shifted. Often, I found myself still there an hour later, recording subtle feelings and realizations in my notebook that were only waiting for me to quiet down a little so that they could be heard. Over time—as I did this faithfully several times a week, either in the morning or the evening—I found that I was experiencing less crises in my life, and that when I did have a life crisis, it was more easily made meaningful and resolved because I had an established place to sit with it and find my true center in the midst of my life's chaos.

Sometimes, when I did not have anything in particular to work on, I just sat there, letting my body relax, muscle by muscle, until I was so pleasantly calm that my breathing itself seemed the only thing moving in the entire world. Other times, I found that my mind would not stop at all. At those times, my first impulse was often to try to force myself to shut up. Of course, this never worked. Before long, I would remember to just let myself feel all that I was feeling. Inevitably, I would then discover myriad physical sensations and subtle emotions attached to the thoughts that would not let me be. They were messages from my faithful old unconscious. When I listened to them and recorded them in my notebook just as they arose, inevitably the thoughts lost their compulsive power and I found myself feeling more balanced, comfortable, and clear.

It is, in fact, exactly this process that brought me into a clean, loving relationship with my son, Chris, after so many years of mistrust and hurt feelings. By the time Chris reached the age of sixteen, he had become expert at getting under my skin. I often found myself arguing with him in my own mind late at night or during a lull in the day, obsessing over what I wished I had said in our last confrontation, enraged at times by his insensitivity and lack of respect for what I had done for him and been to him throughout his youth. I could not seem to let these inner dialogues go, even when it became obvious to me that nothing I said to him would make a bit of difference in the way he responded to me or lived his life.

Recognizing the telltale indicators of a neurotic obsession, I brought the internal conflict into my meditation. One night, instead of agonizing over the anger that stirred up in me, I just wrote everything down. I wrote about how I felt and what I wanted to say to Chris and what I wanted from him. I wrote until there was nothing left in me to write. This in itself seemed to help, but I knew there was more, something else that was hidden that still needed saying.

I read through what I had written, and then let myself relax, letting my body get quiet, watching my breathing a while, until I was still. I just relaxed, knowing that I would get back to these feelings presently. Then I recalled to mind all the feelings and thoughts that were insisting themselves upon me through my anger at my son. I watched as more thoughts and feelings arose, allowing my body to relax every time I felt it tighten against the emotions. I let the subtler awarenesses—which tend to get out-shouted when I get carried away by such intense thoughts and emotions—have their say. *What else?* I asked myself. *What else?*

As I listened with my total awareness, letting the peripheral issues float up from my unconscious on the tide of association that was driving my obsession with Chris's defiant attitude, something clicked into place as though out of nowhere. It was my own childhood voice, the voice of a younger David in me who was disappointed at the failings of the father I turned out to be. It was a hurt, idealistic, discouraged young boy who wanted to become a more powerful, successful, smart, and popular father than what I had been able to be. Chris's disappointment in me had triggered my own, unrealized self-doubt, guilt, shame, and fear about being a father, a man, and an imperfect being that could not live up to what the little boy he had been had imagined he would be some day.

As the voice of that hurt, abandoned, disappointed young boy in me became more clear, I wrote down everything he had to say to me. Later on, I wrote a letter to that boy I had been. I told him that although I could never be perfect, I loved him and would never abandon him no matter what, and that I would keep trying to become the best father that I could be for as long as he needed me. What I could not get across to Christian at that point in his life turned out to be something that a long-forgotten part of me needed to hear.

After this session, my compulsive responses to Chris and his defiant behavior became a beacon leading me back to myself and my own personal disappointments. As a result, Chris and I fought less often and the arguments stopped escalating into a war of words as they had done. Chris continued to be angry and disappointed with me, and he left home not long after his seventeenth birthday. However, I was able to let go of him with compassion and an open heart. Three years later, he came back asking for help and to be returned to the family fold. I was ready. I had already made space for him inside my heart.

Before long, I was using this meditative process, which is very much like what we went through in the Ice Caves of Neurosis during our journey through the high country, on a regular basis. Whenever anything was bugging me and would not let me go, I would write it out fully, then relax and recall the turmoil as completely as possible, allowing myself to sink into the emotions completely. As subtler realizations and images came up, I would record them faithfully, without edit. Inevitably, as I reviewed what had come up in context with what was going on in my life at that time, new, powerful, healing insights would pop up from "nowhere."

Eventually, I found a sort of shorthand for this pathway for "spelunking" into my own frozen depths: Write, Relax, Recall, Record, Review. This is a path that I follow time and again as my life offers new opportunities to become clear in my own mind about who I actually am. No single trip into these depths will ever leave me enlightened wholly and permanently, but having a reliable access point to this aspect of the high country within me keeps real life within my grasp, no matter where I am or what is going on.

The Grief of Growing Up

As I go through this spiral process of rounds of expansion and growth, I can see that the unresolved grief that causes my recurring neurosis has a yin/yang dynamic all its own. It occurs to me that the grieving I need to do from my childhood and from everyday life is identical to the grieving that we all have to do around death. I find that Elizabeth Kübler-Ross's famous five-stage grief process—Denial, Anger, Bargaining, Depression, and Acceptance[1]—keeps showing up in all my personal growth work, and the whole process of personal griefwork begins to make sense to me in a new way.

Whenever I find myself caught up in a neurotic fantasy like the one I was projecting onto Chris, I know that I am in Denial. Usually, if I am forced to look at the situation, the first thing I feel is anger or some related emotion such as self-pity or resentment. Sometimes I just bounce back and forth between Anger and Denial for a long while, until I can't stand it anymore.

Often, I will attempt to strike a bargain with my grief by, say, admitting that I am in the wrong but refusing to make it right until the other person admits that he is wrong, too. Other bargains I use include the use of coffee, alcohol, television, and food. Anything to make me feel better without having to feel my fear, anger, and suffering directly.

Eventually, though, I find that I have no choice but to feel my pain. This realization is depressing, and I often have to allow myself to just feel depressed for a few days or weeks until I get saturated enough with my true grief for the unconscious to offer something meaningful by association. That's what happened with the Chris problem. I suffered for months with that one until it finally gained enough power to, as Jung would say, push through the threshold of consciousness.

I like the way that Kübler-Ross speaks of depression as grieving. She tends to use the words interchangeably. That helps me realize the value and validity of feeling depressed. It helps me to remember that my depressions are purposeful, and that they will lift as soon as I come to an Acceptance either of the my responsibility to change what ought to be changed (such as my attitude toward myself as a father and toward Chris as a confused, frightened kid), or of the fact that the loss is one natural to Human existence and therefore unavoidable, even right.

That is what happened with my anger toward Chris. Even when I just tried to let it go, knowing that I could do nothing to regain his respect, I could not stop obsessing about it. It was not until I recognized the *repairable* part of the loss I was feeling—the loss of self-respect that arose from the hurt child inside *me*—that I was able to resolve the grief. Chris's moving away from me, of course, was a loss that was appropriate to just accept and let go and, as such, it soon resolved on its own as a natural process of the grief of his growing up.

My new understanding of the process of grieving in everyday life has really helped me to accept my own spates of anger, resentment, and envy when they come along. I can see them as natural stages that I need to go through sometimes as I process my life's disappointments. I don't have to be ashamed of these Human emotions, and I realize that they do not mean that I have forsaken my high-country life. In fact, the whole spectrum—from denial to anger and its related emotions, to the bargaining I do against my own suffering with the use of all sorts of diversions, to the acute depressions I experience during hard times—all of these emotional reactions and attitudes are simply part of my Human response to life's changes. As Jung noted, it is only when I do not acknowledge these feelings for what they are that they become a neurosis.

This understanding itself helps me to keep from getting trapped in my grief. Whereas before I might have felt so ashamed of my anger that I could not bring myself to recognize and feel it, now I find that I need not repress my true feelings that way. Neither, of course, do I need to act upon them. I find that the best thing to do with my feelings is simply to feel them. They are e-motions. Their nature is to be in constant movement, and they come and they go on their own momentum when not "fearfully guarded."

Understood from this point of view, all of my interpersonal conflicts, my unpleasant dream experiences, my secret fears and failings, and even the mistakes of my past become a lot more manageable. I can see them as grieving, and I can see the grief process as, essentially, the process of my getting over my fear of sorrow and loss. In that sense, all of my "negative" emotions appear to me as simply fear-based emotions, and I begin to notice that I never become angry when I am feeling comfortable with myself and confident in my life. It is only when I feel fearful in some way or another that I get angry or resentful or even envious at all.

This insight changes the way that I respond to other people's anger, as well. I find that I can often diffuse their anger if I can address their fear. Sometimes, it works just like magic. Sometimes it doesn't work at all. Either way, I find that I am more and more able to maintain my access to the high-country perspective on my life and a high-country environment in my life when I perceive the hurtful and unpleasant aspects of everyday life in this way.

Celebration

When I do not run away in fear from my own suffering, I become more comfortable with myself in general, and I find that Life flows through my everyday living with increasing ease and unceasing vitality. Even when my personal life is very hard and I feel as though I cannot go any farther, vitality manages to arise from within my discouragement itself, as long as I do not abandon my own true, immediate experience of being. Something new is always created at every ending, and my life moves in ever-expanding spirals, generating a self-sustaining high-country environment in which I can create and celebrate my real life.

Indeed, celebration itself has become an indispensable aspect of the art of high-country living as I have learned to access more and more of the innate vitality of life. I have met new friends who know about the high country and who are living out their real lives. We walk and talk together, joke and share our fears. Even our failings tend to become cause for celebration of our friendship and of the magical renewing of life that occurs just from our saying "yes" to it all.

Sometimes, we gather to play music and drum. I think of this as "play" in the highest sense of the word. There are times during our "jamming" when something beyond our individual abilities appears to raise our playing to another level, carrying us along on its own momentum into a realm of light ecstacy.

Indeed, the general act of creativity seems essential to high-country living. Art in one form or another lends expression to our openness to life and to our excitement in the face of the emerging unexpected. Creating art in our lives—whether in writing or drawing or music or simply in painting the walls of the house in a creative manner—is play and celebration, although it often is also hard work. The high-country approach to art, of course, is not about becoming an artist or making a living, although that does sometimes happen, too. Instead, it is about engaging in a conscious, constant "yes" to our lives and to the

Life Force that moves so freely through us when we do not allow our training, our habits, or our fears to interfere with our sense of Spirit.

We do not need to be artists or musicians, however, to celebrate our lives and to play and create. We can celebrate our lives in how and what we eat, in sharing food together, and in growing our own food. We can celebrate by consciously honoring that something has forfeited its own life that we may live, and consciously acknowledging the life that it gives us. We can celebrate in how we bathe and dress, in how we start the day and end it, and in how we respond to the dreams we dream at night. Little by little, our lives can become a celebration in themselves, and our homes, our pastimes, our friendships, and our lovemaking can all become vital, sustaining points of access to the high country that lives within us each.

Especially now—in the age of the solo seeker, of we who must move on beyond the support of mother church, beyond the monastery walls, beyond the cloistered ashram—our willingness to seek out and to develop the artful, playful expression of the Spirit is essential to the ongoing of life in the high country of our Human Nature. Facing our suffering as it arises and developing a lifelong conversation with the unconscious is the very foundation upon which we may build our higher points of view. An artless, unplayful life, where what is highest in our Human Nature is not both accessed and expressed, is not a real life at all. It is, after all, the dynamic dialogue with the unconscious that brings us into real union with our true selves, and that dialogue is exactly what happens in high play and in all creative acts.

Within our everyday lives, therefore, the unity of opposites has to prevail if we are to keep growing. We each must access and accept our legitimate suffering. This means also accepting the responsibility to heal that suffering wherever possible. This deep and conscientious "yes" to Life, sorrow and all, however, does not mean life will be filled with suffering and unhappiness. On the contrary, our acceptance of the whole truth about Life and our individual lives gives us deep access to art, to free-form celebrations, to real relationships with other people, and to a sense of fearlessness that lets us play with abandon and untainted joy. We will find that, more often than not, sorrow gives way to joy, fear gives way to love, and the quiescent silence of Non-Being in the depths of our receptive meditation generates the more pure, more powerful levels of our own Being.

As we each accept this awesome adult life responsibility, our lives become transformed from tedious, neurotic melodramas into creative, spiraling cycles of internal griefwork work and expressive celebration. We become available to one another in ever more profound and enriching ways, and our lives begin to reflect all the vitality that is so evident in the high country itself.

There is an eternal source of creative vitality coursing through each of us, just as it does through all Creation. We have the great gift of our being capable of realizing it in consciousness and of creating something alive out of it, if only we will make the effort to make room for it in our everyday lives. When we build our personal lives upon that realization, we find ourselves living increasingly in direct contact with the high country of Life and of our Human Nature. We find ourselves living as members of a vital, ever-changing community of fellow travelers, in celebration of all that Life brings and in heartfelt compassion for all that, inevitably, must pass away.

In short, we find ourselves naturally living our real lives.

ENDNOTES

. . . .

Introduction

1. Karen Horney, *Neurosis and Human Growth*, Chapter Three.

2. See the introduction to Archie Bahm's *The World's Living Religions* for a discussion of "high" religion as that which says "yes" to life, just as it is.

3. See Carl Jung, "The Transcendent Function," *The Portable Jung*, 273-300.

PART ONE

Chapter One

1. *The Wisdom of China and India*, ed. Lin Yutang, 586. According to James Legge, in his *The Texts of Taoism, Part One*, 51, the "spirit of the valley" refers to the activity of the Tao. The valley is an ancient Taoist symbol for vacuity and, therefore, refers to the invisible power of the Tao, which moves all things but has no particular form of its own.

2. For a more complete discussion of the nature of yin and yang, see *The I Ching*, trans. Richard Wilhelm, lv-lviii.

3. This analogy appears in Stephen Hawking's *A Brief History of Time*, 127.

4. "The Nameless is the origin of Heaven and Earth; The Named is the Mother of all things." From "The Tao te Ching," *The Wisdom of China and India*, 606.

5. Capra, *The Tao of Physics*, 205-210.

Chapter Two

1. Jack Kornfield offers a very accessible discussion of the Four Foundations of Mindfulness as they relate to psychological healing in *A Path with Heart,* 40-55.

2. Source material for Jung's contribution to the discussion of the four functions of conscious awareness that follows is drawn from *The Portable Jung,* 25-51.

3. See Freud's *A General Introduction to Psychoanalysis,* 46.

4. See Jung on Freud in *Memories, Dreams, Reflections,* 114, 146-147. See also "Sigmund Freud in His Historical Setting" in Jung's *Collected Works, Volume 15, Spirit in Man, Art, and Literature.*

5. See *The Portable Jung,* 71. "In addition to the repressed material the unconscious contains all those psychic components that have fallen below the threshold [of conscious awareness], as well as subliminal sense-perceptions. Moreover, we know, from abundant experience as well as for theoretical reasons, that the unconscious also contains all the material that has *not yet* reached the threshold of consciousness. Equally, we have reason to suppose that the unconscious is never quiescent in the sense of being inactive, but is ceaselessly engaged in grouping and regrouping its contents."

6. Paraphrased from *The Portable Jung,* 146.

7. *P'u* literally means an uncarved wood. In Taoism, it has come to represent simplicity, plainness, genuineness. See "The Natural Way of Lao Tzu," in *A Source Book in Chinese Philosophy,* 147.

8. See "Instinct and the Unconscious," in *The Portable Jung,* 47-58.

Chapter Three

1. This classic Jungian concept is discussed concisely by M.L. von Franz in her essay "The Process of Individuation." See Jung, *Man and His Symbols,* 230-234.

2. See Jung, *Memories, Dreams, Reflections,* 198-199.

3. Ibid., 279. See also Jung's *Collected Works: Volume 9, Part Two: Aion.*

4. See Jung's *Collected Works: Volume 9, Part One: Archetypes of the Collective Unconscious,* ¶ 85, footnote 8. "One must, for the sake of accuracy, distinguish

between 'archetype' and 'archetypal ideas.' The archetype as such is a hypothetical and irrepresentable model, something like the 'pattern of behavior' in biology." See also Jung's "Psychological Aspects of the Mother Archetype," *Four Archetypes*, 13, where he explains: "Again and again I encounter the mistaken notion that an archetype is determined in regard to its content, in other words that it is a kind of unconscious idea (if such an expression be admissible.)"

5. Jung, *Collected Works: Volume 9, Part One: Archetypes of the Collective Unconscious*, ¶ 151.

6. Source material for Jung's discussion of the advent of the ego is drawn from "Aion: Phenomenology of the Self," *The Portable Jung*, 139-141.

7. For a concise discussion of the nature of the superego, see Freud's "The Dissection of the Psychical Personality," in his *New Introductory Lectures on Psychoanalysis*, 57-80. Jung's essential agreement with Freud's superego theory is evident in, for example, Jung's *Collected Works, Volume 16: The Practice of Psychotherapy*, ¶ 245-248.

8. For a more complete discussion of Jung's views on the relationship between the social persona and the fully realized self, see "Relations between the Ego and the Unconscious," *The Portable Jung*, 70-138.

PART TWO

Chapter Four

1. Jung's entire career may be offered as reference enough to support the notion that he considered the unconscious an unbounded storehouse of unrealized potential, which no one could ever exhaust. See Carl Jung, "Instinct and the Unconscious," *The Portable Jung*, 52.

For Jung on the unavoidable accumulation of unconscious material in childhood, see "Individual Dream Symbolism in Relation to Alchemy" in his *Collected Works: Volume 12, Psychology and Alchemy*, ¶ 81.

2. See Jung, "Relations between the Ego and the Unconscious," *The Portable Jung*, 83-121.

3. Jung's entire theory of active imagination and his lifelong work with images from the unconscious as intrinsically meaningful are reflected in this fictional dialogue.

4. See Berne, *Games People Play*, 23.

5. A simplified version of Jung's "active imagination."

6. In his youth, Jung actually wanted most of all to be an anthropologist, but he could not afford to travel to Egypt, where he would have liked to study. See *Memories, Dreams, Reflections*, 84. His later work in the psychology of archetypes, in myth, and in alchemy betrays this lingering bent.

7. See Jung, "Relations between the Ego and the Unconscious," *The Portable Jung*, 83-85.

8. Ibid., 83-138.

9. See Jung, "Aion: Phenomenology of the Self," *The Portable Jung*, 146.

10. Jung often referred to the work of Freud and Adler as complementary theories from which he himself often drew, although, of course, he saw them as limited and underdeveloped compared to his own approach. See, for example, Jung's *Collected Works: Volume 16: The Practice of Psychotherapy,* ¶ 24, 74, 75, 234. See also Jung's "Relations between the Ego and the Unconscious," *The Portable Jung*, 114-115, and "On the Psychology of the Unconscious" in his *Collected Works: Volume 7: Two Essays on Analytical Psychology*. For a more complete discussion of the relationship between the works of Freud, Adler, Rank, and Jung, see Progoff, *The Death and Rebirth of Psychology*.

11. For two of several interesting anecdotes of the expression of a neurosis in physical symptoms, see Jung's *Memories, Dreams, Reflections*, 115-122.

12. Berne, *Games People Play*, 23.

13. Ibid., 116, 117, 120.

14. The fictitious dialogue that follows between Fritz Perls and myself is patterned loosely upon therapeutic Gestalt sessions such as those that appear in Frederick S. Perls's *Gestalt Therapy Verbatim*.

15. For a more complete description of this exercise and of the discussion that follows, see Alexander Lowen, *Bioenergetics*, 71-81.

16. See Progoff, *At a Journal Workshop*, 67-69.

Chapter Five

1. See Alice Miller, *The Drama of the Gifted Child*, for a concise discussion of the roots of chronic depression and narcissistic disorders in unrecognized childhood experiences of abandonment and loss of value as real people.

2. "The swift passage of the years and the overwhelming inrush of the newly discovered world leave a mass of material behind that is never dealt with. We do not shake this off; we merely remove ourselves from it. So that when, in later years, we return to the memories of childhood we find bits of our personality still alive, which cling around us and suffuse us with a feeling of earlier times. Being still in their childhood state, these fragments are very powerful in their effect. They can lose their infantile aspect and be corrected only when they are reunited with adult consciousness." From Jung, "Individual Dream Symbolism in Relation to Alchemy" in *Collected Works: Volume 12: Psychology and Alchemy*, ¶ 81.

3. "Behind a neurosis there is so often concealed all the natural and necessary suffering the patient has been unwilling to bear. We can see this most clearly from hysterical pains, which are relieved in the course of treatment by the corresponding psychic suffering which the patient sought to avoid." From Jung's *Collected Works: Volume 16: The Practice of Psychotherapy*, ¶ 185.

4. See Jung, "Individual Dream Symbolism in Relation to Alchemy," *Collected Works: Volume 12: Psychology and Alchemy*, ¶ 81.

5. For an abridged version of this famous Buddhist legend, see Ananda K. Coomaraswamy and Sister Nivedita, *Myths of the Hindus and Buddhists*, 264-272.

6. See Jung, *Collected Works: Volume 16: The Practice of Psychotherapy*, ¶ 109-110.

7. For a more complete discussion of Jung's view on this arc-like progression of psychological life stages, see Jung, "The Stages of Life," *The Portable Jung*, 3-22.

8. See Jung, *Collected Works: Volume 16: The Practice of Psychotherapy*, ¶ 79.

9. The following instruction in the practice and value of what Jung called "active imagination" is paraphrased from Jung's "The Transcendent Function," *The Portable Jung*, 288-294.

10. Ibid., 279.

11. Ibid., 298.

Chapter Six

1. Jung's comments on the difficulties encountered by novice explorers of the unconscious are drawn from his "Relations between the Ego and the Unconscious," *The Portable Jung*, 83-98.

2. Horney, *Neurosis and Human Growth*, 158.

3. Jung, "Phenomenology of the Self," *The Portable Jung*, 146.

4. Rogers, *On Becoming a Person*, 114.

5. Ibid., 123-124.

6. Ibid., 119.

7. See Maslow's "Self Actualizing People" in *The Self*, 173.

8. Ibid., 166.

9. Ibid., 167.

10. Ibid., 168. [Note: caps on "Human Nature" are mine.]

11. Ibid., 177.

12. Ibid., 186.

13. Ibid., 186. [Note: caps on "Human Nature" and on "Human" are mine.]

14. Carl Rogers, *On Becoming a Person*, 350-351.

15. Jung, *Collected Works: Volume 9, Part One: Archetypes of the Collective Unconscious*, ¶ 84. See Esther Harding's *Psychic Energy* for a detailed Jungian overview of the process of individuation.

Chapter Seven

1. Lao Tzu, *Wen Tzu*, 13.

2. *The Secret of the Golden Flower*, 69. [Caps on "Human Nature" are mine.]

3. See Richard Wilhelm's introduction to *The Secret of the Golden Flower*, XVI.

4. The image of the Orphic bowl and Campbell's discussion of its meanings are drawn from Campbell's *The Masks of God, Volume Four: Creative Mythology*, 10-23.

5. Campbell, *The Masks of God, Volume One: Primitive Mythology*, V. All dates and facts discussed in relation to Campbell's review of mythology are drawn from his four-part *Masks of God* series.

6. Campbell, *The Masks of God, Volume One: Primitive Mythology*, 5. [Caps on "Humanity" are mine.]

7. Ibid., 394.

8. Ibid., 398.

9. Ibid., 397.

10. Ibid., 404.

11. Campbell, *The Masks of God, Volume Three: Occidental Mythology*, 7.

12. Ibid., 70.

13. Ibid., 173-174.

14. Ibid., 507.

15. Campbell, *The Masks of God, Volume Four: Creative Mythology*, 677.

16. See Wilber, *Sex, Ecology, Spirituality*.

17. Fromm, *The Art of Loving*, 6.

Afterword

1. Kübler-Ross, *On Death and Dying*, 38-137.

BIBLIOGRAPHY

· · · · · · · · · · · · · · · ·

Bahm, Archie J. *The World's Living Religions*. Carbondale, IL: Southern Illinois University Press, 1971.

Bhagavad Gita. Trans. Juan Mascaró. New York, NY: Penguin Books, 1979.

Berne, Eric. *Games People Play*. New York, NY: Ballantine Books, 1978.

Brenner, Charles E. *An Elementary Textbook of Psychoanalysis*. Garden City, NY: Doubleday, 1957.

Campbell, Joseph. *The Hero with a Thousand Faces*. Princeton, NJ: Princeton University Press, 1973.

____.*The Masks of God. Volume One: Primitive Mythology*. New York, NY: Arkana, 1991.

____. *The Masks of God. Volume Two: Oriental Mythology*. New York, NY: Penguin Books, 1976.

____. *The Masks of God. Volume Three: Occidental Mythology*. New York, NY: Penguin Books, 1976.

____. *The Masks of God. Volume Four: Creative Mythology*. New York, NY: Penguin Books, 1976.

Capra, Fritjof. *The Tao of Physics*. New York, NY: Bantam Books, 1977.

Coomaraswamy, Ananda K. and Sister Ninvedita. *Myths of the Hindus and Buddhists*. New York, NY: Dover Publications, 1967.

Eliade, Mircea. *Myths, Dreams, and Mysteries.* New York, NY: Harper & Row, 1975.

Freud, Sigmund. *General Selections from the Works of Sigmund Freud.* Ed. John Rickman. Garden City, NY: Doubleday Anchor Books, 1957.

____. *A General Introduction to Psychoanalysis.* Garden City, NY: Doubleday Permabooks. 1956.

____. *New Introductory Lectures on Psychoanalysis.* New York, NY: W. W. Norton, 1961.

Fromm, Erich. *The Art of Loving.* New York, NY: Bantam Books, 1972.

Harding, Esther. *Psychic Energy.* Princeton, NJ: Princeton University Press, 1973.

Hawking, Stephen. *A Brief History of Time.* New York, NY: Bantam Books, 1988.

Horney, Karen. *Neurosis and Human Growth.* New York, NY: W. W. Norton, 1970.

Houston, Jean. *The Possible Human.* Los Angeles, CA: Jeremy P. Tarcher, 1982.

The I Ching. Trans. Richard Wilhelm. Princeton, NJ: The Princeton University Press, 1976.

Jung, Carl G. *Collected Works: Volume 7, Part One: Two Essays on Analytical Psychology.* Ed. Herbert Read. Bollingen Series XX. Princeton, NJ: Princeton University Press, 1968.

____. *Collected Works: Volume 9, Part One: Archetypes of the Collective Unconscious.* Ed. Herbert Read. Bollingen Series XX. Princeton, NJ: Princeton University Press, 1968.

____. *Collected Works: Volume 9, Part Two: Aion: Researches into the Phenomenology of the Self.* Ed. Herbert Read. Bollingen Series XX. Princeton, NJ: Princeton University Press, 1968.

____. *Collected Works: Volume 12: Psychology and Alchemy.* Ed. Herbert Read. Bollingen Series XX. Princeton, NJ: Princeton University Press, 1968.

___. *Collected Works: Volume 15: Spirit in Man, Art, and Literature*. Ed. Herbert Read. Bollingen Series XX. Princeton, NJ: Princeton University Press, 1968.

___. *Collected Works: Volume 16: The Practice of Psychotherapy*. Ed. Herbert Read. Bollingen Series XX. Princeton, NJ: Princeton University Press, 1968.

___. *Dreams*. Eds. Jolande Jacobi and R.C.F. Hull. Princeton, NJ: Princeton University Press, 1974.

___. *Four Archetypes*. Eds. Jolande Jacobi and R.C.F. Hull. Princeton, NJ: Princeton University Press, 1973.

___. *Man and His Symbols*, New York, NY: Dell Publishing, 1978.

___. *Memories, Dreams, Reflections*. Ed. Aniele Jaffe. New York, NY: Random House, 1965.

___. *The Portable Jung*. Ed. Joseph Campbell. New York, NY: Penguin Books, 1985.

___. *Psyche and Symbol*. Garden City, NY: Doubleday, 1958.

Kornfield, Jack. *A Path with Heart: A Guide through the Perils and Promises of Spiritual Life*. New York, NY: Bantam Books, 1993.

Kübler-Ross, Elizabeth. *On Death and Dying*. New York, NY: Macmillan Publishing, 1969.

Lao Tzu. *Wen Tzu*. Trans. Thomas Cleary. Boston, MA: Shambhala Publications, 1992.

Legge, James. *The Texts of Taoism, Part One*. New York, NY: Dover Publications, 1962.

___. *The Texts of Taoism, Part Two*. New York, NY: Dover Publications, 1962.

Lowen, Alexander. *Bioenergetics*. New York, NY: Coward, McCann & Geoghegan, 1975.

Maslow, Abraham. *The Farther Reaches of Human Nature*. New York, NY: Viking Compass, 1971.

Merton, Thomas. *The Way of Chuang Tzu*. New York, NY: New Directions, 1965.

Miller, Alice. *The Drama of the Gifted Child*. New York, NY: Basic Books, 1981.

Pagels, Heinz. *The Cosmic Code*. New York, NY: Bantam Books, 1983.

____. *Perfect Symmetry*. New York, NY: Simon and Schuster, 1985.

Perls, Frederick S. *The Gestalt Approach and Eyewitness to Therapy*. New York, NY: Bantam Books, 1976.

____. *Gestalt Therapy Verbatim*. LaFayette, CA: Real People Press, 1969.

Progoff, Ira. *At a Journal Workshop*. New York, NY: Dialogue House Library, 1975.

____. *The Death and Rebirth of Psychology*. New York, NY: Dell Publishing, 1964.

Rogers, Carl. *On Becoming a Person*. Boston, MA: Houghton Mifflin, 1961.

The Secret of the Golden Flower. Trans. Richard Wilhelm. New York, NY: Harcourt Brace Jovanovich, 1962.

The Self. Ed. Clark Moustakas. New York, NY: Harper & Row, 1956.

A Source Book in Chinese Philosophy. Trans. Wing-Tsit Chan. Fourth Princeton paperback edition. Princeton, NJ: Princeton University Press, 1969.

The Upanishads. Trans. Juan Mascaró. Harmondsworth, Middlesex, England: Penguin Books, 1978.

Wilber, Ken. *Sex, Ecology, Spirituality*. Boston, MA: Shambhala Publications, 1995.

The Wisdom of China and India. Ed. Lin Yutang. New York, NY: Random House, 1942.

Zimmer, Heinrich. *The Philosophies of India*. New York, NY: Meridian Books, 1959.

Zukav, Gary. *The Dancing Wu Li Masters*. New York, NY: Bantam Books, 1980.

INNER OCEAN PUBLISHING publishes in the genres of self-help, personal growth, lifestyle, conscious business, and inspirational nonfiction. Our goal is to publish books that touch the spirit and make a tangible difference in the lives of individuals and their communities.

We have selected for our first list five books that reflect our company's goals, depict the process of personal growth that we encourage in ourselves and others, and express conscious business practices that we embrace. To order additional copies or read about our other titles, we invite you to visit us at www.innerocean.com.
Aloha.

The Soul in the Computer:
The Story of a Corporate Revolutionary
by Barbara Waugh with Margot Silk Forrest
Forewords by Alan Webber and Joel S. Birnbaum

Miracle in Maui:
Let Miracles Happen in Your Life
by Paul Pearsall, Ph.D.
Foreword by Kumu Kawaikapuokalani Hewett

The Paradoxical Commandments:
Finding Personal Meaning in a Crazy World
by Kent M. Keith
Foreword by Spencer Johnson, M.D.

High Country:
The Solo Seeker's Guide to a Real Life
by David M. Alderman
Foreword by Jean Houston

Perfect Madness:
From Awakening to Enlightenment
by Donna Lee Gorrell